To Fred Eaton
With Best Wishes.

Fred Riseman,

15·1x·83,

MY ROAD TO CANTERBURY

MY ROAD TO CANTERBURY

by

Fred Riceman

Ricemans (Canterbury) Ltd
Canterbury
Kent

Buckland Publications Ltd
Barwick Road
Dover, Kent

ISBN 0 7212 0609 3

The photograph of the author opposite the title page is by Fisk-Moore Studios, Canterbury

Published jointly by
Ricemans (Canterbury) Ltd and Buckland Publications Ltd

Printed by
Buckland Press Ltd, Barwick Road, Dover
and 125 High Holborn, London WC1

*To my dear wife Betty
and to David, Jonathan and Elizabeth
whose encouragement and support over the
years has been greatly valued.*

ACKNOWLEDGEMENTS

The author wishes to express his thanks to all those who have helped him in producing this book. He is especially grateful to the photographers for allowing reproduction of their photographs and credit has been given in the captions where the photographer is known; to those untraced photographers not thus acknowledged apologies are expressed. The editorial assistance of Denis Weaver is also gratefully acknowledged.

CONTENTS

FOREWORD

by the Lord Lieutenant of Kent

Fred Riceman's enterprise in founding, from scratch, a new family store is in itself a noteworthy achievement. But this book is much more than a simple description of the creation of a department store. It is a full, yet modest, narrative of rich experiences, persistence in adversity, high moral standards and, I suspect, quiet but well-deserved satisfaction at a life well spent.

There is much wisdom in these pages, and those who seek to follow Fred Riceman and establish their own businesses will find a great deal of helpful advice here. One important lesson that struck me on many occasions as I read this book is that the author has found something of lasting value in virtually every experience in his life: even the darkest cloud has provided him with a silver lining, and he has persisted throughout with quiet determination despite set-backs which would have deterred many of lesser fortitude. His account of his war service, for instance, bears comparison with many much more widely publicised achievements elsewhere.

As Lord Lieutenant of the County, it is a particular pleasure for me to commend the story of a man who has contributed so much to Canterbury and to Kent. But, like so many Kent institutions, Ricemans are now known and respected far beyond the County boundary; and they are rightly proud that their standards and quality draw customers from a very wide area.

This is a fascinating tale of a remarkable man and I am sure that all who have been associated with him, in whatever capacity, will want to read how Fred Riceman set out on his geographically circuitous, but in business terms carefully structured, route from Bournemouth to Canterbury.

Robin Leigh-Pemberton

SCHOOL YEARS

School life for me is not a period which I look back on with any sense of pride or pleasure. From the age of eight to sixteen was unquestionably the worst years of my life.

In spite of trying desperately hard, I was always the lowest or next to lowest, in any subject. For family reasons it was decided best for me to go to boarding school at the age of six. All went well for the first two years, but the next eight were a nightmare. When I was sixteen my parents were told it was pointless to keep me at school as no amount of further instruction would be of any use to me—I just could not learn.

However, my housemaster and teachers omitted to appreciate that even in those days I was observant. There were over sixty boys in our house, each had three pairs of shoes, and if there should be an unclaimed pair, they would invariably ask me, "Whose do you think these are?" I nearly always knew whose! So, I was demonstrating powers of observation which have proved invaluable to me in my business career.

Having left school the problem was what to do, with no qualifications and an inferiority complex. The directors of a family business on my mother's side, Frederick Sage & Co Ltd, foremost shopfitters of their day, were approached but they already had enough members of the family with them—so, no opening there!

My father who was a scholar and Congregational Church minister was naturally disappointed at my poor showing at school. As he had friends in the bank, he thought there might be an opening but, of course, lack of qualifications made this impossible.

However, among my family's friends were the Beale family in Bournemouth who owned two department stores. My father went to see Harold Beale who in his friendly and forthright manner said, "Let him come to us as an apprentice," and so it was that an entry into the world of retail distribution was opened for me.

CHAPTER ONE

My Introduction To
Retail Distribution

It was fortunate for me that although I commenced my business career at the bottom of the ladder, the introduction was made so pleasant for me by the welcome I was given by the members of the Beale family. Herbert and Harold Beale were resident directors at Bealesons, their popular priced store, which they acquired a few years before from a Mr Okey. This was where I started in September, 1920.

To be welcomed in their office and to be told something about store life broke the ice for me and helped me quite considerably to face the unpleasant duties I was soon to have to contend with.

They told me the salary I would receive, indicated how fortunate I was that in the changed conditions of the time parents were no longer called upon to pay fifty or even one hundred guineas premium for apprenticeship, and instead I was to have my lunch, tea and 2s.6d a week rising to 3s.6d after six months.

This settled, the buyer of the linen department, Mr B., was sent for and informed that I was to be his new apprentice. It was almost like going back to school again—Mr B. would have been an ideal Dickensian character doing his best to humiliate me, showing himself up as an outstanding and gifted business personality, indicating that he would expect me to arrive early in the morning, leave late at night and do all the menial duties to his complete satisfaction.

This, in itself, was in order though had he been of a kinder disposition he might have pointed out the advantages my efforts would bring as part of my training, rather than making them appear a menial service to him; but he obviously had no interest in the progress of anyone else.

There was no delay in introducing me to my job; all the sweeping of the department was to be carried out by me, and if a pin or scrap of paper was found after I had completed my round—and this had to take place two or three times daily but finally in the evening—I was for it!

The idea of pins seemed to obsess him; I had to pick every one up and save them for future use, and he used so many for display in the department, and in the windows, that it needed considerable concentration to keep my eyes constantly open for them.

Dusting was the highlight of his instruction. First thing in the morning I had to start at one end of the fixtures, take everything out, dust every item, the surrounds and the shelves, then put them back. When this was finished, I was sent to the fancy linen department where every item, separated by tissue paper, had again to be taken out of the trays, the trays dusted and the stock put back again singly. I often felt that the continual handling must have done more harm than the dust! However, it did introduce me to the merchandise in stock and after a time I must have been as well acquainted with it as any senior member of the staff.

Ticketing was another duty, and this again helped me to obtain a good first hand idea of the value of every item in the department.

The sales staff in the linen deparment were much older than myself, having served in the 1914/18 war. They knew I had been to a public school but they were far more helpful to me than the buyer.

I well remember the occasion when the soft furnishing department, which was situated down a few stairs below the linen department, was having a change round late in the afternoon. Having finished my dusting, I asked the buyer if I could give them a hand. How could I ever forget his answer. "What, no work on my department? Start your dusting again," and he made me finish the whole round before going home—for the second time in twelve hours.

After a few months, however, when the department was busy, the day came when I was given my own sales book and promoted to serving customers. This was a great occasion.

In spite of my backwardness at school, I could do simple arithmetic, addition and multiplication, but the problem was calculating the cost of yards of Madapollam and Tarantulle. They were fine cotton materials from which women used to make their undies and were nearly always sold in lengths that finished with five or seven eighths of a yard and were sold at 3s.11¾d or 4s.11¾d a yard. The answer had to be correct to the farthing.

I suffered agonies trying to record the correct answer for a few days with Mr B. nearly always looking over my shoulder with the caustic remark, "Didn't they teach you arithmetic at your school?" It was not long, however, before I wrote out all the answers in the evening at home, and kept them in the back of my sales book, so that I had no further trouble in that direction.

For the first time in my life, I was achieving reasonable success. Customers seemed to like being served by me, in spite of my limited knowledge. It was not so very long before some of my sales amounted to quite large sums, and on one occasion when I had been looking after a very charming lady for some time, and a large pile of linens which she had selected was accumulating on the counter, Mr B. felt it was time he interfered. He walked behind the counter, came up to me, put his arm across me pushing me aside and said, "Now, madam, I can attend to you."

She replied, "And who are you?" to which he replied, "The buyer, madam," whereupon she said, "I think you are a very rude man and I wish to continue to be served by this nice young man." He crept away and fortunately never again interfered with my selling.

There was one part of my training for which I was particularly grateful to him, and that was in packing parcels. He was meticulously careful in seeing that every parcel that left his department was packed to perfection, and anyone who neglected to carry out his instructions was in trouble. Likewise, in the use of wrapping materials and string. This was closely supervised and it was my responsibility to save all used wrapping and string, together with tissue paper. Not an item was wasted, and I suppose my concern, even today, when I see wastage of any kind under this heading stems from the stringent training I received.

Before the first year was out, I began taking an interest in staff training which we received from the directors. I made a practice of making notes and soon had pages of useful information which gave me a broader view of retail distribution, factors which one did not fully appreciate in the limited training which was received in a department.

These meetings also introduced me to the importance of the staff suggestion box. Every suggestion put in, whether accepted or not, meant a personal interview with Mr Beale. Some months I earned more from suggestions than from my pay.

After some months the change of environment from school life with long holidays, to long hours of work with little fresh air, affected my health, and the family doctor advised my parents that I must take a month off. This distressed me and I asked him whether I could do outside work. He said that was perfectly all right as long as I was not in the store for long periods. I therefore asked Harold Beale if he would allow me to be an additional outside representative.

He had a kindly nature, and did not take much persuading though, looking back I now realise he must have taken quite a risk, as I knew little about the samples that I would be carrying!

Mr B. soon made it plain that he did not expect any orders from me. However, I extracted samples from him and for four weeks I had a most enjoyable time visiting hotels and boarding houses. Incidentally, I surprised everyone with the amount of sales that I was fortunate enough to make. I kept a little book and each day or so, I made Mr B. sign for the total I had achieved.

The highlight of this month was a trip I took by paddle steamer to Swanage where I visited one of the hotels. It was out of season and I was dressed in my best suit, which must have made me look as though I was going on holiday. On entering the lounge I was welcomed by the porter, who was very anxious to help me, taking my bag, and when I told him I wanted to see Mrs "So and So", the manageress, he replied, "Certainly, sir." He showed me to a chair in the lounge without realising that I was not on holiday but on business.

However, the good lady must have been kindly disposed towards youth, because we spent nearly an hour chatting, and I told her what I was trying to do without in any way letting her feel I was an expert.

She let me show her my samples, one of which I told her was a beautiful linen damask tablecloth (so Mr B. had told me), of which we only had twelve left, and which I thought were keenly priced. She was interested in them and placed an order for them all, together with other items. I remember the total order was over £200.

I returned to the store just before closing feeling very pleased. I reported to Mr B. the results of my visit to Swanage. On hearing what I had sold he called the staff—I can hear him laughing now—and told them that I had "palmed off" his old stock of cotton damask tablecloths as best Irish linen.

I pointed out that he had told me they were linen, and it was on this information that I had sold them, so I must therefore go back and inform the lady that, in my ignorance, I had made a mistake. He, of course, said, "If you do that she won't buy them," but I told him it would be better that way than that we should sell them under false pretences.

So I returned to Swanage, apologised for my mistake and asked the lady if I could get some others for her to see. She smiled, thanked me for returning, telling me that she had known all the time that they were cotton, and she was certainly going to have them. They were good quality and she thought well of the store that I had returned to admit my mistake. This resulted in our receiving a large order for carpets.

In the late summer, before my second Christmas at Bournemouth, much to my delight I was transferred to the soft furnishing department for a few weeks and here the buyer and staff were quite different.

They welcomed me and helped me in any way they could. At the same time I took full advantage of all I could do for them. In particular, when the buyer was at lunch, and he went at the same time every day, the other two members of the staff used to leave me in charge of the department to attend to customers, only calling them if necessary.

They each had a shelf in the blanket cupboard, where they went to sleep! This was situated behind the counter where I served so I had no trouble in calling them, if needed, but I usually managed on my own.

It was in October of the same year that my first real chance came. I had noted the previous year that there was much scope for business in the toy department, which operated for some six to eight weeks before Christmas and I had assisted with serving.

I asked Mr Beale if he would put me in charge of the department, under the buyer, as I was sure I could increase sales. This he did, and it gave me the opportunity of applying my mind to the importance of having the right stock properly presented both in the windows and in the department, and also the increase in business that could be obtained by placing repeat orders at an early date when it became evident which items were going to be the best sellers. On the whole there seemed to be plenty of stock available and we had a record Christmas.

This was really my introduction to hard but interesting work. I enjoyed every minute of it, and my enthusiasm must have had some effect on the rest of the staff, who were mostly temporary, or transferred from other departments. I, of course, had no trouble with my arithmetic in this department and the opportunities in the retail trade began to come home to me.

I made up my mind that I was not going to return either to the linen or the soft furnishing departments. I would try and get into parts of the store where I knew I could receive detailed instruction from buyers and staff, and come more into contact with customers and manufacturers.

So, once again I was in Mr Beale's office and my future was discussed. He allowed me to supervise the ground floor from the 1st January, in my second year, it being understood that I would give all the assistance I could to the buyer whose responsibility then covered practically all the departments on the floor. This included all fancy goods, haberdashery, lace, hosiery, gloves, scarves, perfumery, handbags, overalls, knitting wools, etc. Too much for one man and therefore any small help that I was able to give him was appreciated.

This resulted in my never having a dull moment—there was always something to do. I soon got to know most of the customers to the store and made a point of saying "Good morning" or "Good afternoon" to each. I wrote down their names, whenever I could, as I found it difficult to remember them. This, indirectly, gave me an introduction to the fashion departments, as customers used to talk to me about what they were going to purchase or what they had, and I began to feel that I carried some responsibility that was of value to the business. I also found that the senior staff of each department, who assisted the buyers, were able to give me detailed instruction on stock keeping, stock control and pricing.

It was surprising the large range of interest that this appointment gave me. It seemed to be as small or as large as I made it. Therefore, among other things, I came into closer contact with the display staff and discovered the importance of colour, tickets and window presentation, choosing the right merchandise for display at the right time. Then there were the manufacturers' representatives who came to the store. Here again I realised the importance of welcoming them, whatever department they were intending to visit and indirectly obtained a lot of useful information from them. In later years in the same store I found that this friendly contact with representatives was so contrary to what they found practised by many buyers that when they had something that was really good to offer, they frequently gave me first refusal.

My third Christmas meant a return to the toy department and this time to help with the buying, as well as the arrangement of the temporary department and sales. The results were a great success.

Again I was called to the board room to see both Herbert and Harold Beale and it seemed an appropriate time to ask their advice as to what I should do for the future. Where should I go to get further training? Harold Beale was most helpful to me and wrote to one of his friends, Mr Fred Pope, then managing director of the Bon Marché, Gloucester, asking if he would take me for further training.

After an interview, I was accepted as assistant to Mr George Pope, Fred's brother who was a director and bought for the children's and spacious hat departments.

With some trepidation, once again, I launched out into a new sphere, away from familiar surroundings. I am not sure at this stage whether I aspired to having a small establishment of my own, or not. My dreams regarding promotion were always imaginative, and with much in my mind wondering what the future held for me, I took a slow train from Bournemouth West to Gloucester.

CHAPTER TWO

BON MARCHE, GLOUCESTER

Home had always meant much to me, though at the age of nineteen to be launching out on my own, and keeping myself on £3 a week, gave me considerable satisfaction. Living in the city did not appeal to me, and I was fortunate in finding a retired valet and his wife, kind and homely people, who seemed glad to welcome me into their cottage home in the small village of Longford, about three miles out of Gloucester.

The Bon Marché was a wonderful business, almost unique in the provinces. Their trade had been established on merchandise of outstanding value, which needed little, if any, advertising to support it. Everyone from miles around shopped at the store. I could not have found a better trading centre for experience.

It was not long before the reason for the success of the business became clear to me. It had been started by the father of Fred and George Pope, but it was the dynamic personality of Fred Pope that was responsible for the remarkable progress which had been achieved. There were few, if any, like him in retail distribution at the time. He knew everything that was going on in the business and set an example for capacity and speed in work that was difficult for others to keep up with.

When he was walking through the departments he went with such vigour and speed. Yet at the same time left you quite certain that he noticed everything which was not as it should be and he was not slow on commenting on it. George Pope was different—a kindly, friendly personality, who spent most of his time in buying for the juvenile and hat departments, both of which he did with outstanding success. I soon became friends with him and his wife. They were most kind to me during my comparatively short stay with them. Our friendly link continued until his untimely death some years ago.

On taking up my duties at the store, I was placed under his control, and for about eighteen months, I assisted him in the running of the departments for which he bought, though it was the hat department which took up most of my time. There were twenty-one sales assistants under my control, of varying ages, but whatever they may have thought of a young lad being put over them, I never remember any difficulties.

Indeed, it still stands out clearly in my mind that the senior lady who must have been approaching forty, asked my advice, in confidence, as to the best way of dealing with her matrimonial problem. I certainly was not qualified at that time to give her advice, but as she appeared to be so fond of the person concerned, I thought it was a good idea for them to get married—and I heard later that it had all turned out very happily!

There was plenty of work to do throughout the week but the great day was Saturday. The store used to be packed from early morning until approaching 8 p.m. in the evening. It required considerable planning to make sure that the stocks of each price group were filled in throughout the day, to keep a watchful eye for customers, and to see that they were contented if they had to wait for service.

During the quieter days of the week, all the staff were kept fully occupied with stock control, marking off, and sorting out stock for department displays and windows.

It was during this period that I began to feel my feet and to realise the tremendous scope in retail distribution if one had a wide experience and was prepared to work. This was the sort of action that I understood. I enjoyed every minute of each day, in spite of the long hours, seldom getting home in the evenings before 7 or 9 p.m. on Saturdays.

In spite of this I found time in the winter to start the Gloucester Seconds Rugger Team. It was an extremely happy period for me and I made a lot of friends.

The example of Fred Pope had a considerable influence on my approach to work. His personality was so strong, and the effort he put into his work so great that I soon realised there was no real success without enthusiasm and hard work. Apart from his amazing driving power, he taught me that the instinct and action of a merchant was vital for success.

Although he kept an eye on the whole store, he set standards for all the buyers with the care and skill with which he bought ladies' coats. Few coat departments in any provincial store took more money per square foot than he did, and to me it was an entertainment to see him on a Saturday rushing up and down with piles of garments over his shoulder, either replacing stock sold, or filling up windows.

There were a few incidents which will always stand out in my mind, which I feel may be of interest, during this period.

The first was the winter of the great floods, when the Severn, as it does so frequently, overflowed its banks—but on this occasion it covered a far wider area than ever before in living memory. I was awake about 6 a.m. and although it was dark I could see the reflection of the water as it was rising and gradually coming up the main road through the village. Before breakfast it had reached our front door and was still rising rapidly.

Mr and Mrs Watts told me that I would have to spend the day with them, as nobody would be leaving the village, it was completely cut off. This had never entered by mind, and I told them that fortunately I had my swimsuit with me, and would, with a bit of luck, be able to carry my clothes in a bundle over my head and walk through to the outskirts of the city.

At 7.30 a.m. I set off—complete with towel! The villagers from their windows gave me a splendid send off and I told them that when I returned I would take the children for a ride across the flooded meadows on a big tree which I thought would be afloat by then. I was able to keep my promise the next day.

It was no easy matter proceeding for over a mile through the flood waters, because, in places, the current was extremely swift, though the hedges on either side did break the flow to some extent. The month was January—so it was cold!

When I reached dry land I went into someone's garden, had a rub down and dressed and arrived at business as usual at 8.30 a.m.

Soon after I heard Fred Pope racing through the juvenile department calling out to them, "Riceman will not be here today because of the floods," and the staff replied with some pleasure, "He arrived ten minutes ago, sir."

Another incident, was an idea I had for a Christmas attraction. I thought if I could build a model of the Tower Bridge of London, with a lift going up and down in one of the towers and the bridge rising and falling, with railway lines running across it, as well as traffic and ships underneath it would be bound to be a big attraction.

So, I went to Fred Pope and told him of my idea, to which his quick reply was, "What do you need to make it?" I told him, "Meccano". "How much do you want to spend?" "£50." "Right, order it up." So I did, and in the late spring the large crate of meccano was delivered to the home of Mr and Mrs Watts.

It will demonstrate the kindly people they were, when I record that they gave me their best front room which was normally only used on Sundays, to carry out this work. Anyone knowing what this meant to them will realise it was a considerable sacrifice on their part.

I had no picture or plan for the construction, except that which I had in my head, and I had certainly never built anything worth looking at before in Meccano. However, I was confident it would be something quite outstanding, and every spare minute of my evenings was spent working on it.

When completed in the early autumn it stood over six feet high and looked something like the real thing. It was only in my imagination that I had added the lifts and railway lines, etc. Now problems which I had not thought of before started to arise. One was that I could not get it out of the door, so it had to be taken down and moved in sections. This was possible, but it took time.

Then, it had to be made to work. I thought Fred Pope would deal with this for me. On receiving my request, he instructed me to contact the best firm of electricians to carry out this work. Unfortunately, after examining it, they reported back to him that it could not be done—so he told me it would have to go into the window as it was. I remember saying, "But that would be useless, it will not attract anyone unless it works."

I spent several days giving a lot of thought to this problem. I never had been mechanically minded, but the matter was so important to me that I felt something must be done.

In the end, I went to the store electrician and asked him for a fan. Then I went back to Fred Pope asking if I could spend some more money on some cogs of various sizes and yards and yards of link chain. Again he agreed. When it all arrived, I built a box in Meccano, the interior of which was open to view, standing about 2ft high by 10in wide and 14in long.

Then within the Meccano frame, I geared the speed of the fan down to a large wheel which turned about once every three quarters of a minute. This wheel was then attached to the end of the bridge, and both sides of the bridge were linked together so that when one side moved the other did the same. The lift was also linked with it, so that it went up and down. I had overcome my major problem.

Fixing this up in the window, later in the evening, when people were leaving the theatre, attracted a large crowd, covering most of the pavement outside, and I think it proved almost as big an attraction during the course of erection, as it did when the lights were on and the window fully dressed.

It had not been on display for more than a few days before Fred Pope was approached by the police. It was attracting such attention that the public were causing an obstruction and we had, therefore, to move it up to the toy department on the second floor. Here again, however, it proved a great attraction, for as many people came to see this as visited Father Christmas. What the majority of the boys were particularly interested to see was the machinery which worked it.

This was the first of my many efforts to introduce something entirely different for Christmas trading as a means of attracting the crowds to enter a store, and I feel sure that this, my first effort, made Fred Pope as pleased with the results as I was.

The last specially interesting item was when Fred Pope pulled me up in one of the departments and talked to me about my future. Incidentally, I never remember seeing him in an office; I do not know whether he even had one as he always seemed to conduct his business either in the coat department or around the store.

"I am going to make you buyer of the dress department, Riceman." It was not a question of what I thought about it, though I did say to him, "What do I know about buying dresses?" I well remember his reply was to the effect that if he thought I could buy dresses, I could buy them!

I then asked him if I were his son, would he give me this appointment or would he send me to London? His brief reply indicated that I would have to go.

I then asked where. "To Barkers of Kensington. Get on their display department, you will learn a lot."

"Who should I see?"

"Go straight to the top. Ask for Sir Sidney Skinner and mention my name."

"Would you be good enough to write to him for me?"

"Certainly not. If you cannot get in to see him, and get an appointment, you don't deserve to go there."

I then asked him if I could come back and see him later, and he told me when I had more experience and had achieved some success by my own efforts, he would certainly be glad to have me back, and he would watch my progress with interest.

I was sorry to leave his brother George and indeed all the friendly associations that I had built up in such a short period, but I had learned much and felt in the circumstances it was better I should look for further experience. London was obviously the place.

CHAPTER THREE

My First London Experience

Fortunately for me, I had no idea that when going to see Sir Sidney Skinner I was doing something quite out of line with normal practice. It was unknown to me that large stores had a staff office and in particular a staff controller who in those days at John Barker & Co Ltd was a most important gentleman.

Further it had never entered my mind that junior applicants would seldom, if ever, be interviewed by the staff controller himself, but by one of his assistants—so when I arrived at the store, I had no idea of the disturbance my unusual action was going to cause.

I went straight up to the managing director's office and saw his secretary, only to find he was leaving the next day on holiday. I remember that she was extremely nice to me. I told her I would not wish to trouble him before he went, and that the matter I wanted to see him about was important, but I felt he would be better able to deal with it after he had been away for a while. She, therefore, told me the day he was returning and fixed an appointment soon after for me to see him.

When the day arrived, I was there on time and shown in to see Sir Sidney Skinner. A most remarkable man. His approach to me was very like that of Fred Pope. You could tell he had risen from the ranks by hard work, dynamic drive and imagination. The progress of Barkers was due to his live control.

When he heard who had suggested I should see him, and I had told him Mr Pope had told me that I had to make the approach myself—no word was going to be put in for me—he seemed to like the idea, especially that I had found my way in to see him. He gave me about fifteen minutes of his valuable time, questioning me on the little I had done, and my aims and objectives, during which time he was obviously assessing my potential. It was not until some eight years later that he told me what he thought it was!

On closing the interview, he threw the question at me, "You want to come to Barkers?"

"Yes please, sir"

"What do you want to do here?"

"I would like the opportunity of working in your display department."

"Right," he said, and picked up the telephone asking for the staff controller, Mr Pegg.

He was up in Sir Sidney's office in no time—a tall man, severe looking, in a black frock coat carrying a top hat. I had to sit and listen to a conversation between him and his managing director. Something on these lines: "This is Fred Riceman. He wants experience in our display department. Have you a vacancy?"

"No, Sir Sidney, their staff complement is full."

"All right, Pegg, make an opening."

Then Sir Sidney, turning to me, asked, "How much do you require?", and I replied, "Since going to Gloucester I have not been an expense to my parents, and I feel it would be difficult to live in London on less than £3 per week."

"Right, Pegg, see that he has £3 per week."

A short conversation followed that this was too much, and would put the costs out of line. Sir Sidney had the last wold, and so I became an unwelcome intruder to John Barker & Co Ltd, having offended Mr Pegg and soon to find out that Mr Dawes, the display manager, was equally hostile to having an extra pair of hands on his staff, knowing that it would put the costs out, at least for the time being. However, neither of them dared to question their managing director's instructions, as it was quite apparent that his word was law.

It did, in fact, only take me a few weeks to settle down, in what was to prove one of the most instructive years of my training.

A word about my lodgings—even in those days, £3 did not go very far in London, when board and lodgings, travelling, and all meals had to be paid for. I found a small room in a poor district in Putney; it was clean, but very plain. The accommodation was owned by a hunchback workroom hand in a London factory, and her two sisters who were, I believe, similarly employed.

The point which I am not likely to forget was there was no bath in the house; I had to use a tub in a shed in the garden. Water had to be carried out in pails from the house, which was quite a job in itself, and the shed leaked, was very cold and draughty, especially during the winter months.

They always had their clocks twelve minutes fast and when they were rushing to catch their bus in the morning they stopped to subtract the twelve minutes, to make sure that they were not ahead of time! No amount of persuasion on my part would make them put their clocks right and save all these calculations.

I frequently walked a mile and a half to Putney Bridge, to save paying the bus fare, which could then be added to my lunch money—for this I allowed myself sixpence a day. The menu was rather plain, usually a glass of water, a sausage roll and a roll and butter.

I have never regretted the care I had to exercise over my spending, as it has made me far more understanding of the needs of those who later were looking to me for their employment.

Now to the main part of my training during this period. Mr Dawes, after a week or so, had me as his junior assistant in the windows, which resulted in fetching and carrying to and from departments for him, and helping in the preparation and carrying out of particular types of displays for which Barkers were famous in those days. They were open, and yet attractive selling displays. Apart from Christmas-time, there was seldom anything in the windows, other than stands, merchandise and tickets.

The procedure for dressing most of the windows was roughly as follows: first, ascertain from the buyer of the department concerned the merchandise to be shown, and if colour was included, Mr Dawes or one of his senior assistants, would select them.

While the goods were being brought to the window, stands were positioned on the floor of the window, then piece by piece the display took effect.

Change in design of windows was largely dependent on the replacing of the same stands at different heights and positions each time, but seldom were different stands included, though occasionally a chair or a table was introduced—a most economical procedure.

Mr Dawes specialised in the dress fabrics and fashion windows and it was not long before I knew how to dress a model, though it was some time before he would allow me to do any of the fashion drapes, which he prepared with meticulous care; each colour was carefully selected and each fold had to be precise before it was pinned to perfection.

The second in command was a man named Jock Ellson who had quite a different personality. I could talk to him and he was good enough to help me in many ways. He specialised in the fancy windows and hosiery, the latter being among the finest in London.

As the months passed, I was learning in the best school the importance of good window displays, and the instructions I received proved invaluable to me in later years.

Their ticket libraries, and the method of sanctioning the wording and prices for all tickets throughout the store was, in itself, an education but perhaps best of all was the knowedge I began to obtain of merchandise.

Our windows were usually completed by lunchtime, and during the afternoon I was not allowed in the display room, which was across the road. This was reserved for the display manager, and according to those more senior than myself, during the afternoon he used to retire for a rest until about 4 p.m.

Knowing that he was out of the way, most of the other display staff seemed to follow likewise, and all too frequently, I was the only member of the team available. This resulted in the buyers coming to me when they wanted items changed or taken out of a window for a customer, but in return they always answered any questions I might have about the merchandise, which was a great help.

So much for my introduction to the display world.

Again there were a few items of interest that I remember in connection with Barkers, and which I feel are worthy of recording.

For instance, the directors daily paraded through the store about 10.15 a.m. led by Sir Sidney Skinner, all with their top hats. I always wondered if they saw anything as they marched through the main gangways. My guess is that Sir Sidney did, and at the conference which no doubt followed, suitable instructions would be given.

Their sale periods were terrific occasions. It was hard labour so far as displays were concerned, putting an entirely different type of window in, when so much stock was involved and it had to be dealt with in so short a period.

Remnant days were equally important, and I doubt if any store in London at the time attracted more business for this part of the sale promotion.

I usually had to help during the first day, and it was non stop from 9 a.m. until closing time.

Retail distribution at this time was beginning to suffer from recession, but not so at Barkers. While other establishments were going bankrupt, Barkers seemed to profit more than any other store by buying up stocks at a big discount. I, therefore, noted for future reference that a store without sufficient capital in reserve is likely to suffer severely, if not cease to be, when difficult trading periods have to be faced.

Anyone who can remember Barkers exciting advertisements during the twenties will realise how they turned a depression, so far as general trading was concerned, into a success, by their clever buying and promotion, which created a big selling feature without lowering their quality standards.

The fifteen months passed all too quickly and by then I felt I was able to dress windows in my own right. The knowledge that I had gained of merchandise would help me if I could obtain more detailed experience elsewhere—so back to Harold Beale I went for further advice.

This time he suggested I should contact a Mr Vesey who always called himself the governing director of John Dyers & Co Ltd, Southsea.

After thanking Sir Sidney Skinner, Mr Pegg and Mr Dawes for their help, I told them the time had come for me to move on for more experience.

CHAPTER FOUR

John Dyers & Co Ltd, Southsea

Looking back on this period it was the most disappointing and least effective part of my early training. John Dyers was a good class store in two buildings, fashions and gift departments in the main store and furnishing just across the road. I did not like this arrangement at the time as the staff in the main building were not as closely linked with the furnishing as I would have liked. However, I learnt that the presentation of furnishing requires entirely different treatment to that of fashions and gifts.

For the latter a constant flow of shoppers is good and for the former, so long as there is a good window frontage and attractive sales features within, the shoppers on the look out for home furnishings find it easier to select in a quieter setting. This probably is the reason why a number of stores have been developed with home furnishings entirely separated from the rest. When this has not happened it has been found that too many people on a furnishing floor can distract from intending shoppers and prove harmful to stock.

The store itself was off the beaten track, although when it was first established it was in the main shopping centre. The general trend of the shopping public had since moved nearer to the sea. It is interesting to note that particularly during the first fifty years of this century a number of well established stores with first-class management gradually declined through no direct fault of management but merely because shopping habits of the area had changed.

Later I was to realise that it is usually better to pay an excessively high rent in the best position just as it is false economy to save on rent by occupying a secondary site. I believe there are a few cases where management having noted this have moved to a newly developing area. To have done this must have demanded great courage and foresight. However, John Dyers was not seriously affected by this until some years after I had left.

My first meeting with Mr Vesey was one that I shall always remember. With his white hair, he looked like a member of the clergy and had a kindly soft voice. Our conversation was such that I thought his intentions were most altruistic. My responsibilities were to help him put his good ideas into practice, which I found most difficult. Once again I was also to cover the ground floor of the main store, assisting the buyers, managing the staff and developing staff training.

My duties, therefore, developed in a quiet, and to me, unimpressive way, until by accident one day I picked up a business magazine which I have since felt had more effect on my future career than any other single incident. It was a yellow backed cover of the *Efficiency* magazine owned, edited and mostly written by Herbert N. Casson. It was the first time I had ever read a publication that provided ideas and inspiration.

I read it from cover to cover and sent in a life subscription, as reading the first issue, it really put new life and excitement into my every effort. It is a great help to a young man to look forward to the beginning of each month in anticipation of obtaining encouragement and some guidance to make the best use of his efforts.

I also took an equal interest in the books he frequently published and I still have most of them on my shelves at home. Titles such as *Thirty Great Lives, Efficiency, The Joy of Life, How to Succeed, The Importance of Correct Letter Writing, The Art of Showmanship*, stand out in my memory. His exciting approach to business activities followed on the lines of Lord Beaverbrook's success story, which must have likewise encouraged many a young man to do better.

As his office was in Regent Street, and I was passing with a few minutes to spare, I called in on the offchance of seeing him. He was there, so I thanked him for the help his *Efficiency* magazine and writings were to me and it started a friendly link which lasted until his death. He often took me to Swan & Edgar's department store for a coffee and I would just sit and listen to him expounding on the principles of efficiency and how to apply these to put life and fun into business, ideas which he had learnt in a hard school, both in Canada and America. A similar approach by someone equally gifted today could be of great help to young people setting out to meet severe competition in all walks of life and would complement our more advanced training schemes.

The one benefit that John Dyers received from this, was that it had a marked effect on my approach to staff training. I no longer have copies of the notes from which I spoke to the staff, but I remember a new excitement and interest entered into all I had to say to them, and as a result their interest in these lectures seemed to be correspondingly greater.

I soon found myself taking far more note of successful men in retail distribution, and did everything I could to find out how and why they had achieved their success. Studying the lives of great men in the store world, who seemed to have worthwhile objectives, made me dream of eventually becoming a managing director of a department store, or better still to have one of my own.

I did not want to leave the pleasant surroundings. I got on well with the buyers and staff, my salary was all I needed to live in pleasant accommodation, and provided me with a motor cycle so that I could return home at least two weekends a month. I don't know what happened to my health, at that time, as I was always looked upon as being fit; however, I continued to miss the fresh air, as in my previous appointments, but this was the first time it had affected my health to such an extent that the family doctor advised my father that I should go for a sea trip.

This, of course, I thought was a wonderful idea, and when asking my father where he would send me, he wisely told me that I was old enough to look after myself, and that when he was a young man, he had worked his passage, and I could not expect him to provide me with a free ticket. This attitude which my father from time to time showed to me, althouth I did not like it, I later realised was a great help as it put me on my mettle.

In this instance, it resulted in my going to see my favourite aunt in London who knew lots of influential people, and I asked her if she knew anyone in shipping. She did, and made sure I was invited to a party at which the representative of a large shipping company would be present and his daughter was to be my partner for the evening.

I must have presented my case to him in a suitable manner, because without any further meetings, he kindly placed at my disposal a free ticket that he was permitted to use once a year, but in this particular instance he was unable to use it himself. The next day I was at the shipping company's offices and found for a nominal payment of £10, I could go to the Middle East, first class for three months.

Although the experiences of the next three months were not a direct help to me and my chosen career, indirectly it brought me face to face with some of life's difficulties when I had to stand on my own feet. The following are one or two instances that stand in my mind:

It was a modern ship powered by steam but only of 5,000 tons. There were two other passengers, a Colonel Coke and his wife. It took us nearly three days in the teeth of a gale to cross the Bay of Biscay! The captain told us it was the worst trip he had ever had and we would be lucky if we reached harbour safely! We were battened down below deck and I can still smell the leather upholstery which made it difficult for us to enjoy our food! However, I managed.

We were in Alexandria Harbour for about fourteen days and, as I left London with only £10, I realised that this would have to go a long way. So there were no outings and I spent most of my days walking around the harbour and the town and the evenings talking with the steward.

This we were doing one evening, when the glasses and cutlery on the table were thrown up in the air. Thinking something had hit us and we might be sinking, we rushed on deck to see the front of large buildings crashing to the ground. An earthquake that had struck the Far East had moved through to the Middle East. It was obvious that there was panic among the people, so I thought it would be a good time to walk into the town as nobody would be interested in me. The destruction of buildings was terrible and wherever I went rubble was being searched for individuals who had been buried.

I eventually returned safely on board and there were no further instances although I had feared the possibility of a tidal wave following the trouble and this, no doubt, was one of the reasons why I walked up on the higher ground in the town. After cruising up as far as Joppa where we rowed ashore in small dinghies, I spent a small amount of my limited resources on a trip to Bethlehem and Jerusalem.

Unfortunately, on returning to Alexandria, I had to change to another ship and spent over three weeks anchored in the harbour. One day to overcome boredom, I accepted what was supposed to be a fishing trip with a party of young men who I soon realised were only interested in taking everything I possessed, which was not much. Before we had travelled a quarter of a mile I realised that if I didn't do something drastic, I might not return safely, so I stood up in the boat and shouted at them that the captain and crew knew who I was with (they were a party who regularly supplied our vessel with fruit and vegetables) and if I did not return within a given time they would know where to look for me. By my shouting and pretence that I was not in the least afraid of them (though I was quaking) they eventually turned round and took me back with no fishing and I never accepted any further offers from local inhabitants.

Incidentally, on our return trip there was a member of the crew who was working his way home. He had been an officer on another ship who had been lured away to the poor end of the city, attacked and stripped of everything he possessed. During the unforeseen delay, he had missed his sailing and so had to work his passage home as a seaman.

On a quiet and peaceful evening walk around the harbour I suddenly felt two bare arms around my neck. I knew what was happening, so I went slack and gave a terrific kick behind me. I caught the man in his stomach and, as he fell, I ran as fast as I could back to the ship and decided no more evening walks!

The return trip was uneventful, the only problem being when we were approaching Lands End. The captain received instructions to proceed to Manchester instead of docking in London. This at least gave me the enjoyment of travelling through the Manchester Ship Canal but by then my money was running short and after I had taken out the cost of a rail ticket home to Bournemouth, there was little left for the steward, but he was a good sort and understood. And so I returned home safely.

CHAPTER FIVE

HOLDRONS OF PECKHAM

After three months' exciting travel, I was naturally anxious to return to work, but soon found, as many others have to their cost, that when you are out of a job it is much harder to obtain an appointment than when you are in one.

A few weeks passed and nothing suitable had turned up; my father was beginning to get the idea that I was not trying to obtain anything and, as on previous occasions, his attitude towards me was such that, in spite of my disliking it at the time, I could not really have been dealt with in a more satisfactory manner. He did, in fact, suggest that I should go away and not return until I had found something. I left the same day, and was fixed up before the evening was out!

It happened like this: I had been advised that I should try and get into another well situated, busy, popular priced store where there would be plenty of action. The name of one such store had been given to me by someone who was well acquainted with the managing director, Mr W. J. Hopton of Holdrons of Peckham.

Only knowing South East London vaguely, I found it difficult to picture such a store in that locality. On arrival at Rye Lane, Peckham, my wonder increased for the trading carried on there was mostly of the 'market place' standard and yet, I found this enormous emporium, spreading over many thousands of square feet round an important corner opposite the railway station. There was nothing else comparable with it, and I wondered how ever it existed in such unlikely and drab surroundings.

Once inside, however, I felt quite different. The place was humming with life; long gangways on the ground floor with counters on either side, packed with merchandise, interspaced with display cases which made room for better grade stock, and seemed in turn to enhance the appearance of the lower priced ranges.

Most of the trade was carried out on the ground and first floors and there were two large arcades providing about 180 windows in all. Later on, I discovered that, like many other stores, they were dependent on attracting shoppers from almost the whole of South East London, which was also covered by a comprehensive delivery service.

While I had been at Barkers, I had not even heard of this store, which was probably because very little press advertising was done, apart from sale times.

They relied mainly on large hoardings on the side of prominent railway bridges crossing the roads in South East London. You could not miss the *Holdrons of Peckham* spread across them in large letters—particularly when they were linked with sales and special event announcements.

From advice I had been given, I knew that John Hopton was the genius who had contributed most to the splendid development of this almost unique business.

So, it was to Rye Lane, Peckham, that I made my way and after walking round the windows and the departments, I felt as I proceeded to the management offices that this was the place for me. Once again, I was fortunate in finding the managing director's secretary helpful and it so happened that she was able to arrange for me to see Mr Hopton.

It was with some excitement that I was shown into the board room. It is difficult to describe my reactions to the atmosphere of this spacious room, so different from the display of bargains throughout the store—more fitting to be found in Buckingham Palace, than in Rye Lane, Peckham. Long, expensively panelled, with two or three photographs, or they could have been paintings, everything of the very best, the carpeting, the long table surrounded by leather chairs, and the enormous desk at the far end, at which sat John Hopton.

He struck me as a man who was sympathetic, wise and kind—more like an Archbishop of Canterbury than a dymanic personality who was controlling this enormous and profitable business. Not the sort of gentleman I had expected for one minute. Smartly dressed in a black frock coat, silvery white hair with a slight wave in it, a cheery face and eyes that welcomed me as though I was somebody really important.

He stood up, shook hands with me, and gave me a seat. Immediately putting me at my ease, he looked at me as though I had only to ask for what I wanted, and it would be given. I soon found out this was not so! He had merely put me at my ease so as to extract all the information he could about me, of my past experience, and at the same time to gain an inkling of my ambitions. This interview was so thorough that it must have lasted for half an hour, and by the end of it, he looked at me with the same benign disarming smile, unfortunately not to offer me an appointment although saying I was just the sort of young man he wanted but they were fully staffed throughout the store at the present time.

Although this came as a shock to me, I can clearly remember saying, "If you had a vacancy, you really mean that you would be looking for someone like me?"

He replied, "Yes, certainly."

I then made a proposal, one that I am sure he had never received before, and perhaps later he may have thought he replied too quickly; anyway it worked, for I said, "If you cannot afford to engage anyone with my limited qualifications, I will come to you, as soon as you like, and work for nothing for two weeks. You can test me in any work that you have to offer through the store and I will do my best for you. If, at the end of the fortnight you think that I can do better than some that you already have with you, then, no doubt you will find a temporary niche until you can fit me in on a permanent basis. If not, you will be under no obligation to engage me."

Without hesitation he replied, "Be at this office at 9 a.m. tomorrow morning.

Punctually at 9 a.m. I reported, and he told me that he had thought about the talk we had had, and he was going to give me a free hand on their large ground floor. I was to make myself useful in any way I could, so long as I did not upset the buyers! Thus began another eighteen months or so of varied and exciting experiences—quite different to anything that I had done in the past.

Within a fortnight I looked upon myself as chief supervisor of the floor and gave more attention to departmental displays than anyone else had previously done. Mr Hopton, as promised, sent for me at the end of the fortnight and said he would like me to stay, though he still had no opening for me, but he was sure he could find one, if I would be patient for perhaps a few months. In the meantime, I was given a wage of £3 per week.

Apart from my duties on the ground floor, I was at the disposal of the buyers, and set out to win their co-operation by helping in any way I could. On Saturdays it was literally a free for all; apart from directing the hoards of people as they flowed through, I had to make sure that disgruntled customers who had waited too long for service, were kept happy, and I well remember among the many items that I dealt with was the counter which was devoted to fleecy lined knickers; our sales in these were tremendous!

And so, a few months passed, until the day arrived when they were short on the display staff, and I was asked if I would help. Fortunately, I had kept my eyes open for staff in the store who used to fetch and carry to the windows, trying to assess if any of them had any special qualifications so far as colour and style were concerned. When I was given a fashion window to dress, I knew immediately the junior who would be of special help to me, as I had noticed her natural gift for wise choice in both colour and style.

With her help we put in what proved to be a good selling window. Others followed, and never was a window put in that Mr Hopton did not notice and if it was not up to standard, you knew you were for it.

It was at this time that I discovered that Mr Hopton had an extremely fiery temper, but I took no notice of it, and tried to learn from what he was telling me. Gradually I realised that his reaction was not so much on the appearance of the window, but on its selling qualities. If the wrong merchandise was displayed, or the right merchandise in the wrong way, you soon knew about it. This, incidentally, is a lesson that quite a few managers in the retail trade have still to learn, though today many stores are depending less on windows and more on departmental features.

One day, to my surprise, Mr Hopton asked me in the store if I would like to go home with him to dinner that evening. Naturally, I gladly accepted, and was welcomed by his wife and members of his lively and happy family. They had a beautiful home at Streatham Common, where he and his daughters used to ride. For the further year or so that I was at Holdrons, their home was open to me. An interesting sidelight to this enjoyable episode was the numerous introductions I was given to the principals of family department stores who were personal friends of the Hopton family.

After about six months, my opportunity came. The display manager was taken ill, so I contacted Mr Hopton and asked if I could be of any assistance. He asked me to help plan the Christmas windows, and in particular the Christmas hosiery window on the front. It appeared that this was the highlight of their Christmas display, and the turnover from it was out of all proportion to that which resulted from most of the other windows.

Previously, they had been dressed on old fashioned lines, with stockings stuck to the window pane. I thought I would utilise the display methods of Jock Ellson who had taught me so much in this direction while I was at Barkers. It required a quantity of glass shelves and pedestals, and took me nearly two days to dress, but it introduced a more modern display note to the presentation, and made everything look so much more attractive.

The display had been finished on a Friday evening and on the Saturday morning when Mr Hopton saw it and found that his usual presentation had been altered, he was furious, and I felt the full force of his sharp temper. He wanted the window changed immediately. I told him, being Saturday, we must leave it until Monday, otherwise we would not sell anything. So he had to agree to this, and the matter was left until he saw the trading figures for Saturday which proved to be excellent—and the window display stayed! Instead of receiving further displeasure, I had the benefit of the charm that came so easily to him. That was the end of his old fashioned displays and a step towards a more modern presentation. The other windows also appeared to satisfy Mr Hopton. Incidentally, at no other time had I noticed any other director displaying similar interest in such details.

The display manager returned to work after a few weeks and I told him that I hoped he would find everything in order and returned to my ground floor supervising. Little did I realise that jealousy was to rear its ugly head, but I was amazed to discover a suggestion made by him that I had been trying to usurp his appointment while he was absent. Fortunately, I ignored his attitude and said nothing about it to Mr Hopton either in or out of business hours.

However, after a fortnight or so, I was requested to go to the board room and found the display manager already there. It was quite evident from the extremely annoyed expression on his face that he had been to Mr Hopton with his allegation that I had been trying to usurp his authority.

Mr Hopton was, as usual, sitting in his comfortable chair at the end of the board room and he let Mr E. talk. When he had finished he asked if I had anything to say, and although I was stunned by the foolish, petty and misguided attitude of Mr E., I felt it wisest only to say how sorry I was that my actions had been misinterpreted. I had only tried to be of help both to him and to the interests of the business, and I hoped, on reflection, he would appreciate this.

Mr Hopton then turned to me and said, "Riceman, if you were given the opportunity, could you look after the windows here?" I replied without fully realising the implications of his remark, "Yes, I could, with some guidance." So, without any further to-do, he turned to Mr E. and said, "Your presence after one month from now will no longer be required. Riceman, you are the display manager from today," and my salary was immediately adjusted accordingly.

With a large staff under my control, and the display of some 180 windows to be attended to, there was little spare time for me over the next twelve months. Gradually we introduced new ideas, which so far as I can remember must have been effective, as no adverse comments were received from the buyers or Mr Hopton. In the meantime, apart from the closer study of display, I was learning more about merchandise.

During this period, I made a suggestion that we should start a social club. A meeting was called, and as the idea had originated from me, I was invited to be the first secretary. I mention this as later it indirectly resulted in my taking on additional responsibilities.

Towards the end of my period at Holdrons, I began to sense that Mr Hopton had some important move on hand; he was excited and seemed less interested in the small but important things that went on in the store and which previously he would never have missed when he was on his round of inspection.

The reason for this was soon made known, when the staff was called together after business and Mr Hopton announced that the directors had decided to sell the company to the Selfridge Provincial Stores. Although he was staying for the time being, he might be leaving later, but all the staff would be retained.

This came as a shock to the staff at all levels—a shock from which the business never fully recovered; it seemed as though the heart had gone out of it, and everyone feared that its unique character would be changed.

A further meeting was called a few days later, when both Gordon Selfridge and Gordon Selfridge Jnr, came to meet us, and I well remember the interest I took on this occasion in trying to weigh up the father, who was a remarkable man. I still think that his achievement in putting up that great store, facing the difficulties he had to contend with, was an unsurpassed feat in the history of retail distribution in this country during the first half of the century. He surmounted every difficulty that came his way and introduced to this country a framework of store life and procedure which to a very large extent, was to be adopted by his best competitors. There are many who share the view that if he had confined his energies to his great store, and had not frittered them away in other directions, he would have died a happy, successful and worthy man.

Naturally, as display manager, receiving a satisfactory salary, I did not want to leave, and I discussed the matter with a personal friend of mine, Trevor Smith, who at that time was our personnel controller (we shared a car together). He later became the managing director of the Thomas Wallis furnishing store when it was opposite Gamages in Holborn, and in which appointment I believe he achieved marked success.

The outcome of our talk was that we should get to know Gordon Selfridge or his son. I, therefore, turned my thoughts to the Sports Club and decided it would be a good idea if we planned a sports day on a large and exciting scale, to which we would be justified in inviting some of the staff of Selfriges and also Gordon Selfridge Jnr. The staff, also, fortunately thought it was a good idea, I am sure they were pleased with the results. It certainly proved to be one of the best days of its kind with which I have ever been associated.

The large park at Dulwich was crowded and the programme for the afternoon and evening went like clockwork. I had arranged for Trevor Smith to look after Gordon Selfridge Jnr as I would be busy seeing that everything went smoothly and that I would not, on this occasion, go out of my way to speak to him.

However, it was understood that Trevor would see that he knew who was responsible for the planning of the arrangements and the appointment that I held in the store, in the hope that he might send for me to see what I looked like, and to assess my potential for use in other directions.

I think the interview that followed a week later was due rather more to Trevor than to myself; however, the plan had worked. I received a request to report to his office at the Bon Marché, Brixton. Fortunately, I had had a good look round the windows before entering and after receiving a few words of congratulations on the sports day, he asked me what I thought of the Bon Marché windows. I was able to reply, without hesitation, that they were dreadful! It was obvious that he was a man who wasted little time on long conversations and all he said was, "Please let me have a report within a week about them."

I took a notebook and went round them again, recording what I could find of merit and adding all the points which I felt would be helpful to the proper presentation of their standard of merchandise. Trevor, who was far better than I at preparing anything of this sort, went through my notes. I am sure it was again largely due to him that a day or two later, after these had been delivered, I was instructed to make my second visit.

The interview was short and to the point. I arrived for a 10 a.m. appointment just before the striking of the hour. Gordon Selfridge Jnr had not arrived. However, he turned up two mintues later, rushed through the door saying, "Morning, Riceman. Are you early or am I late?" This short phrase in some measure described the approach to business of this young man, who, at that time was assumed would be one of our top men in retail distribution.

"I have considered your report, Riceman, and I am prepared to make you Director of Display of the Selfridge Provincial Stores—would you like the appointment? The salary will be **** and you can start your duties on Monday." I replied in the affirmative and received no further instructions, nor did I run into any difficulties except those which were self created, until a few months later when I handed in my resignation for reasons still to be disclosed.

All I asked for was the names of the managers of the stores in the Group and their addresses. Although this appointment sounded attractive (perhaps the title director appealed to me), I soon realised that I could easily fall between two stools. I had no facilities at that time for planning displays on a large scale. The requirements of each of the stores were quite different from one another, and I still had to continue with the detailed responsibility as display manager for Holdrons of Peckham; this should have claimed all my time but I was not permitted to engage another to take my place.

My car was put to good use travelling round the country, and I found it interesting visiting the other stores. However, as there was no organisation behind me, I am sure if I had not left I should either have been dismissed or offered another appointment.

Fortunately for me Mr Fred Pope had heard of my promotion and in keeping with his promise of some few years back, wrote asking if I would see him. This I did, and when he heard of my varied experience, the outcome of the conversation was that he felt I now had the qualifications he considered suitable to justify my being appointed branch supervisor to the Edwin Jones & Co Ltd group which operated from Southampton.

This meant a further increase in my salary, and once again enabled me to return home, which to me was as important as the opportunity of earning more money. So I told Gordon Selfridge Jnr of my plan; he was annoyed and told me that I would never have the opportunity of joining any store again that operated under the direction of Selfridges. I was sorry about this and I would have liked him to understand that I had not sought this appointment to Southampton, but that it was too good to be missed, offering me experience in management. (Incidentally, I was approached some years later, with a view to my considering a senior appointment at Selfridges in Oxford Street.)

(1) An Air Sea Rescue Launch like others captained by the author during the war.

(2) The founding of the Independent Stores' Association: the author, Gerald Bentall, Goss Grant and Roger Day, the ISA controller.
Photo by *The Drapers' Record*

(3) Welcome to Heelas of Reading by Charles Hayes the retiring managing director.

(4) The opening of the Jacqmar fabric floor at Reading in February, 1949.   Photo by John C. Thackeray

(5 & 6)   Father Christmas arriving at Reading.   Photos by C. E. May

(7 & 8) The Herne Bay store before and after the face lift. Note the early telephone number.

Earlier photo by Tower Studios

(9 & 10) The Whitstable store in normal weather before Ricemans took over and in abnormal weather afterwards.

Photos by Douglas West

(11) Part of the Deal store before the facelift.

(12) Norman Wisdom cutting the tape at the replanned and extended Deal store.   Photo by *The Drapers' Record*

(13) Felder House, Worth, the author's home near Sandwich.

(14) A presentation to Fred and Betty Riceman by the staff at Deal to commemorate
ten years in Deal. On the left is Denis Hedges, Bill Dawson on the right.

Photo by Francis Day

(15) Celebrating the topping-out of the Canterbury store during which the author persuaded the men to speed up building to allow the store to open in September as planned.

(16) The old and the new: Canterbury Cathedral looks across the city to Fred Riceman and his new store.

Photos by *Kentish Gazette*

CHAPTER SIX

BRANCH SUPERVISOR—
EDWIN JONES & CO

Fred Pope was no longer managing director of the Bon Marché, Gloucester. He had taken over larger responsibilities and was now chairman of the Drapery Trust Group of Stores of which Edwin Jones & Co formed a part. This Group later became part of Debenhams.

Mr Moat was the managing director of Edwin Jones, Southampton, and although I was to work under his direction during the two years I was with them, we only met occasionally and it was Mr Pope who took a personal interest in my responsibilities. However, he had to oversee the expansion of much larger stores, so I was left much on my own.

Apart from the reasons I have already mentioned for accepting this appointment, I am sure if it had been in the north of England I should still have done so; I had such admiration for Fred Pope that I should have been glad to take a responsible position under his direction wherever it had been. His very presence and personality seemed to inspire one to achieve success.

To be in charge of four small stores, gave me wider scope in management responsibilities, and to be free to take whatever action I felt necessary to bring them up to date, and to improve their service under every main heading— staff, merchandise, layout, display and promotion. All these came under my supervision. Little did I imagine at this time the sort of difficulties with which I would have to contend. However these were soon made clear to me when I made my first round to meet the managers.

The stores themselves were old fashioned; the managers had obviously been having an almost free hand for far too long; their expenses were out of all proportion to their turnover, and the businesses needed new life instilled into them, otherwise they would soon cease to be. My office was in the main store at Southampton, though I was to spend little time in it.

After ascertaining the facilities that were placed at my disposal for expansion of trading, which of course included expenditure on lay-out, new display windows, money for increasing stock and general improvements, I then obtained the necessary information regarding the use we could make of the main store for the system which would enable us thoroughly to control buying, selling and expenses. Apart from this, I was free to spend and act as circumstances dictated. Therefore, my first objective was to get to know the managers all of whom were old enough to be my father.

On arrival at Dunsfords, a small store in Southampton situated almost opposite Plummer Roddis, I found the manager to be a kindly person. The business had been ticking over smoothly for a number of years, but it was not large enough to justify planning any major improvements, therefore my task in this case was an easy one, particularly as he had the facilities of the main store near at hand, from which he could draw additional stock.

From my first observations I felt that the site was not suitable for operating as a department store and should be split into speciality shops. It was interesting to find that this eventually was done and dealt with as a property transaction. However, during my stay this particular store caused me no serious problems.

On arrival at Bournemouth the situation was very different. Here was an old fashioned store trading under the name of Edwin Jones & Co Ltd situated at the wrong end of the town. Though it had a large frontage, it did not attract enough business to justify large expenditure.

It was here that I met my first real problem; the manager had obviously enjoyed almost complete freedom of control for some years, and I well remember him looking at me severely as I approached him for the first time. He told me that he had been in Bournemouth for many years and had managed very well without any assistance, and he was sure the business was not going to profit because of a young man with only a few years' experience coming on the scene—not an encouraging start! However, fortunately for me, I had learned not to feel or look important on such occasions, but to give a person of this nature his head. This I did, and it enabled me to know exactly what was in his mind. I did not tell him what was in mine until our next meeting!

His attitude was not entirely unreasonable, but although he was not anticipating retirement, he was no longer young, and he had settled down far too long to find it easy to re-adjust himself to changed conditions. The store obviously needed new life and impetus; a wider stock selection, and a new interest given to the staff who, like their manager, had naturally been just ticking over in a business that had made little progress for a number of years.

Plans were already in hand for a new frontage but the building was such and the windows had been planned in such a way that they really could never do justice to the site. However, my efforts were concentrated on encouraging the manager to co-operate with me in introducing a policy that would increase the sales and popularity of the store. With patience and considerable understanding, on both sides, over a period of some weeks we were able to work together quite well. During the second year we had no trouble and were thinking along similar lines. In fact, he constantly amazed me with the helpful information that he gave me regarding merchandise in certain departments and he, in turn, appreciated the ideas I had to liven up others.

I well remember the staff training meetings we had after business hours, when he sat beside me while I addressed the staff for about twenty minutes on subjects which I hoped proved helpful and encouraging to them and to my surprise he seemed quite glad to arrange these.

A sales campaign was drawn up and, once he found that when set in motion it resulted in increased turnover, there was no difficulty in persuading him to deal with such plans on a permanent basis.

My next visit was to the Bon Marché, Poole, situated in the centre of a busy shopping community, trading on a lower level than in Bournemouth. Here we had to carry out considerable alterations to make it possible to increase turnover. The manager, though somewhat unimaginative, was reliable, and created no problems for me.

He had no fashion sense, but in other departments he had an extremely good sense of value and knew how to buy at the right price. The results of our re-planning, to bring this store into line with more progressive selling, were most encouraging.

We were unexpectedly helped by the son of the founder of a store in Bournemouth who had acquired premises with an excellent frontage only a few hundred yards from us.

My manager was very worried about this but I remember telling him it was a wonderful opportunity, and I arranged to go north with him on a big buying spree, returning with a wide range of bargains. He was not to advertise them, nor to put them in the windows until the day before the new store was opening.

I knew our competitor was going to spend a lot of money on advertising and that the crowds would be in the area, so that all we had to do was to have values in merchandise that would attract extra business. This far exceeded even my expectations and the new store helped our progress for many months to come.

The fourth store was at Weymouth. I met the manager who had been there for many years, and assured him I had come to wish him well and would be glad of any help he could give me. He later told me it had been his intention to hand in his notice to me as he was not going to be under the control of a young supervisor. However, instead of saying that, he gave me a good chicken lunch!

The two years of this appointment passed all too quickly, with no serious troubles to contend with. It was again a most helpful period to me, as I gained considerable insight into the difficulties of operating small department stores profitably.

It had never occurred to me to look for another appointment, but again the approach came from outside and, though the attraction of remaining at home was strong, I could not resist the challenge nor the terms offered. It came from

W. J. Hopton who wrote asking if we could meet; this was arranged and he surprised me by giving me full details of the responsibilities he had taken over as managing director of what he described as going to be one of London's largest stores.

After showing me the plans, and indicating to me his enthusiasm over the whole project, he asked if I would become his merchandise manager at a salary which, with bonus, was to exceed £3,000 p.a.

This was an opportunity no young man of twenty-seven could miss and, although I regretted leaving Fred Pope after only two years, I felt he would understand when I explained the position to him, as of course he did.

Having agreed on terms, I asked Mr Hopton to confirm the details in writing. He assured me that there could be no possible misunderstanding, and he asked me to arrange to start with him as soon as possible after my return from a sea trip. So the date of my leaving was arranged and a day before sailing the letter confirming my appointment arrived from John Hopton. Although the terms were quite clear in my mind, they had obviously not been clear in his; the details were quite different!

To be fair, one must assume that with all his other responsibilities at the time a genuine error had been made, but it was one that would be so costly to me that I was not prepared to allow it to pass. I therefore wrote to him outlining the terms we had verbally agreed and perhaps rather rashly added that if I did not receive a telegram by the time I sailed would he please assume that I should not be joining him on the date agreed. The telegram arrived confirming the details we had originally agreed!

I enjoyed a happy farewell from each of the stores I had been supervising and I still like to think that they were as sorry to part company with me as I certainly was to leave them.

CHAPTER SEVEN

HENRY GLAVE & CO LTD

It would be difficult to express my feelings as I approached the store to take over my new responsibilities. A rebuilding programme had commenced and there was dirt and dust all over the place. Part of the new building towered above me, and my imagination was working overtime, picturing, after a few years' hard labour, the building completed and attracting shopping crowds from near and far.

Though the new building was beginning to take shape, there were still large sections of the old remaining, and the merchandise and presentation was still in the past. It was an old fashioned business with a long frontage but insufficient depth as like many other stores of its type it had expanded by taking on additional adjoining premises which were linked together on the ground and first floors.

There was a narrow service lane at the rear, and the main part of the new store was to be erected beyond this lane as the rebuilt front section was inadequate in depth. This site later became the headquarters of the YWCA.

First of all, I had to see Mr Hopton and find out the extent of my responsibilities. Seeing him in his new office came as quite a shock. Having always pictured him in his palatial room with expensive panelling and pictures, here he was in a pokey little office looking somewhat out of place in the West End. I say this without meaning to deprecate his fine qualities, which were ideally suited to the store he had operated so successfully in Peckham; but nevertheless from the first day of my arrival at Henry Glaves, I felt that he had made a great mistake in coming to the West End.

After he had given me some idea of the expansion programme and the system he had initiated for buying, I had to settle down quickly, get to know the buyers, some of whom had been there for decades, and plan the merchandising policy in such a way as to conform to the slowly expanding premises and business, which was no easy task.

Although about half the ground floor and part of the first floor in the new building was already open for business, on completion it was planned to have seven floors. A national advertising campaign had already been commenced, mostly on the front page of the *Daily Mail* and we were beginning to attract people to the store, before we were ready to receive them, and this created its own problems.

When at Holdrons of Peckham a kindly couple had welcomed me into their home as a paying guest and now that I was returning to the West End, I contacted them once again and they were pleased to have me back.

Although I had a car, it had not entered my mind to use it frequently when starting in the West End. Travelling on the buses and the Underground gave me time to think. My early training had left its mark on me, and though I bought good clothes and do not think I was mean, I was certainly careful. It cost me little more to live during this period while I was in Oxford Street than it had done when I was working in Peckham.

The days were long and arduous, leaving Dulwich soon after 7.30 a.m. and returning home about the same time in the evenings. It was certainly a testing period and I found little time for outside interests and amusements though once again Mr and Mrs Hopton were to welcome me frequently to their home and to join them in visits to the theatre.

My responsibilities were to cover more than the merchandise. They included planning displays, advertising and much of the general management of the store. Initiating our buying policy is worth mentioning for it raised many problems which had to be dealt with; probably the most difficult was gaining the confidence and co-operation of those who had been with the old company for so many years. In particular there was Miss Grace, the buyer of the lingerie and corset departments. At first, she refused to speak to me, after having expressed the view that no one in his twenties could possibly tell her how to buy. I could understand her feelings and in large measure agreed with her, though it took me the better part of a year to gain her confidence and help, in the end it proved well worthwhile. No one could have given me better support, not only so far as her own department was concerned, but also with other senior members of the staff with whom she had considerable influence. The new buyers were a lot easier to work with.

It soon became evident to me that it was necessary to have something on in the store practically all the time. It was a new lesson for me, as the bulk of my experience in the past had depended on the merchandise to attract business and trade in each case had been largely built up by the value and selection offered.

When the main front was nearing completion, and there was a good restaurant on the top floor, much of my spare time was given to planning features that would attract the crowds. Quite a few were adaptations of those that were already being carried out in other stores but some had a distinct mark of their own. One, in particular, coincided with the opening of our fashion floor at the commencement of the spring season. We planned a Fashion Festival Fortnight, with the primary intention of filling the main part of this large floor with new potential shoppers, and to get the store talked about in the national press.

Apart from the fixtures on the walls, we turned the floor into a miniature theatre. There were seats for about 500 people plus standing room, with a stage, appropriate lighting and the usual raised platform down through the audience. There were two performances daily on five days of the week. Seats could be booked and they were usually all taken. The programme was not so much a normal fashion parade but rather special scenic displays with a tableau by the team of models.

For example, swim and beach wear would be shown against a beach background, suitable music helping to create a holiday atmosphere. I used to walk up and down with the girls, talking to the assembly, mostly women, but what I actually said, or did, I have no idea now, except it would have been to encourage sales!

I was able to obtain the help of a leading stage personality without cost, to open each show. This I managed by spending a number of evenings before the festival commenced, walking from theatre to theatre, in my evening dress and opera hat, and whenever I saw an attractive picture with a name under it, I went in and enquired about him or, mostly, her!

My next move was to get to know the stage door keeper and through him the dresser of the person I wished to see. Having once gained their co-operation it was easy. Usually I was allowed in the dressing room between scenes and in most cases managed to make arrangements for them to come for lunch or tea and help me with the opening of the show. Among these famous names were Diana Wynyard, Bobby Howes, Constance Carpenter and Merle Oberon.

On one occasion, only a few hours before the afternoon performance, a telephone message came through to me from the theatre that the star was unable to come. It had been widely advertised, all the seats were booked and I knew a dreadful situation could be created. She just had to come. I took a taxi to the theatre, found her there and discovered that she had no other engagement, neither was she indisposed—she was just terrified of making a speech! So I told her I felt far worse and invited her out to lunch in the store restaurant suggesting we should both try to forget about it. After lunch, I asked her advice as to what she felt was the best way to deal with the problem we both had. In the end she thought I should open the show, to which I replied, only if she would accompany me. She did and the result was the success that I knew we could expect with her sparkling presence.

That fortnight really helped to establish our fashion business and, given a few more years of similar expansion, I am sure we should have held our own against our competitors. The turnover of the store was now increasing and we were overcoming most of our difficulties by expanding departments and opening new ones as the space became available, at the same time improving our methods to cover security during some of the most difficult moves.

Sometimes the excitement of gradually taking over space as it becomes available in a new building is an attraction to shoppers—they want to know what is happening. However for a considerable period we suffered by selling in two buildings, new at one end and the old at the other, with steel girders in the centre part. This led me to do a foolish thing. I was in a hurry to get from an upper floor in the new building some eighty yards or more to the building at the other end. To save time I decided to take the short cut and walked carefully across the girders. I have never been too good with heights, but there was no turning back, so I kept my eyes fixed on each upright column in turn and reached the other side safely—but never again!

Towards the end of the second year I began to note a great change in John Hopton. It was quite obvious he had to have more turnover than we could possibly give him in the space that was, at that time, available.

The foundations had not even been commenced on the main building at the rear, and we were faced with being asked to cut down stocks at a time when our ranges should have been increasing, coupled with the fact that we had great difficulty in operating in a top heavy building with insufficient depth but an excellent frontal façade (which incidentally still stands out as an imposing building almost adjoining the Dominion Theatre on the north side of New Oxford Street as you leave Tottenham Court Road going towards the City). On seeing this, one would naturally expect to find something quite different inside, not just the shallow floors which were then all that was available to us. However, every effort was made to try and overcome the difficulties and everyone hoped the building programme would not be stopped. It was about this time that I was invited to address the Drapers Chamber of Trade Summer School at Oxford. It is an occasion I am not likely to forget, as it taught me a lot. My address received a very mixed reception from those who attended. The title of my subject was *Opportunities in Retail Distribution* and so far as Henry Glave was concerned, it proved a great success with good write-ups in *The Times* and several other national papers, some good but others not so complimentary.

Apart from bringing the store into the news, it did result in a number of applications for appointments, one of which came from as far away as Australia. Incidentally, about this time I was responsible for interesting two young men in entering retail distribution. Both became managing directors of prominent store groups.

Among the points I referred to was the wage structure in retail distribution and how in some cases the pay that was offered was not adequate for work expected. At the same time there were opportunities for department managers and buying appointments giving an intelligent ambitious person the chance of earning £1,000 or more a year, a fair salary for the late 1920s.

It was this reference which caused such wide interest and criticism; Percy Best was the chairman for this occasion and he even forgot to thank me for my address in his anxiety to criticise it severely, although later we became good friends. At the time he was managing director of Shoolbreds a large and well known London store which was shortly to cease trading. This was largely due to the position of the store becoming off the beaten track.

Soon after this it became evident to me that John Hopton's launching into the West End store life was to fail. I think I was even more upset about this for him and the staff who had been connected with the old establishement, than I was for myself. I knew he must have invested a considerable amount of his capital in it, and now the chairman of the company who was giving him financial backing had run into serious trouble in other directions, which meant that the resources were not available to complete his dream. He took it very well but it must have been a terrible blow to him.

After expressing my concern for him personally I asked his advice about my own future, and he thought the wisest course would be for me to leave before the store finally had to be closed. We parted but with great regret on both sides.

In spite of the trading difficulties, I must have found some favour with the staff for at a farewell meeting in the restaurant I was presented with a gold watch and a card which indicated that every member of the staff had contributed towards it. This meant a great deal to me, expecially as I was still a young man, although of course at whatever age, such a gesture is valued.

A short time before I left, Miss Grace, the buyer who had been so difficult when I joined the store and who later became one of my most loyal supporters, came to me to express her concern at the way things had worked out. She must have either saved or acquired a fair amount of capital, because she did her best to persuade me to allow her to advance me sufficient money to buy a successful and well known baby linen shop, trading in large premises in Oxford Street.

As she was likely to be retiring in the near future, I felt that the financial risk was too great for her, though I would very much have liked to take advantage of her offer. I add this little postscript as an indication of the happy and helpful relationship that we had established after all.

So ended another chapter in my business life. I never anticipated this would be for such short duration when I took over my responsibilities with Mr Hopton for the second time some two and a half years earlier.

CHAPTER EIGHT

AIDS TO SUCCESS

About this time (1930) I was beginning to realise that hard work alone would not ensure success. I had been fortunate in obtaining key appointments that offered me scope and salaries well above the expected rate for my age but my knowledge of the basic principles of retailing that ensured success was limited. So, I set out to find the qualities which anyone out to succeed should strive to possess. They might well be termed quick lines to success. They included:—

Honesty: in buying, selling and advertising.

The Seeing Eye: To develop the natural aptitude of walking round any store, window displays or studying advertisements to see anything wrong, out of place or worthy of note. This is a quality in management that is often overlooked. Yet no store can operate at its best without alert management which in turn encourages staff right down the line to be on their toes.

Ideas: The success of many a business both in manufacturing and distribution has to a large extent succeeded because of the bright ideas that have supported products or merchandising standards. It is too easy for management to settle down and live on its past records, instead of attracting new ideas that encourage the development of new life and continued progress.

Friend makers. Sometimes people reaching management level become elusive, difficult to approach. At worst they attract dragon type secretaries that keep everyone at bay. The most successful key men and women in business are approachable. This can prove invaluable both with anyone associated in the business as well as with suppliers and potential customers.

Vision: Seeing ahead, not just living in the present. This is not only all important in the realm of fashion, but also most aspects connected with management of a successful store.

Enthusiasm: When a project is good, whether it be a promotion, new merchandise or any idea that would encourage expansion of profitable trading, management must tackle it with enthusism. This has to be fired from the top.

Energy: It was said of Gordon Selfridge in his young days, though his ideas roused opposition, that the pace of his energy was such as to flatten any such opposition out of existence, earning him the store's nickname of "Mile-a-minute-Harry".

These qualities are all essential attributes to success but they have to be supported by knowledge of merchandise and financial control, study of world markets, and the most effective methods of buying and selling.

In my personal training scheme I realised that the more I could learn from the success or failure of others, the better chance I would have of promotion so I set out to study the lives of early pioneers in the development of stores in the second half of the last century and the early part of this century. How some had failed, not because of bad management but because the store was in the wrong position or a movement of interests, transport, etc., had lessened the trading potential and so the store had either to cease operating or move to another site.

The successful development of stores in this country and in America intrigued me. Some had started with one shop on a prime corner site and had grown step by step acquiring adjoining premises. J. E. Beale of Bournemouth was just one example. For a year or more on my return to Bournemouth, as he lived just around the corner from my parents, I used to drive him and his wife on Sunday mornings to Richmond Hill Congregational Church where he and his family were active members. The way he had developed his business so that he could retire around fifty intrigued me. When my father bought his first car from a garage in Pokesdown the manager complained that Mr Beale had opened a shop for car and cycle accessories in competition with him and other garages; as new departments were added to the developing Beale store, which had started with gifts, toys and trinkets, others affected by this new form of competition no doubt joined in complaining. Mr Beale won through successfully and his efforts helped to make Bournemouth an attractive holiday resort. Whenever I had the opportunity of meeting anyone who had contributed to the development of a successful family controlled store, I tried to learn from them how their business had started, and what they were doing to secure its continued success.

All this led me to think back further to the earlier forms of distributors. I prepared a talk under the title of "Distribution through the Ages" and the following is the basis of the notes I made. Unfortunately, I omitted to record the sources from which I obtained my information but I believe some were from the writings of Gordon Selfridge and also Herbert Casson.

CHAPTER NINE

DISTRIBUTION THROUGH THE AGES

Notes for a talk I gave at Henry Glave

Production and distribution is taken very much for granted by the average person today. All that matters is securing what is wanted without difficulty and at a reasonable price. Where it comes from and how it is made is not of much consequence. Yet the story of the development of production and distribution through the ages up to the present time makes an exciting story.

From our earliest historical records, trade and barter has been associated with the lives of all nations. Every nation and nearly ever person in them has something someone else wants, and they are willing to part with it at a price, so all men become traders.

We confine the title of traders to those who buy and sell goods but surely the scientist, the writer, the artist, the lawyer, the doctor and the statesman are all traders—they part with their knowledge and their work for a consideration and if they did not do so, the wheels of life could not revolve. The dignity of business in whatever direction it is conducted is judged by the manner in which it is carried out.

Adam Smith wrote about 250 years ago that "All original wealth comes from the soil"—hard work upon it brings rich crops but it is the wheels of commerce that turn the golden harvest into golden coin or its equivalent.

It is one thing to produce; it is quite a different thing to create a demand for what you have produced. Many fine inventions and ideas have been scoffed at by the crowd. The inventor often being treated as a criminal, imprisoned, hampered at every turn and sometimes killed, the ideas being looked upon as evil magic. It was the commercial instincts in men that eventually overcame the incredulity of the ignorant crowd. However, the crowd is no longer ignorant, and in the world's struggle for truth, our ideas must keep ahead of the masses.

It is not the crowd alone that has held back the commerce that brings wealth to a nation. History tells of kings, rulers and governments who have also restricted the activities of men who would bring them progress, not by conquest of arms, but by trading. Commerce has often developed in spite of foolish legislation. The cause of such restrictive laws is the old story of meanness, jealousies and fear of change. Human weaknesses are much the same, but fear of change is no longer a problem. Our problem now is to see that change is for the better.

DISTRIBUTION THROUGH THE AGES

Trading does not mean getting the better of others, though there are always those who will abuse it in this way and thrive on it for a time, but these low standards never survive for long. History proves that the most successful traders have been the honest traders who believe in the practice of the golden rule, whose integrity has been backed with imagination, courage and drive.

What was it that made Britain great? It was our merchant adventurers, supported by craftsmanship the like of which was not to be found elsewhere in the world. We must not forget the lessons of our bold forefathers. We need to recapture the spirit of the old merchant adventurers. It is not enough just to be free from controls, we also need to be possessed with their bold and imaginative spirit.

Cheap, shoddy and ordinary goods for home or export will never bring a higher standard of living to our people. Our designers and producers must be encouraged to think of making something new in the field of colour, fashion, power, transport, something exciting—with the old stamp of reliability and quality. *Made In Britain* was for centuries a welcome sign all over the world—it must be so today. If the fine old spirit is maintained, then we, as a people, shall not want.

The story of commerce through the ancient civilisations, and how it has progressed through the ages under the leadership of merchant adventurers, makes an interesting and at times exciting study against the background of modern distribution.

CHINA

When we look into the distant past, we, of course, think of China. These oriental people were trading before we were cave men. If they had not been the most conservative people in the world, they might have become richer and happier.

Many of our modern inventions are not new; the Chinese thought of them thousands of years ago and then forgot them. Printing and the mariner's compass are just two examples.

They could have had department stores before Britain was born but they were content to go on in the same old way. They had inventive minds, but they kept their discoveries to themselves—they had no merchant adventurers.

4,700 years is a long time ago. Then China was far ahead of any other country in the world. A wonderful discovery was made about that time by the emperor and his wife, Hwang Ti and Lui Tsu. Their discovery has been the delight of lords and ladies all down the ages—the use of the silkworm.

Silkworms had spun their little sleeping robes for many years but nobody had taken any notice until Lui Tsu (called the Goddess of the Silkworm), with the aid of her husband, found how to unwrap the silk from the cocoons and make beautiful fabrics.

Though civilisation advanced in other parts of the world and traders began to move between countries and continents, the Chinese kept this discovery to themselves for about 2,300 years. Then Alexander captured great quantities of silk and had it taken to his palaces in Greece and Macedonia.

China introduced standardised currency about 600 BC and mined gold, copper and tin about 1800 BC. While China was holding back from trading abroad, other smaller nations were getting busy.

It is said that civilisation sprang from that great territory east of the Mediterranean, which was inhabited by some wonderful races and some progressive countries. We will first take a glimpse at two.

BABYLON

Under Nebuchadnezzar II and his successors Babylon became a great trading centre. It covered an area of up to 200 square miles, filled with multi-storeyed houses, beautiful palaces and wonderful gardens, among which were the famous hanging gardens which were one of the seven wonders of the world. Their height has been recorded as 335 feet and 85 feet wide.

The amazing city filled with so many wonders was built up from the wealth derived from agriculture and trade. The soil was so fertile that farmers raised three crops a year.

Their trading spirit led their merchants to take long caravan expeditions, carrying articles of necessity and bringing back new found treasurers. It is recorded they went as far as India and competed with that masterly little race the Phoenicians.

PHOENICIANS

These hardy and venturesome people were the first great systematic traders in the world. They were not only successful inventors but they were also adept at making use of the inventions of others. Their home was 200 miles of the coast on the eastern shores of the Mediterranean, with a depth of up to thirty miles. In this little land they built the cities of Tyre and Sidon. They were specially famed for the art of dyeing fabrics, the dyes being obtained from shell fish found off Tyre in the Mediterranean. They also made beautiful glassware and pottery.

They sailed the seas, even through the Pillars of Hercules (Gibraltar), across the Bay of Biscay to the Tin Islands (now the Scilly Isles) and to Cornwall for tin. It is said they circumnavigated Africa 2,000 years before Vasco da Gama.

They sailed without charts to discover goods for their market places. They did it without the sword; they became rich through trade, they were friend makers; they were the chief contractors for Solomon's Temple; they provided the shipping facilities for the Egyptian traders. One writer has said of them, "They won their great reputation by always giving full weight and measure and setting the highest standards for quality. Success was theirs by right of commercial conquest, not by war."

Isaiah (23 viii) spoke of her traffickers as "the honourable of the earth" . . . and Ezekiel (28) gives a good description of the trade of the "city of beauty that dwells by the sea".

This small nation prospered for over 2,000 years but their wealth was, in the end, too much for them and they ceased to trade, their shores became barren and their cities were no more.

GREECE

Now let us cross the Mediterranean and look at Greece. We think of Greece in terms of her orators, writers, philosophers, sculptors, architects and statesmen. These gifted leaders and artists set standards which, in many directions, this twentieth century has failed to equal. Yet Greece's foundations would have been weak without her commerce though she did not have the enterprising merchant adventurers of the Phoenicians.

Plato himself made reference to the place of trade in the structure of a city and in his sayings we find this reference, "The first and greatest want is provision of food; the second, lodging; the third, clothing." Then he includes a list of various occupations which form the background of distribution, thus: "In the city itself how will they exchange with one another what each has produced? They will do so by *buying* and *selling* . . . a market place and an established coinage as a symbol for the purpose of exchange must spring up from hence."

Their markets conformed to a set design, rather like that of a chess board. It is surprising that such architecturally-minded people, who proved themselves capable of setting standards which we have been unable to equal, should not have applied these to their commerce. With the wide range of merchandise they had for distribution, they did not provide the Greeks with stores as we now know them. Perhaps this was partly due to the climatic conditions?

A few hundred years BC she had her trading centres, or small colonies as we would now call them, as far away as Spain and also on the present site of Marseilles. Her navigators were skilful and her mercantile laws were outstanding for those days. Her business principles were recognised to be so high and sound that rich merchants from other countries sent their sons there to learn the art of trade.

Quite a number of well-known Grecian personalities or their families were connected with trade. The father of Socrates owned a flute factory; the mother of Euripides was a grocer, and Solon the law-giver was himself a commercial traveller. After he had composed his famous code he left Athens on a ten year journey with two objects in mind (i) to persuade people to try out and appreciate the value of his laws, and (ii) to sell oil.

ITALY

In this fleeting glimpse of long ago, place must be given to the people of Italy and the one-time Roman Empire. Although the Romans occupied these islands for some 450 years, they never settled here. Theirs was a military occupation and the occupational force was continually changing—unlike the skilled refugees from the Netherlands in Elizabethan times who settled in Norwich and helped the development of the cloth trade, or the German miners who commenced mining copper in the remote parts of the Lake District.

From the ninth to the fifteenth centuries, trade played a prominent part. Venice, Florence and Milan in the north, and Naples in the south were the key cities that brought to Italy the distinction of being known during this period as the mistress of the world's commerce.

The development of Venice dates back as far as the fifth century. The Venetians gained the reputation of not only working conscientiously for themselves but also for the city they loved.

As Europe developed, these traders, gifted with the art of collecting, exchanging, financing and distributing the merchandise that the people wanted, both at home and abroad, had connections with all parts of the civilised world.

Giovanni and his sons Cosimo and Lorenzo dei Medici, were one family whose remarkable trading gifts not only enriched the Mediterranean cities, but also many other trading centres as well. Possibly no single family has ever gained such authority and power as did the Medicis and they did it through their ability, courage and enterprise.

Integrity was woven into the very foundation of their house and their wealth was wisely and intelligently controlled.

Giovanni was the real founder of the House of Medici, and in the early part of the fifteenth century he had his agencies all over the civilized world, including Constantinople, France and England.

The Medici arms are still a familiar sign in many countries today. Three of their six golden balls hang over the entrance to pawnbrokers' shops.

The Medici headquarters were in Florence which made it the richest of the Italian cities. They dealt in all types of merchandise, but finance was the main pillar of their commercial enterprises.

During the Middle Ages certain traders in Northern Europe were first in the field of co-operating to protect their own interests. They were suffering through action by overbearing kings; then there were robbers by land and pirates by sea—so the Hanseatic League came into being, and for over three centuries it was the most powerful of the old combinations of merchants for the control of commerce.

The Hansa towns in the twelfth and thirteenth centuries were Hamburg, Bremen, Cologne, Wismore, Lubeck and later Antwerp.

Now to bring the story nearer home, let us note the development of the methods of retail distribution in this country.

The merchant has always had to deal with the problem of how to acquire his goods and then how best he can reach his public for distribution.

Before the introduction or modern transport, when journeys had to be made on horse-back, on foot, or in small boats, each of which was accompanied by dangers, the problem was not easy.

Each small town had its individual craftsmen and in rural villages they produced their own food, and almost all their clothing, furniture and farm implements were home-made either by peasant or by village craftsmen.

As the mediaeval age ended (about the fifteenth century), new opportunities opened up for enterprising traders. Fashion played an important part—for once it was in menswear. The change in men's outlook was reflected in their change of dress. Chaucer, like Dante, was still clothed in the dignified long gown and plain hood, but those of Chaucer's fashionable contemporaries, who could afford it, abandoned the gown for a short coat and jacket and tight fitting trousers or hosen, thus introducing for the first time our present familiar coat and trousers—but by no means as drab and monotonous as they were earlier this century. They enjoyed bright colours. Some of the more conservative men still continued with their gowns, until the Tudor period some two centuries later.

With the change in fashion, more comfort was introduced into the home and this increase in luxury meant an increase in trade. The merchants of the time must have rejoiced at the possibilities opening up before them in the field of fashion, furniture and even food; and incidentally, the extravagances of the feudal lords helped the rise of the trading community.

The growth of the cloth trade was of paramount importance to the merchants from about the thirteenth century. In Chaucer's time (fourteenth century) the production of broadcloth in England was trebled. The enormous advantage that England had over other countries as the producer of the best wool gave her merchants the opportunity to command the pick of the world's cloth market, as she had for previous centuries commanded the European market for raw wool.

This development which took second place to agriculture created new classes in town and country, adding to the luxury of the manor house, at the same time relieving the poverty of the cottage.

The cloth trade held such an important part in the life of the community that our speech and literature acquired many phrases and metaphors which were taken from the manufacture of cloth, e.g. spin a yarn, unravel a mystery, web of life, finedrawn, home spun, thread of discourse, while all unmarried women were called spinsters.

FAIRS

Fairs played an important part in distribution. I have been unable to obtain any certain knowledge of when they were introduced into England, though they go back as far as Alfred the Great who helped commerce and encouraged fairs.

Henry I granted to the citizens of London, that they should be free of tolls throughout England when they were going to sell at fairs.

In the Magna Carta, King John was forced against his will to agree that, "Merchants shall have safety to go and come, buy and sell without evil tolls, but by honest and ancient custom."

Thus in England, as already on the continent, fairs became the market place for the exchange and distribution of merchandise. Many fairs were actually religious in origin but commercial in practice and nearly every county had at least one annual event. Some fairs continued for many weeks.

During the famous fair at St Giles at Winchester which lasted sixteen days, all trading in every other place within seven miles' radius was prohibited.

Fairs were generally held in large tents, erected in rows so as to form streets. Many of the traders were foreigners and every kind of known commodity could be purchased at them; kings, princes and barons sent their agents to them.

There were the Bartholomew Fair of Smithfields, the Sturbridge Fair near Cambridge and many others. The Sturbridge Fair traded from the twelfth century but as the primitive methods of lighting gave way to gas and electricity and the stage coach to the train, so the methods of distribution changed and the fairs had to give way to a more permanent form of distribution. The Sturbridge Fair lingered on until 1882.

During the fifteenth and sixteenth centuries, the government of London was conducted largely by the members of the great merchant companies or guilds—the mercers, grocers, drapers and to a lesser extent the fishmongers and goldsmiths and nearly all the mayors and aldermen of London came from these great companies.

William Caxton was a member of the Honourable Company of Mercers and he made enough money during thirty years trading to be able to retire from business and devote his later years to literary pursuits. It was then that he discovered the new mystery of printing with movable types. In 1476 he set up the first printing press in England at Westminster.

Out of these stories of the past we find that early in the nineteenth century retail distribution was still being carried on in small shops, each confining themselves to a particular type of business. Retail trading under these conditions was in consequence at this time considered a petty and insignificant type of trading carrying with it little risk, little profit and needing limited ability; so shopkeepers during the early part of the century were considered to be low in the social scale.

Dickens gives a good illustration of this in *Pickwick Papers* when he depicts the visit of Mr Tracy Tupman and the Stranger (Mr Jingle) to the charity ball at Rochester:

> "Wait a minute" said the stranger, "Fun presently—nobs not come yet—queer place. Dock-yard people of upper rank don't know Dock-yard people of lower rank, Dock-yard people of lower rank don't know small gentry—small gentry don't know tradespeople . . .

That was how Dickens summed up the social standing of the tradespeople of his time.

This standing continued until a few shopkeepers with imagination supported by a return of the spirit of the old merchant adventurers, felt the public could be better served by taking on additional shops and carrying different types of merchandise, and at the same time improving their method of distribution. So the idea of the modern store in its early stages appeared.

Curiously enough the idea took effect in Paris, London, New York and Boston about the same time. In Paris, the Bon Marché was opened in the early 1850s.

In London, Shoolbreds was functioning as a store in the early 1850s and Hitchcock & Rogers, later Hitchcock & Williams, and a few other city houses were trading as small fashion stores during the same period; these later became wholesale businesses. Quite a number of our modern stores were in being as small shops a century ago.

In New York R.H. Macy's was founded in 1858 and A. T. Stewart's also about the same time. Incidentally Macy's started as a fancy goods store. In Boston Jordan Marsh was established as a store in 1858.

The greatest progress had, however, been made during this present century when stores have come into being in all our large cities and towns and they now offer the public enjoyment, service and advice.

The spirit of the old merchant adventurers still lives on in us as a people and you will find it expressed in many ways as the years pass.

The British public will never be satisfied with a stereotyped form of distribution. They look for change and variety to support the ever changing pattern of goods produced in our twentieth century factories and they will welcome new forms and settings for distribution that will make the most of the wonderful variety of every conceivable product that appeals to the discerning shopper—and those who have chosen retail distribution as a career will see that the public are not disappointed.

CHAPTER TEN

An Interlude And Its Lessons

There had been little time for thought about my future as I had worked at full pressure until the day of my departure from Henry Glaves. The time had come for me to find an appointment that offered scope, where I could settle down permanently; there had been enough moving about to gain more experience.

Our trading conditions in the West End had been hard but they had given me confidence in myself. There would always be much for me to learn in the constant challenge which was to be found in retail distribution. It never entered my mind that a suitable opening would not be found. It proved to be a month or more, however, before successful arrangements were completed and the experience during this period was quite enlightening. There were several possibilities for me to think about.

1. A business of my own—already the idea was formulating in my mind. It would have given me great pleasure to operate a small business which offered scope for development. So, like many other optimistic young men, I went to two leading agents and obtained a folder with particulars of small businesses that were in the market. On selecting one, in North London, I fortunately had the sense to consult a distant relative who had experience in this field and he joined me in going to see the business which on paper looked to be of interest.

It did not take him five minutes to convince me that I was not, at that time, properly equipped to launch out on my own, nor was the proposition all that exciting when examined in detail. Though it was a tempting idea, it had to be given up at least for the time being. I realised that to start a business I needed more experience and more money than I had saved.

2. So my mind turned to a management appointment in a department store and I went to see Sir Sidney Skinner again, for his advice. There was no difficulty in arranging a meeting, and in spite of his being such a busy person who met so many people, he remembered me from our first meeting and had also noted, with interest, some of the moves I had made since leaving Barkers.

The thirty minutes or so I spent with him were most helpful. It intrigued me at the time to try and discern the purpose of his detailed questioning of both my experience and my hopes for the future. He was not the only one who started off by saying, "You are far too young to have been merchandise manager of a West End store." I agreed with him!

However, he was encouraging and helpful, and I had what may have been a rare experience, when he related to me some of the difficulties he, in turn, had had to contend with when he was a young man and how he had to fight his way up step by step.

I had no intention of returning to Barkers, and I think he must have guessed this, for towards the end of our chat he bluntly told me, "There is no opening for you here at Barkers". Having made this rather severe statement, he went on to say that it was not made out of disrespect but because he felt I might find a more suitable appointment elsewhere.

He then added these words, which greatly surprised me and which I have since often recalled: "Riceman, if I had £150,000 to spare, I would make out a cheque for you now, and you could go and buy a business with my approval, and run it under your own name."

I was then just twenty-nine, some twenty years before this dream was to come true. As we parted, I felt I was privileged to know one of the most outstanding and vigorous personalities in retail distribution who contributed much to the establishment of our modern department stores in this country.

3.   My next meeting arose as a result of an invitation received from the chairman and managing director of a large well known department store and an appointment for 4 p.m. was fixed on an agreed date.

Arriving early to have time to have a look round the windows and departments, I was impressed with everything I saw; it was evident the management was keen and progressive and a note of anticipation of further expansion was in the air. As four o'clock was approaching I made myself known to his secretary. She proved to be a very good introduction to the person I was later to meet. Though she offered me a seat there was no indication that I would be shown into his office for some time to come. He was attending an important meeting, she told me, and she was uncertain as to whether he would be able to see me at all. I pointed out that, as I had come at his request, he must have wanted to see me and therefore I would wait. Without receiving any apology or explanation for the delay I waited for well over an hour before his secretary returned to say that Mr X was free but he could only spare me a few minutes.

On entering the large office, I saw plans spread over the table and desk and was confronted by a dynamic personality whose mind seemed to be far away from any useful discussion with me. He did not offer me a seat nor even a word of welcome, and I remember feeling that, however successful this genius was, I was not the type to work with him—so I told him so, adding that I was amazed that somebody of his standing should have requested someone to see him at a given time, and then after an hour's delay not even apologise or have the courtesy to offer him a seat. However, as he was so busy, I would not trouble him any further.

Instead of taking offence, he immediately gave me an insight into the more charming side of his character, which was quite illuminating. From that moment on, I was offered every courtesy and shown the plans of an expanding business by the master of all that was taking place who would never find himself in the predicament of my good friend at Henry Glaves. Anyone with ability who joined this company could anticipate a successful future. Indeed, looking back over the years and having met others like him since, I now feel confident that I should have been happy and successful with him. He offered me a good executive appointment but ultimately I turned it down, as two other more interesting openings came quite unexpectedly my way.

4. While at Glaves, I had listened with interest on more than one occasion to talks given by Sir Frederick Marquis who later became Lord Woolton. Here was a gifted man, largely responsible for the development of the Lewis Group of stores in the north of England. On my buying visits up north I always allowed time to see these stores in either Manchester or Liverpool. This led me to write to him, and to my surprise he replied saying he would be pleased to see me at his London office. This was my first personal meeting with him and from the moment we shook hands, I felt he was a man I should be proud to be associated with. Again I was closely questioned as to my past experience and future hopes. Though he expressed surprise at some of the appointments I had held, he did not attempt to belittle them, or to question my apparent inadequacy through age to justify having held them.

However, he made it clear to me that I could not expect to start at the top in one of his stores, for they had a strict ruling that all general managers had to work their way up from a lower level. My reply to this was, "Although I have much to learn, I do feel that I have reached the stage where I could expect to find an appointment as a deputy to a general manager, or merchandise director, with a view to promotion if my efforts proved successful."

It was evident that this raised a problem for him, but he indicated that he would give careful thought to the points we had discussed together and see if he could find me an opening which might be of interest.

5. After this interview I returned to my parents in Bournemouth as they were naturally interested in what I was planning for the future. As usual, I visited the family store with which I had such happy connections, and it so happened that one of the Beales (at that time there were four brothers controlling their two businesses) asked if I would like to come and have a word with them when they met the following day. This I was glad to do, though not expecting it to be more than a pleasant talk on what had happened since I had

left them and the progress they had made.

This, naturally, formed the first part of our conversation. Then one of them put an unexpected question to me, "And what do you think of Bealesons?" to which I replied, "Well, I think there is room for improvement."

"Can you give us some indication of what you mean by this?" So I tried to indicate that they needed to introduce a more progressive sales policy, and that I had been surprised to see that an advertisement in the local paper of some days previous had advertised they had *Fifty only of a special offer of blouses @ 5/11d each* and that the previous evening the same advertisement appeared giving the same number of blouses. I thought it was unwise to let the public know that the first advertisement had entirely failed in its objective!

Whether this was the case or not, it started an interesting discussion. The outcome was an invitation to a further meeting the next day, when I was asked whether I would consider returning to them. Now this needed careful thought because it is not always wise to return to a business where you have started your training. Further it might be some time before sufficient progress could be made in this particular business to justify receiving what I then looked upon as a reasonable income.

However, it was a great temptation to return home once again and to the many friends I had in Bournemouth. The salary I was offered was smaller than I had received for many years—only £400 p.a. but it was understood that as the business progressed this would improve, and also I would receive an interest in the increased turnover and profits. I then asked if apart from being general manager, would they be prepared at a later date to consider my becoming a director? They saw no reason against this, if everything worked out according to plan.

Being single, the first objective in my mind was not necessarily money, and I had managed to save a reasonable amount during the previous four to five years, so I gladly accepted their proposal. Indeed, I like to feel I still have the same friendly link with them to this day, that we forged over the coming years.

The following day, after agreeing to their proposals, I received a letter from Sir Frederick Marquis, telling me he had found a way out of the problem which had arisen from our discussions, and he was prepared to offer me an appointment as assistant general manager in a store under their control, which did not operate under the name of Lewis. As it so happened, their ruling did not apply to this particular store.

The commencing salary was £2,000 per annum plus bonus, so I did sacrifice a considerable amount by returning to Bournemouth, but I never regretted it.

CHAPTER ELEVEN

FULL CIRCLE

Perhaps it was the thrill of returning home that accounted for my overlooking some of the difficulties. However, I was soon to find them out.

Reference has already been made in an earlier chapter to the unique department store, Beales, that the Beale family had built up in Bournemouth. It had so many distinctive trading features which had not appeared elsewhere in this country.

Some of their most successful departments in the twenties and early thirties were those which are often the weakest, and all too often, unprofitable sections in many other establishments; included among these were toys, games, sports goods, stationery, books, printing and book binding, wool and art needlework.

Bealesons, on the other hand, though operated by the same family was not, at the time, so distinctive or successful.

In fact, great care had been taken to see that it was run entirely separately, and there was no buying link or shared information in the field of merchandise between them. The trading potential of this company was nowhere near as good as that of the parent company.

Then again, I was still young with much to learn and I was returning to a store where I was known from my apprenticeship days. Fortunately, this did not create any problems, though I half expected it would as a few of the sales staff who had given me instruction were still in their same positions. I made certain that the blanket cupboard was no longer available for mid-day rests!

No one could have received fairer treatment than I did from Herbert and Harold Beale, the two resident family directors. Herbert concentrated his attention on general administration and maintenance. Apart from this he was also responsible for the rebuilding of the main store between the two wars and I was intrigued with a large scale model he built of it, I believe out of matchboxes. Harold Beale for his part, gave most of his time to merchandising

The first year was, naturally, a difficult one. Big changes under every heading were long overdue, including merchandise, display, and general promotion.

I did not know whether I was being too careful, or whether friendly persuasion kept me from moving too quickly, or, more likely, the general slump in trading at that time was the cause; any way after the first full year's trading, the results proved to be one of the worst they had ever experienced since acquiring the business! I remember we all took a percentage cut in salary from the managing director to the lowest paid assistant.

It never occurred to me that we would not succeed, or that I might be requested to leave. We pressed on with our new programme and the second and third years began to show marked improvement.

Our buying methods improved, we cut our losses on our furnishing workshops, where too much had been spent in dealing with unprofitable contracts, often at the loss and expense of normal trading. We were not big enough to handle both satisfactorily.

February, as in most stores, was the worst month of the year, and we decided to promote a fourteen-day household event for which large purchases had to be made; this attracted much business where previously staff had been stood off during a normally quiet period. On returning from one buying trip to the north, I remember reporting that we would need at least ten sales people in the overall department for the first day of the event—whereas normally one was more than necessary. As it proved, we did need them for the value and price of the overalls offered must have been exceptional for the result surprised even myself.

It became normal procedure to travel to London, Witney, the midlands and Belfast on frequent occasions so that we could remain in the forefront in offering values which began to make us more widely talked about as a store.

On one occasion I learned the lesson that you can offer goods at too low a price. We had sold quantities of bedroom suites at £8.19.6d and £12.19.6d upwards, but I thought if only we could get one at £6.19.6d, we would have a tremendous queue.

This was not an easy matter, and required considerable negotiating and adjustments with purchases of other numbers in similar furniture to make it possible; anyway we offered one hundred at this ridiculous price, and it took us some months to sell them! They were, however, indirectly responsible for enabling us to sell a considerably increased number of higher priced suites.

We paid special attention to a Christmas attraction each year, always something different. Though I thought out the main scheme, the credit for the final results should be spread among a number of enthusiastic helpers.

The results attracted large crowds to the store and were in no small measure responsible for the increased turnover during this busy shopping season. I will mention only three of these, as they were rather different to anything which was normally presented in a department store.

The first was an interesting and instructive feature *With Scott to the South Pole*. It told the story in scenic displays, and took some minutes to pass through—with Father Christmas, of course, waiting at the end.

The second was bolder, and it would be difficult to describe the reaction of the four Beale directors when the proposals were put before them. They certainly were long suffering with me, for they allowed me a free hand. I cannot imagine the principals of other family businesses doing so!

Anyway, I was responsible for cutting a hole in the roof with a temporary roof above down through the floors at various angles, so that we finally had an alpine slide, which commenced on the roof, through the second floor and terminated on the lower ground floor.

It was well constructed and a local firm of shopfitters made frames for us, which after positioning at the required angles from the top to the bottom (there were sharp corners to turn) on which were placed ceiling battens running from top to bottom covered in white lino, the latter being laid from the bottom to the top and then highly polished.

There were scenes on the way down and at the parts where there were steep slopes and equally sharp corners, there were mirrors to add to the excitement. The fact that 42,000 travelled down the slide during the first season (and more adults than children!) indicated that it was a success. One party of soldiers used to come in from the Wareham area most Saturdays to go on it! There were no accidents during the two seasons in which it operated, and only one complaint — a laddered stocking!

Seldom have I been able to introduce an attraction to exceed the draw of this one. On a busy Saturday it was quite an undertaking for those at the exit, stationed on the lower ground floor, to take the passengers off the run before those following caught up with them.

Then there was Chipperfield's Circus. I happened to come into contact with Dick Chipperfield, and at that time he specialised in the handling of lions. I persuaded him to come to us for about five weeks. So we had a real live circus in our despatch department at the rear of the store. The seating was arranged around the big cage and accommodated about 500 people. This was more difficult to control, as it necessitated handling queues of people ready to go in for each fifty minute performance, and on a busy Saturday this created serious problems. Another difficulty was the noise that the lions occasionally made at night which frightened local residents but we managed to get by. Although I would not attempt to repeat this particular attraction, it was a wonderful way of bringing us into the news.

Then tragedy came to the business. One afternoon Herbert Beale asked if I would see that everything was all right, as he was not feeling too well, and was going home but he was sure he would be better in the morning. One of his delights was his car and I remember he took details home with him of a new one he was intending to buy. We never met again; in spite of the best medical advice which was available he died within a few days.

Being a family business, this was a great shock to us all, particularly to his brother Harold, and to me as I had really begun to feel one of the family. Inevitably this brought us closer together and we shared the responsibility of running the store which proved to be a happy association.

In the hope of easing Harold's sense of loss I suggested that we should buy a small cruiser. To my surprise he jumped at the idea, and for the next few years until I was married, we had great times together at sea, in Christchurch Harbour, and later in Poole Harbour. The dual ownership worked splendidly; he was chief engineer and I was usually navigator. A unique understanding developed between us, and I felt that my future was tied up with the Beale family.

The hard work that had been put into the business over the previous years was now beginning to take effect and the trading results started to increase and this was encouraging to us both. I was learning fast in the hard school of experience.

The Beale family kept their promise, and without any persuasion from me I was made a director, at which time it meant a great deal to me and they were equally generous in the remuneration I received.

An amusing incident occurred in the early thirties which indicates how often the almost impossible can be achieved if one has confidence and the nerve to try hard enough.

The Beale family gave all the staff a Christmas party at the Pavilion, Bournemouth. It was a great occasion with a good meal, sometimes light entertainment and an excellent band to lead the dancing. There was always an interval for prize giving.

It so happened on the evening in question someone came to us early in the proceedings telling us that the traffic was held up outside as the crowds were so large to see Jessie Matthews who was appearing at the Regent Cinema opposite. This gave me an idea! I put it to Harold Beale. How about getting Jessie Matthews to present our prizes. This shook him and he replied to the effect that we could never get her. I said I would have a go and if I returned with her would he see she was suitably welcomed and entertained. I am sure he didn't think for a moment this was probable as we knew the Regent Cinema management was paying a lot to get her and we would never get them to agree to release her—however, he humoured me, and wished me luck.

My evening tails, white front and white carnation were a help for although the road outside was packed with people and the police and commissionaires were in force at the doors they must have mistaken me for one of the management for they made a passageway for me to get into the cinema where every seat was taken and people were standing all around. However no one stopped me so I quietly worked my way through to the entrance at the rear of the stage to the dressing rooms behind. I soon found the special one allocated to their star visitor—who fortunately had already made her appearance.

I knocked on her door and found her alone. I welcomed her, telling her how pleased we were to have her in Bournemouth and that there was a big crowd at the Pavilion who would be just thrilled to see her. How would she like to pop over and say hello and present their prizes. I would see her safely there and back. She came, entering into the fun of the surprise and I might have been the mayor conducting her through the crowds with the cheers of a delighted public following us. Her manager and the cinema management were not so keen but with her help they were appeased as I promised to see she soon returned.

She received a tremendous welcome from the staff and of course from the Beale family. She presented the prizes, danced with Harold Beale and myself before returning to the Regent Cinema. I can't remember what Harold Beale said when I introduced Jessie Matthews to him, but I am sure it was fitting for the occasion!

To be part of a happy family is one of the best aids to success. For me it started at our wedding at Richmond Hill Congregational Church, Bournemouth in September 1936. There were over 700 in the congregation —personal friends and friends from church and business. Many favoured us by travelling long distances to give us a good send off. The wedding ceremony was led by that great preacher and spiritual leader, Rev Dr J D Jones, MA, PhD, CH.

My wife, Betty, and I had met some eight months previously when I had shown her and her mother into a seat at morning service. It never occurred to us there was anything more to it than that. It was a month or two later when we had both been persuaded to attend a meeting to which neither of us was keen to go, but out of consideration for the speaker we did. Betty was with the Abbott girls (whom I knew); I sat in front of them and after the meeting I was introduced. I casually mentioned I was riding the next afternoon in the New Forest and asked if any of them would like to come. My wife to be couldn't refuse anything to do with horses and she was the only one who accepted my invitation, so a weekly engagement followed and I soon realised how wise I had been to wait until I was thirty-one to find the right partner.

Our family tree on both sides was an interesting one but suffice it to say as soon as I met my future parents-in-law, Dr and Mrs Vincent Howell, I treasured them. He was a wonderful doctor gifted at diagnosing and she was a lovely person who soon became set on seeing our marriage was launched successfully.

We have always been fortunate in our homes, first of which was "The Moorings". Having saved enough money to buy the furniture with £800 over I had difficulty in persuading the builder who was starting a new block of houses at Ferndown surrounded by heather. This proved a problem as the builder required £1,000 and I did not intend to borrow, so I pointed out to him that this was the first of a large building venture and if it was occupied and the garden laid out, it would help as an introduction to the others, as a result of which he eventually let me have it for my £800. So we had no capital left but we had our first home which was a happy one.

Trading results for this year of 1936 continued to be encouraging. One of the grandsons was soon to enter the business; he was John Beale and in my own age group. This presented no problem as he was to go to the parent store, Beales. However, at the end of this period I saw the possibility of my happy link with this family not proving to be permanent, for within the next five years, there was likely to be another three or four grandsons of the founder, who would be old enough, and most likely wish to enter the family business.

This could present problems not of my asking. Though I had enjoyed much freedom of action, I was not the type of person who would take kindly to suddenly finding my responsibilities questioned by a younger man, who might not only have different ideas on how to operate the store, but might also demand seniority to myself.

My wife and I discussed the matter, and it so happened we were told of an old-fashioned store that was for sale in Andover, where my wife's uncle and aunt were stationed (General Sir John and Lady Crocker). We went and sought their advice and found them most enthusiastic and more than confident that we would do well. However, we did not want to move; our friends and all our interests were in Bournemouth, but as I saw it, my position could only be counted safe for another few years.

So I told the three family directors at that time, Bennett, Harold and Cyril Beale. They listened, as always, to what I had to say, and after some discussion they were all convinced that my fears were entirely unfounded. We were, of course, delighted, but I must admit I still thought they were wrong, and I am afraid circumstances proved this to be the case.

In the meantime I found myself taking more interest in merchandising, discussing buying arrangements before each season with buyers and frequently joining them when special purchases were likely to be made. Three points stand out in my mind, which helped in the profitable development of the business.

1. More attention was given to discounts for prompt payment, and there was also the possibility of seasonal and quantity discounts.

2. The founding of the BMC (British Merchandising Club) of which Harold Beale was a founder member in the early thirties, the membership comprising the principals of a number of family owned department stores throughout the country. I took a special interest in this and was elected chairman for a period prior to the war. It was at these meetings that we soon saw the opportunity of increasing our bargaining power with manufacturers and obtaining extra discounts or special prices.

One particular incident which proved a success was the introduction of a special "Guinea Gown" department. The gowns were bought from Simon

Massey of Peggy Page Ltd. The styles and selection were the finest value on the market at that time, but the price we had to pay gave us a low mark up. So the BMC members were persuaded to promote them and as a result obtained an extra 5% discount which then gave us a reasonable margin.

3. Looking out for new suppliers—there is nothing wrong in seeing the same people each season, but the most successful buyers are those who are continually on the look-out for someone better.

There are several ways of doing this—to see all manufacturers' representatives, even if only for a minute; to study advertisements for new names of suppliers and also by just walking into a showroom or agent's office with whom no previous contact has existed.

A number of new and successful firms opened up in the thirties and I came in contact with quite a few who later did much to help our trading interests.

One, in particular, was Percy Trilnick. Reference to his new venture appeared in the *Drapers' Record*. He was not only going to produce fashions in this country but aimed mostly at bringing in the best for ladies and children from the United States and Canada, all at reasonable prices. So I called at the address given, in Regent Street, only to find bare floor boards, no furniture, no stock. Just one lively little man and his partner who I believe was a Mr Rubinovitch who later was to leave him and return to the United States.

Percy Trilnick had a dynamic personality, eyes that sparkled, always with a white carnation in his button hole. He welcomed me as though I was the prime minister and the drab surroundings seemed to disappear, such was the change this gifted little man made. "Mr Riceman, do you realise you are my first customer? You will never regret it." Nor did I!

Standing up, for there were no chairs, he told me of his plans. I liked them and what is more he stood by all the promises he made to me. We did considerable business together and he was constantly giving me helpful advice on buying, particularly when I went to the United States and Canada.

He was one of the most colourful and helpful business friends I ever had, until he died, all too young, a few years after the war. Some said he worked himself to death; he was like a candle that just burned itself out—a never to be forgotten personality.

Another useful habit which helped to keep me up to date with my knowledge of merchandise was that, when visiting one of our regular suppliers in London, I was on the look-out for names of other businesses in the same building or street, and when I saw one that looked interesting, I used to pop in and see what they had to offer. If I liked their ranges I then automatically asked if they could give me the name of some of the stores they dealt with. I made many useful discoveries this way.

I was to make quite a few visits to the United States and Canada while in Bournemouth and I think I turned them to good account. However, it shows the consideration the three family directors gave me, for as far as I can remember they never once refused my request to go, and the business always met my expenses.

Looking back on those occasions, I would like to think that, in their place, I should have been as generous, for not one of them went with me, nor did they go on their own during this period.

In those days, most of my time on the other side of the Atlantic was spent in visiting stores, their principals and, of course, manufacturers. In the evenings, on trains and in planes, I wrote copious notes on all that I had seen, sorting out my ideas under most appropriate headings—merchandise, display, staff, staff training, general promotions, layouts, fixtures and fittings, and colour schemes.

Though seldom referred to, these notes helped me to put more colour and finish into my own ideas. For anyone making similar trips, particularly when young, at least for the first few visits, I would commend the advantage of writing full notes of all the useful information that has been gathered.

On the buying side it was also useful, particularly in the middle and late thirties, for during this period they were forging ahead with new ideas in fashions, lingerie, hosiery and fancy goods.

There was the occasion of my first big buy of hosiery and lingerie from New York and Montreal. Having some idea of the lingerie we could sell, and also the prices we were paying in London, I had no trouble in making a suitable selection, and they gave me some big reductions, especially to make my trip worthwhile!

The hosiery buying was quite different. I was not too sure of my ground and this perhaps was an occasion where I was more fortunate than clever. The scene was in a large office in a Canadian hosiery factory. The sales director welcomed me and told me he had collected a wonderful parcel for me. Bringing out the first item, I looked at it, felt doubtful, but said nothing except, "Thank you," putting the sample box on the long empty table.

Then I asked to see the next, and so it went on, and the pile on the table grew. I was still anxious until a second director joined the first and fortunately, I saw in a mirror a glint of pleasure in his eye and began to sense I was being trapped.

However, I continued to act as though in complete ignorance. Soon there were four directors present, and the pile on the table was getting higher and higher. The time eventually came when they had nothing else to bring out, no more bad lines.

"Is that all you have?" I asked.

"I'm afraid so, Mr Riceman. Now what about giving us your order?"

Then they received what I am sure was an unexpected shock—"These, gentlemen, are the items I do not want. They will do no good to either your firm or ours. May I come into the stockrooms with you and find some items that are really good which will make my visit worthwhile?"

The silence was acute for what seemed far too long, However, they proved to be great sports, and before I left I doubt if anyone could have been more helpful and generous to me.

The other occasion tied up with one of the early trips of the *Queen Mary*. I had spent about £5,000 and the purchases were specially crated with our firm's name in bold letters outside.

The idea was to have them photographed at the docks at Southampton at the side of the *Queen Mary*. This was done and made the centre illustration of our large advertisement in the *Bournemouth Echo*. "A personal visit to the United States and Canada brings this wonderful collection of . . . to Bealesons." Then some of the items were illustrated individually. It proved to be quite a successful promotion. It was different, it happened to be timely and it certainly made people talk. I had signed a few thousand personal letters which I had taken with me and posted mostly to account customers from New York and this also created interest. By then the future success of the store was assured with Marks and Spencer on one side and later British Home Stores on the other. The company owned considerable property at the rear, and I was all for developing this and gradually adding to the store's selling space.

We had long and arduous arguments about expansion but it was always three to one and therefore I usually lost. They were probably right at the time to be satisfied with steady and sure progress.

One of the arguments that was used against mine, was that the population of Bournemouth was only slowly expanding and it would be years before it would increase enough to stand another large department store—there were already five, and they looked upon that as one too many!

As it turned out, it would have been a wonderful investment to add another 20% to our selling area, for the war was soon to come and this would put a stop to building for another ten years; but they were not to know this and nor was I! The only point in mentioning this is that it indicated that I was looking ahead with confidence and enthusiasm to the future.

My wife and I returned to Bournemouth after a visit to the World's Fair in New York, only a short time before war was declared. The second time in our lifetime when the lights were going out all over Europe.

The post-war generation can have no idea of the feelings every father and mother went through at that time. How long would it last? Would we, and our children survive it? Would life ever be the same again? We were standing in the lounge in our first home when these solemn thoughts and many others passed through our minds as we stood almost dumbfounded in the silence, after listening on the radio to Mr Neville Chamberlain announcing that war had been declared.

It started as a phoney war and had a curious effect on our business. We thought it might almost close us down, but to our surprise things went on very much as usual. We still obtained our supplies and people still appeared to have money to spend.

Conscription had not yet started, and I remember I had a chat with John Beale (my own age group) about joining up. He was thinking along the same lines, so on the next of my London visits I went to the call-up centre for the Admiralty, only to be told that at thirty-five I was too old, and that in this war my age group would not be wanted! I would serve the country's interests better by carrying on my present occupation. So back I went with a clear conscience for the time being.

In 1940 when it was realised that hostilities would eventually start a few people, when circumstances permitted, made plans to move out. The Spanish Ambassador and his family were among these. They lived in a beautiful house with a minstrel's gallery and a large garden with a lawn running down to its own private mooring in Christchurch Harbour. The news was so black that there was no market for a property of this kind but when my wife and I saw it we both had enough confidence in the future to take a chance. We knew we would never again have the opportunity of buying such a beautiful house at a price we could afford. We bought the house for £3,500 and lived there for about six years. Our elder son, David, had been born in 1938. Jonathan was born in our new home "Shoreacres" during the Dunkirk evacuation. Our daugher, Elizabeth, arrived in 1945.

I joined the AFS (Auxiliary Fire Service), and was stationed at Christchurch some one and a half miles from our home. I had my busiest time of the war when the blitz came—hard work all day and all too often out at night as well fighting fires. Of these the Southampton blitz was the worst. In the evening of the attack the extensive fires could be seen clearly from Bournemouth as well as the sound of explosions. From a distance it looked as though the whole city had been obliterated. Some of us were called out early in the evening to help—I was to drive a truck carrying a large water butt, as some of the water mains were already out of action.

It was a pitch dark night and our dim lights made it most difficult to see on the road. However, we happened to lead the whole convoy and I had a little man to help me. I don't know who he was, or where he came from, all I remember of him was that he constantly asked me, "Where are the shelters?"

All went well until we were approaching the central area and we stopped just in time facing a large bomb crater in the road. We had to get through, so I had, unfortunately, to drive the truck through a wall of an undamaged house, through their front garden and the next one and back on to the road. Eventually we reached the corner site where Plummer Roddis used to stand. My partner then said he must leave me, but could I pick him up at 8 a.m. in the morning? I told him, if he was lucky, I would.

So, I was on my own. There was chaos everywhere. Tyrrell & Green (now a John Lewis Partnership store) was on fire as were most of the buildings on the opposite side of the road down to a large insurance block on the right-hand side. There seemed to be no one around. There was a fire hose in the road but it could not be used as there was no water supply. So after having a look at the extensive damage to Tyrrell & Green, I knew there was nothing I could do there.

Fortunately, when I was back in the road again a little further down, a water supply started. There was a large fire in the building before one of the main insurance blocks, so I thought it best not to try and save the one burning furiously but the one beyond. It so happened that I had been soaked with the unexpected supply and while trying to put out the fire on one side of the street, the raging inferno on the other behind me helped to dry my trousers! And so, until the early hours before dawn I saturated it and the adjoining fire infested building. Eventually the fire subsided and the building was saved.

The bombing had ceased and I kept busy until about 7.30 a.m. next morning when all was quiet, so I picked up my truck and a little before 8 a.m. found my partner at the Plummer Roddis corner and he jumped on board telling me that he had had a comfortable night in his shelter!

Just down the road there was a party waiting, and I picked one up who had obviously come from his shelter, and drove him to (I assume) near his home on the outskirts of the city. I asked him where he worked, and he told me an insurance company. On enquiring the name, it was the very building I had been instrumental in saving; I told him he would find his papers rather wet! An extraordinary coincidence.

Another incident which stands out was one of the many miracles which were enacted at that time and which I feel I must mention.

I was on call at the AFS station one evening when they phoned through from another station to let us know that bombs had dropped in the centre of Bournemouth but there were no fires. However, they thought I should go as they knew one had been dropped near our business.

I was soon on my way, and as I approached the square which is the centre of the town, I looked down St Stephen's Road which branched off to the right. There I noticed a crowd had gathered, and traffic had been stopped. So, I parked the car, and being in uniform had no difficulty in making my way through to the scene of the disaster.

My father and mother lived in a top flat, the fourth floor of a new building on the right hand side of this road, and as I drew near it became apparent that it was this building which had been hit. The half of the first section of flats, from top to bottom, had been demolished by the bomb, including half of my parents' flat.

There was no sign of life in the building and all that was left was a huge pile of rubble and dust on the ground. I went up to one of the wardens and asked, "Has anyone been rescued?"

"Not yet, they are just going to start moving the rubble, but I doubt if anyone could be alive in it."

My father was away but I told the warden that my mother was there, and he promised to watch for me and let me know if there were any survivors if I returned in half an hour. I then found another bomb had been dropped on our church opposite; although it had been considerably damaged, fortunately the building was not destroyed.

Harold Beale was already at the business when I arrived but all was well, so I returned to see the warden who had been on the lookout for my mother.

He told me the only person who had, so far, been rescued alive, was quite an extraordinary woman, as when they moved her out of the rubble she insisted on walking to the ambulance—but they didn't know her name.

I replied, "That's bound to be my mother," for she had always been an independent person, and if she could walk, no one would be allowed to carry her! I think the warden was somewhat surprised that I could be so certain but there was no doubt in my mind.

She had been taken to Boscombe Hospital where I found her, and although she had a nasty cut on her head and nose and had been covered in dirt and dust, there was not a bone broken in her body, though grit was frequently to work its way out of her head and nose for over twenty years!

When you next see a block of flats—look up at the fourth floor and imagine the whole section being demolished by a bomb, and then for someone to be picked up without any serious injury from the rubble and you will know what I mean by a miracle.

She was not a bit concerned about herself, or her own safety. All she could say was, "Who is going to make the coffee for the Forces Canteen tomorrow?" She ran this with my father, for servicemen in the hall of our church. She was then sixty-seven years of age and she lived to be ninety-six!

Business prior to this period had been most exacting, though we were operating in most unorthodox ways. We were free to buy what and where we liked, though I knew it could only be a matter of time before stocks would either dry up or be rationed.

Although we had no intention of hoarding, we nevertheless agreed that if stocks were not likely to be available, we would have to act as best we could to cover our requirements for a reasonable time.

This covered a number of special items, but three stand out in my mind. Firstly, blackout material, the need for which came early in the phoney period of the war. We searched the markets and bought roll upon roll of material from the most unexpected places; one was rubber backed sateen from a rainwear manufacturer.

Secondly, the blanket situation which developed more slowly. I found they were still available, but the prices had rocketed, and I was advised to place orders before stocks were exhausted. To pay more to the mills than retailers were selling them, seemed to me to be absurd, but such is the strangeness of business habits that it was thought to be quite out of order to buy from any other source than that of the accredited manufacturer or wholesaler. It was a case of buy at the inflated prices and store principals had no thought of obtaining their supplies in any other way.

Until restrictions were imposed, either by the retailers themselves or the government, I wanted to buy in the cheapest markets. With this in mind, I discussed the matter with Harold Beale; I am not sure of his first reaction, but anyway, he agreed that we should go ahead and this is what happened.

I spent a day in the blanket departments of the West End stores and bought from the assistants who, in most cases, were still on commission. They were offering a reasonable selection at both pre-war quality and prices, so there was no restriction on my buying if I was accepted as a normal customer.

Instead of placing orders for £5,000 with the mills for inferior quality and inflated prices, I spent about the same amount in placing orders, spread over four or five West End stores; the purchases were made in my own name and were delivered to our home in Mudeford. I expect they thought it was a hotel, but they were not really interested; in each case they had a good order, and that seemed to be all that really mattered.

This unorthodox procedure brought home to us that our own sales must be controlled and I am sure other retailers adopted the same practice later.

Anyway we could offer pre-war quality blankets for some months longer than most of our competitors at prices lower than those appertaining for the inferior qualities which were then being produced by the mills.

Some might look upon this action as unpatriotic but I still do not think it was. Knowing what was going to happen with the market, store management should have been quicker to control their sales.

Thirdly, silk stockings. It was officially announced that no more were to be made available to retailers from a given date. I had been away from business and on my return about eight days prior to this taking effect, found that we had only placed normal orders, nothing extra.

We had a quick management conference and it was agreed that we would buy all that we could get but by then the market had nearly dried up. Stores had been quick to obtain all they could put their hands on. Anyway I went to Leicester and London rather despondent that this time we had missed the boat.

Perhaps I was lucky but a personal friendly link with a number of good suppliers came to my aid. At the end of the week I returned having spent about £8,000. Harold Beale took charge of the sales and made the stock last for some months after our competitors' supplies had run out. Even in those alarming days, the difficult customer, as usual, turned up demanding more than the two or three pairs to which he had limited them. Needless to say he stood firm.

This sort of business could not last. Dunkirk had passed, the blitz had started, and the main threat of invasion had been passed. In 1942 call up for my age group was still a long way off, so I had another talk with John Beale and found that he had decided to join up.

I therefore discussed the matter further with my wife and Harold Beale and my duty became clear to me. I attended my last directors' meeting until hostilities were over. The three of them, Bennett, Harold and Cyril released me from my business responsibilities and generously kept me on the pay roll while I was absent.

There was still no appointment for me for duties at sea in the navy, so I applied for a commission in the ASR (Air Sea Rescue) service of the RAF and was accepted. After training, I spent the rest of the war serving in this capacity.

Some men like service life—but although I enjoyed the active life at sea, I found much of the time on shore tedious, missing home and the constant challenge that competitive business life offered.

CHAPTER TWELVE

AIR SEA RESCUE

(13th May, 1942 to 11th May, 1945)

I regretted having to leave my interesting work with the Beale family but I look back on the following three years as a chapter in life which provided me with excitement and brought compensations particularly as I was on rescue work which attracted me far more than the unpleasant but essential actions that so many of our friends had to undertake during the war.

I was at sea, which I had always enjoyed, but my wife was left with the responsibility of looking after our two sons without a car. She had to take them shopping and to school on my bicycle, one on the front and one on the back. Our home overlooking Christchurch harbour was on the direct route for enemy planes attacking the RAF base a mile or so away. Bombs at times were far too near our house, indeed one fell in the garden by the water. My wife sometimes used to meet me at Christchurch station with the pram so that we could more easily carry my luggage and perhaps some extra rations home.

Before the war practically all rescues at sea were effected by the lifeboats stationed all round our coast, and worked largely in conjunction with the coastguards. Air Sea Rescue had not been taken up seriously, although a few launches had been built but towards the end of May 1940, a rescue service was started, operating mainly in the Dover area. In the next five months, when the Battle of Britain was fought and won, some thirty airmen had been rescued by every type of craft available.

By this time it was found that the existing service of the lifeboats, floats and a few RAF craft were quite inadequate. The following factors were found to be essential for success: — (i) Speed in all weathers; (ii) Long range craft; (iii) Communications and aircraft co-operation; (iv) High Speed Launches with fully trained crews at bases all round the coast.

These entailed big planning, building new types of launches and opening new bases all round our coast and overseas to patrol the waters over which the RAF functioned. As flying increased, so did our losses, although between 1st June and 30th September, 1941 some sixty lives were saved.

Coastal Command would, with increasing force, operate over the enemy's shipping lanes, round Norway, Denmark and the French and Belgian coast. Also they had to keep a constant watch for enemy submarines and aircraft endangering our Atlantic shipping.

Bomber Command had to cross the North Sea and English Channel in its steadily mounting attack on all parts of Europe. Fighter Command had to protect our shipping and coasts from enemy attack and later join in aggressive work as well as protecting our bombers whenever possible.

It took months of training before a pilot and his crew were ready for action and, apart from the lives involved, it was essential to save as many as possible. Planes could be replaced but men could not, until the Air Training Scheme got fully going.

One early spring Monday morning in March, 1942, I entered Adastral House, Kingsway, London, the RAF Headquarters, to ask if they would accept my services.

"Sorry, you are too old to be a pilot or air crew," a bright young lady told me, but I didn't like to be turned down as useless because I was over twenty-five, so I stayed and asked questions.

"Are you sure the Air Ministry wouldn't like me for any other purpose?"

After looking up some notes and then speaking to someone on the 'phone, she asked, "Do you know anything about catering?"

"Yes," I replied meekly, "But it doesn't interest me."

I was just leaving when, as an afterthought, she said, "I don't suppose you know anything about the sea?"

I was all ears and eventually the story of ASR was revealed to me. Forms were filled in and the day came for me to go before the selection board which would decide if I should have a commission. Although I was used to handling small craft in all weathers having possessed a thirty foot launch I knew little or nothing about navigation or signalling. During the three weeks prior to the interview, I read books and took lessons from an expert. Then I wrote the little I knew down on paper and it just filled one foolscap page.

I was determined to avoid being asked questions I couldn't answer on navigation, so, on entering the board room to face the experts around a large table, I was quick to get in the first word.

"Good morning, gentlemen, I realise how valuable your time is and so to avoid troubling you to ask me a lot of questions, which I could not answer, I have written on this paper all I know concerning navigation and small craft. If this is the sort of ground work you can use and train for ASR work, then I am your man."

It was my lucky day. I was out of the room within fifteen minutes, having only been asked questions about some of the more exciting trips I had enjoyed on my own launch.

War is a dreadful business and, although it often brings out the worst qualities in human nature, it also brings out good. ASR did that for we had to be thinking continually about someone else's danger, and so forget our own. Ours was not a mission of destruction, our job was to save valuable lives, who, without our aid, would perish. This responsibility gradually began to sink in during my early training days.

The qualities needed for success were: — (i) always to know your position at sea; (ii) always to know your average speed, especially in bad weather; (iii) to understand the effect of wind, tides and tidal races on one's course; (iv) to be able to make a quick and right decision in an emergency and, at such times, to keep a cool head; (v) to have confidence in yourself, your craft and your crew; (vi) to be able to handle a launch yourself in an emergency.

At last came the day when we were considered fully trained and we had to spend three agonizing days while the knowledge we had acquired was put to the test, both afloat and in the examination room. I shall never forget with what relief I heard that I had passed!

AIR SEA RESCUE EXPERIENCES

It was my good fortune to spend most of my time on the south-east coast, but one of my earlier postings was to the Bristol Channel area. It seemed a long way from the fighting but it proved an excellent finishing off ground to my training.

The Bristol Channel has one of the largest rise and fall in tides in the world* and spring tides flow at eight knots. This added considerably to the difficulty of finding anyone in distress, especially in bad weather. We frequently took our crew out for exercises so as to get used to overcoming these disadvantages.

The method we adopted was simple and effective. A small flag mounted on a float was dropped overboard. Then we would go under way for an hour or more, altering our direction three or four times, after which we received an imaginary crash call, "pilot in water". We estimated his position, took our own, then estimated the time it would take to reach him, added that to his position at the rate of the tide and wind and so obtained our course and ETA (expected time of arrival).

There was a prize for the member of my crew who spotted the flag first—we would have to be within a few hundred yards before it could be seen. Their keenness was tremendous. Only once did we fail to find it and that was in a rough sea and I think it must have sunk as it was never returned to us although it had our unit's name on it.

---

*When my high speed launch was in harbour, particularly during full spring tides, I became aware of the massive power available when water rose and fell well over thirty feet twice a day. Many years later, when there was much talk of the need to find alternative sources of power, I devised a scheme to harness the tide to produce electricity. My son David refined my ideas and produced a plan which I sent to the prime minister of the day, Harold Wilson. He sent me an encouraging letter and put me in touch with a professor in Cambridge who closely investigated my ideas with his colleagues and decided that the scheme was practical but too expensive to be viable.

If we had travelled fifteen miles from the position of dropping the marker and there was a tide of seven knots running, it meant the flag could be twenty to thirty miles from our position. These experiences proved valuable later on.

One gruesome experience in the Bristol Channel was to recover the dead pilot from a crashed American Thunderbolt which had landed in shallow water at low tide. The Americans asked us to recover the body so that it could be identified and we spent two very uncomfortable days in bitterly cold water finding the plane and then lifting it to release the pilot trapped underneath.

THE NEED FOR CO-OPERATION WITH PILOT AND CREW

Our objective was to save life but our real usefulness could only start when men landed safely in the water. Could fatal accidents be reduced? This same concern was felt by higher authorities and ASR schools for air crews were started, where the men were trained in the correct use of all their rescue equipment, Mae Wests, parachutes, inflatable dinghies and emergency rations.

It wasn't long before I found myself talking to pilots and air crews on the importance of their being prepared for an emergency, and giving them hints to adapt devices of their own to aid them in an emergency.

They were supposed to carry a whistle to attract our attention when they were in the water, yet, from experience, it was found to be impossible to hear it while our engine was running. Therefore, I suggested that they should carry a toy balloon or any other object that could be held above the water to attract attention. It is surprising how difficult it is to pick out a man at sea with only his head showing, even at only fifty yards range, especially when it is rough.

Whenever I was invited to visit a fighter or bomber station to talk to the officers and airmen, I always accepted if circumstances permitted and so did a number of my colleagues. We found the American pilots good listeners. They had good equipment but it was often missing when wanted, or crews hadn't been instructed what to do in an emergency. We found many of their dinghies had failed to open on contact with the water, or the food, knife and torch were missing.

I like to think that the talks we gave to the Americans may have, indirectly, been instrumental in saving lives. Another useful link we had was to take pilots out to sea with us whenever possible. We were permitted to do this by arrangement with the CO concerned, except for a period immediately before and after D-Day.

This brought home to them what an unpleasant thing it was to land miles out at sea, especially in winter. It gave them a first hand view of how we functioned and how, in an emergency, they had every chance of being rescued if they were able to carry out a few simple duties.

AIR SEA RESCUE

Only a few asked to come out a second time, unless the weather had been very kind to them. During 1944, the peak year for ASR, it was rough most of the time. If, therefore, they had a touch of sea sickness, together with a reminder of the wash and spray from the sea as we carved through the waves, it was usually sufficient to send them back to their bases glad that their job was in the air and not at sea. I never found one who wanted to swap jobs.

As the rescues began to mount—I believe over 4,000 had been saved by early 1944—a fine spirit began to spring up between the pilots and ourselves. Many of them assisted us in searches for their friends who had run into trouble and were unable to make for home.

These are the links that bind men together, and nations too, and there was no sea that ever prevented us from answering a call from these young heroes as our air attack intensified.

RAMSGATE, 24th August, 1943

There is nothing like expectancy for tickling up one's nerves. To be suddenly posted from ferrying with orders to proceed immediately knowing that over twelve other officers and crews were receiving the same instructions, made us think that invasion days were on hand.

I was given command of a new HSL 2626, latest type power boat. Three 500 h.p. Napier Sea Lion engines, fitted with every new device made for rescue work including sick bay, refrigerator, wireless cabin, large wheel house and bridge, two gun turrets containing twin Brownings and an Oerlikon aft.

A brief talk to my coxswain and crew of our opportunities ahead, a rush getting our equipment on board and we were off from Calshot, reaching Dover five and a half hours later.

One of my crew, Corporal La Blanche was a Frenchman and when we sighted the French coast as we passed a few miles off Dungeness, his excitement was terrific. A few minutes later he cooled down when some tracer bullets came right across our bow. Fortunately, they came from one of our own boats on patrol nearby, captained by a rather wild fellow from the south seas. I never discovered whether the shots were fired by accident or intent! Anyway, the officer in question was found a shore job a few months later.

On arriving at Dover, I realised my troubles were really beginning. Only my wireless operator had previous active ASR experience. My coxswain had never handled an HSL before and on entering Dover, I found if I didn't watch his every movement we should be smashed up.

On reporting to the CO of the RAF Unit, I was ordered to proceed to Ramsgate, fifteen miles away. We sailed early next morning. It was one of my lucky days! My coxswain fell down the engine hatch and was laid out on a stretcher for a few hours, so I put my second coxswain on the wheel, except for entering Ramsgate, when I took over.

The number of HSLs on the unit had been increased from three to nine, complete with officers and crews and nowhere could have been found a keener set of fellows. Our crews had quarters at our unit headquarters on the front landing at *HMS Fervent,* the naval HQ. The officers resided at "Shalimar" a large house owned and run by a kindly Mrs Debbling. She called it her piece of war work to look after us. She was a real good sort and must at times have lost money by it as she only charged us 45/- p.w. and was lavish in her kindness. There was always a meal ready for us whenever we came ashore, even at midnight! And what a meal. Always two eggs at a time, sometimes fourteen a week. Whenever we were ashore, her supper table was a sight worth seeing.

So started my happiest days in the service. The exacting work, the risks we shared all helped to bring us together. The whole atmosphere at the time seemed electrified with expectancy. Something was going to happen. None of us knew what. For a unit suddenly to become three times its normal size and to know that similar increases had been made at Newhaven and Dover, looked as though something big was in the offing.

We arrived in August 1943. Duties started in earnest within a couple of days and for a month we were kept going at high pressure.

Sweeps by fighter planes were on from dawn to dusk almost daily and we began to feel our ASR training had not been in vain. Our motto was *The sea shall not have them* yet I recall an incident when lives were lost which might have been saved.

Bombers were returning from the Calais direction passing over the Goodwin Sands. We were positioned at various points outside the Goodwins when we picked up a message that a bomber was ditching. She was losing height, having left the French coast and was proceeding on a course to take her about ten miles north of my position. Fortunately, two HSLs were on the spot, south-east and to seaward of the Goodwins. The bomber passed so low over them that it nearly knocked their masts off, dropping to only a few feet off the water. The HSL captains were signalling to it to ditch before reaching the treacherous Goodwins but, unfortunately, the pilot managed to get one more spurt out of his engines and the bomber rose a few feet, passed over the Goodwins, crashing into the sea a quarter of a mile on the north shore side of the Goodwins. It sank almost immediately. The nearest launches were a little more than two miles off, yet there was a distance of six miles for them to get round the sandbank, through a narrow rarely used channel.

Then the rush started; launches from all directions cut all the corners they dared to reach the scene of the crash. The one from the north made it first. Those nearest to the crash were right out of it. Six out of the ten crew were saved but they might all have been saved had the pilot ditched three miles sooner.

AIR SEA RESCUE

THE PILOT WHO PLANNED HIS FALL

Another incident on an unpleasant day, wet and rough, was when we were sent up the coast to a position off North Foreland, in company with HSL 2688. After an uncomfortable five hour wait, a call came through. An American fighter pilot was out shooting up trains on the continent. When, owing to his limited petrol supply, it was time for him to turn for home, he spotted another train fifteen miles away. He couldn't resist the temptation, knowing full well that it would mean that he couldn't reach home.

Having done his shooting successfully, he started to plan his own rescue. First he notified his own station of his plight, giving them his course and the expected distance he would cover. We were informed. The next message came when he reached the Dutch coast and the final when he jumped from his plane.

He was one of the pilots who knew all about the correct use of his rescue equipment. It was all in order and as his feet touched the water, he disconnected his parachute and pulled the cord to open his dinghy, which he was sitting in before the water topped his waist.

He was picked up within twenty minutes, smoking a cigarette. All he had to say was, "Oh, boy, am I glad to see you." F/O Cooke my colleague on our accompanying HSL 2688 had the privilege of taking him ashore.

Block busters were just starting to be used. If the bombers were unable to drop them within the target area, they were usually dropped at sea on the return trip and how they used to shake us! The sight of the water spouting up in the air was quite something, especially at a distance.

These Ramsgate days were often times of endurance tests. Two days stand out especially in my mind. Both were rough with bad visibility, drizzle and no moon.

On the first occasion we left harbour after breakfast and were sent to a position about nine miles off the North Foreland. It was too rough to cook a meal, but we made good use of our tins of self-heating soup which automatically warmed up as the tin was opened. Our RTB (return to base) came about 15.00 hours and, in spite of a heavy south-westerly sea running, we were soon back in harbour, all of us having visions of a good meal which was long overdue. I had a mental picture of Mrs Debbling welcoming me with two fried Dover soles, together with a smile across her broad generous face and just waiting for us to chaff her.

After making fast in harbour, entering up the log, checking up fuel and oil, we raced for our quarters. Before I was halfway along the harbour wall, a messenger interrupted me. The instructions were, "Put to sea immediately." All other boats had a similar message. The weather was deteriorating, it would soon be dark and we had to punch our way for thirty-five miles to a position off Dungeness as quickly as possible. These were the times when we wished we could take some of those in authority ashore, who had no regard for our feelings, for a trip under such conditions. We wondered if they would then occur so often.

It was wonderful the way the launch stood up to the buffeting. We had to cling on for dear life. The sea was short and steep. Fortunately, we had no casualties, though I was a near one. I was just noting my time for altering course while on the bridge, when a large wave caught our bow and instead of cutting through it, we went over the top, dropping down in the trough the other side. It sent me half somersaulting across the bridge and down into the wheelhouse. Fortunately, I was only bruised.

Off Dungeness was a bunch of destroyers, keeping us company. For us all to be out on such a night made us certain that something big was in the offing.

Our recall came about 22.00 hrs. We did well on the return trip until we were well past Dover. Taking the inshore route, inside the Goodwins, I gave the coxswain the last course and told him to look out for a green light flashing twice.

I went below, leaving the lookout for just three and a half minutes. On returning to the bridge, I asked the coxswain if he had spotted the green light. "Yes, sir, right ahead."

Visibility, I thought, must have improved as I didn't expect to see the light for another three minutes. I had a look at the light. Yes, he was right, yet instinct told me something was wrong.

"What is your course, coxswain?" I asked.

"050° sir." This gave me a shock for we were 54° to starboard off our course—another of the many times this poor coxswain landed me in trouble.

I immediately gave the order to close down and stop port, centre and starboard engines. On checking our position, I found we had crossed a shallow shoal which I wouldn't have even risked crossing on a crash call. We were near two dangerous wrecks, there was a five knot tide running and the night was black. Unfortunately, I didn't know the exact time the coxswain had altered course so I was uncertain which buoy was ahead.

All I could do was to proceed on one engine at low revs. Fortunately, we reached it safely and our position was then ascertained. We still had another twenty minutes run when, by right, we should have already been safely in harbour.

Our troubles were not over. On reaching a position one mile from the entrance to the harbour, I saw a light; in the right direction but it seemed too high for the entrance light. I called up on my Aldis lamp but there was no reply and this made me more suspicious. My coxswain was, of course, certain that all was well. I checked its direction once again; it was correct so I gave the order to proceed at 1,000 revs—slow speed (about 12 knots). So we approached the light; I felt convinced we were running into danger yet I couldn't account for it as we had received no challenge or warning from naval control. Only this one light was visible, everything else was pitch black, though fortunately the wind had eased. At last, after a minute and a half, in spite of my coxswain's continued assurance that all was well, I gave the order "hard to starboard, astern starboard engine". This was for a quick turn, almost in our own length and as we did so we were challenged not 200 yards away.

We had just passed the harbour entrance within 150 yards and had got to within a less distance from the rocks. All lights had been out because of a raid and shelling warning. The light we had seen must have been shown by an enemy agent. The harbour lookout had, for once, been attracted by an explosion ashore and had missed spotting us.

When we were ashore, everyone had gone to the shelters but such were the dangers that we had already passed through that, for once, the bombs and shells held no terrors for us, or we were too exhausted to worry about them. It wasn't long before I groped my way through the black-out to "Shalimar" where Mrs Debbling came up from her shelter to provide me with my long overdue meal.

The other endurance test that stands out in my mind during this period was on the big day itself, Thursday, 9th September, 1943. The whole atmosphere was electrified with expectations as to what was about to happen, all of which were wrong.

As it happened, it was just a large scale attempt to persuade the Luftwaffe to come off the ground so that our fighters could shoot them out of the sky and give our future increased bombing programme the freedom of the sky. But the whole project was a flop.

My launch was the nearest to Calais for over fifteen hours and I never saw an enemy plane all day. Hundreds of our own machines were going backwards and forwards all the time but the Luftwaffe remained grounded. Their intelligence must have given our idea away.

As the day advanced, the weather deteriorated and by 15.00 hours we had to keep the engines running so as to maintain our position as the set and drift of wind and tide were so strong. It was a short, steep sea, at times so bad that I feared we would capsize, especially while turning to maintain our position.

The fighters were returning so low that at times I thought they would hit our mast as they whizzed past, though we couldn't see them. This we had to endure, until we were finally ordered to RTB at 20.30 hours

ASR EXPERIENCES AT FELIXSTOWE

On returning to Calshot from a long ferrying trip, I was told to take over a new HSL to fit her out and leave within twenty-four hours for Felixstowe. Other officers and crews received like orders.

No skipper could have wished for a finer set of men and they did great service during the following months. We sailed from Calshot on 30th March, 1944 knowing that this time it was bound to be invasion, for our ferrying experiences had shown us all the preparations which had taken place in every harbour round our coast and we knew they were almost completed.

On arriving at Felixstowe I made it my business to get my crew and HSL 2690 prepared and fitted out for any emergency. There were six HSLs, which were later increased to nine. We linked up in the north with Lowestoft and in the south with Ramsgate.

Off the east coast there are many navigational dangers and various sets of the tide, due to the banks. I noted every different experience I encountered, also those I was given by other skippers. The most useful was a list of courses to steer at various states of the tide and weather conditions to almost any position to which we were likely to be sent.

As each week passed our bombing raids and fighter sweeps increased in intensity. Before we left harbour we were informed of their course out, also the direction from which they would return. We proceeded to our positions in the North Sea, varying from ten to sixty miles from the coast. There we stayed on continuous listening and visual watch. What a sight it was to see those fleets of bombers go out in formation, followed by their fighter escorts. At times the sky seemed just filled with them.

They had a bad habit, when leaving our shores, of trying out their guns by firing a few rounds. They seemed to forget that although there was no shipping way out in the North Sea, we were there, and every bullet and shell they fired had to come down. I was always expecting that we would have casualties in this way but, fortunately, we escaped. The bombers themselves were not so fortunate.

I saw two shot down in this way. One happened very high up and it came down at a terrific speed, breaking up as it fell, before crashing into the sea. It was one of many tragic sights we witnessed.

One night we were duty boat in harbour. This meant that I was beside the telephone to take any message and my crew was ready to put to sea at a few minutes' notice.

Our call came at 05.00 hours for three boats to go out to various positions. As this was not a crash call, we had to contact the other crews and get a relief crew to take our place before putting to sea.

It was a dreadful morning, dark and thick fog. Felixstowe harbour has a narrow entrance and the fog was so thick that it was impossible to see from one side to the other. Visibility was down to about eighty feet and there was a strong spring tide running. All we could do was to steer a compass course from buoy to buoy to the boom defence, then out through its narrow entrance and buoy to buoy again until we were clear of the harbour approach. Our luck was in, we were the only launch that got out, the other two were unable to do so until four hours later.

Our next trouble was a message that had been received from NHQ informing us that E-boats had dropped a lot of mines in the main shipping channels, for at least twenty miles up the coast. I had no definite information as to which course to take to avoid trouble. My instructions were to go to a position about thirty-five miles out. The route I took covered a distance of sixty miles and we actually passed within a few cables from where a mine-sweeper was blown up later in the morning, with considerable loss of life.

The fog began to lift as we got away from the coast and we were soon able to proceed at full cruising speed. All went well until we were about ten miles from our position.

The bombers had been passing overhead when, way out towards the Dutch coast, we spotted a trail of smoke. I called up my wireless operator enquiring if any messages were coming through but the air was silent. By right, I should have continued to my position but it seemed a worthwhile chance to investigate. I listened in on my VHF but still all was silent.

I altered course and went full speed ahead for ten miles, notifying the naval base of my action. After ten minutes we sighted smoke rising from the water and when we reached the spot it was like a roaring inferno rising out of the sea. Petrol was all over the water. We went to within fifty yards of the scene and the heat almost seared my skin. Nothing could have been living there.

Also I had to think of the safety of my crew as the bomber would have been carrying a full bomb load and I hadn't heard them go off! It was a time for quick decision. Was I to search round the position of the crash, or to assume the crew had jumped, and, if so, in what direction had they come down?

I chose the latter course. Fortunately, it proved to be the right one. We picked up the first man six miles from the scene of the crash and only thirty-five minutes after sighting the smoke. The second man was recovered six minutes later eight miles away and the third ten minutes later about nine miles away but unfortunately he had drowned.

We continued the search for some time with aircraft co-operation but no others were found; they must have gone down in the plane.

My nursing orderly worked hard on the third man in the hope of bringing him round and after half an hour, I thought there was some hope but we were still nearly fifty miles away from harbour.

I returned at top speed sending a signal requesting a launch to intercept me with a doctor on board. This was done, but even with the doctor's help, the poor fellow never came round. Another young American had given his life for our freedom.

My first crash call occurred a few days after arriving at Felixstowe. We were out at sea, awaiting an emergency, when we picked up a message for us to proceed to a given position, where a fighter had crashed. Aircraft were co-operating.

Unfortunately, we could seldom go in a straight line owing to the many navigational obstructions and dangers in these waters. This meant a hasty plotting on the chart of the quickest way, making due allowance for the altering position of the pilot in the water, who was of course, drifting with the tide.

Visibility was bad but we made good time to within five miles of the crash when we sighted an aircraft co-operating and directing us, almost on our actual course to the pilot, whom they had already spotted in the water. At the same time a Walrus rescue seaplane had also joined in the search and picked up the message of the position at the same time as we did. Though the distance was only five miles, it was an unequal race and when we reached the spot, the seaplane had already alighted and we had to stand by and see them take the pilot on board. We only recovered his inflated dinghy. He was safe, that was all that really mattered, though we naturally liked the satisfaction of taking them ashore.

On two occasions at Felixstowe, a Walrus had to be towed back to harbour after landing when it was too rough. The second occasion was within ten miles of the Dutch coast, when there were five survivors on board. The crew and survivors were taken aboard by my HSL (another officer was taking duty for me on this occasion), and the plane was taken in tow. She was in a sinking condition on reaching harbour.

There were only a few Walrus in service. Given a fine, calm day they were ideal for rescue work, especially for crash calls a hundred or more miles from our coast, but, unfortunately, such conditions seldom prevailed, so their service, though occasionally good, was nevertheless limited.

SEA FORTS

Off the Thames Estuary and as far north as twelve miles off Harwich, a number of remarkable sea forts were erected soon after the commencement of the war. Their method of construction and erection on the various positions was equally remarkable.

They were built near Tilbury and consisted of a long hollow concrete cylinder with an elongated erection on the top, which was supposed to look like a naval cruiser without funnels.

These enormous objects were floated down the Thames, with the aid of a number of tugs and when over the exact positions at slack water (where the sea bed had been carefully examined previously), the water chambers at the base of the concrete cylinder were, one by one, filled until it sank into position on the bed of the sea; leaving the enormous cylinder tube in a vertical position with the fort in its correct position on the top. Their positioning was a remarkable achievement as they stood over one hundred feet high.

AIR SEA RESCUE

I was told by one of the captains that one of them nearly toppled over with all the men on board while the water chambers were sinking. Their design and construction were a real engineering feat to withstand the buffeting of the gales, with such a heavy superstructure, complete with guns and equipment for a crew of over fifty. The crews' quarters were actually below water level in the large cylinder. There was a proper electrical charging plant on board, also air conditioning and large storage accommodation.

The two forts nearest Harwich were *The Rough* and *The Sunkhead*, the latter being further out. It was sometimes our luck to go out to *The Sunkhead*. If the weather was good, we were able to go alongside and I went aboard, where I was in telephonic communication with the shore. The officers were always welcoming and would give me a meal. They were eager for company and any newspapers we had, as theirs was a monotonous job, doing six weeks' duty at a time.

INVASION DAY

During the night of 5th June, 1944 the whole of the invasion fleet moved out of practically all the large and small waterways of Britain. Before dawn arrived on 6th June I was sent down south to a position sixteen miles from Ramsgate. The circumstances were very similar to the big day at Ramsgate the previous September.

All during the day our bombers and fighters were going south and fortunately not one crashed in our area, though we missed the satisfaction of doing some rescue work. The weather was bad and we were positioned off the Thames Estuary, where the sea and tides all helped to add to our discomfort. We had our exciting moments. One plane nearly crashed a few yards from us. It had been losing height all the way from the French coast, coming in a straight line for us. We were all ready to assist when they gained a little height and maintained it to the English coast.

It was an anxious day, even my crew was serious, spending most of their free time round the wireless operator's cabin hoping for a flash of good news. We knew the weather was bad for invasion and we were wondering how the poor men who were making the first landings were faring.

Our recall came at 19.35 hours, making our time at sea over fourteen hours.

After the first ten days of invasion were over, our bombers and fighters once again started in earnest on their trips over the North Sea. German communications were being continually pounded.

All this meant for us long and frequent periods of duty at sea. To make matters worse, the weather was bad, either rough sea or fog.

MY ROAD TO CANTERBURY

A FOG INCIDENT

One day we left harbour in bright sunshine and only a moderate sea, so we were in high spirits. We had a sixty mile run to our position. All went well for the first thirty-nine miles, when straight ahead we saw a complete wall of fog. The position we were making for was in very tricky waters, well out past the swept shipping channel. An old disused navigational buoy marked the spot and if we saw it we were safe from drifting on to either of two dangerous banks which ran approximately two miles on one side and one mile on the other from the buoy. What chance would we have of seeing it when visibility was down to ten to twenty yards?

However, all I could do was to steer for the buoy and hope for the best. When I estimated we were one mile from the position, I reduced speed and had all hands on deck on lookout, and then ran a further mile and a half. Then I stopped. No buoy had been seen.

Now it so happened I had run my last course directly into an ebb tide so there was still a chance, though a small one, that we should still drift back on to the buoy. I estimated we were half a mile past the buoy, so a double lookout was ordered for the next thirty minutes and after about fifteen minutes, a shout came, the buoy had been spotted just under twenty yards away. I took a quick fix of its position, as we were drifting fast and it took thirty seconds to get the engines started, then we had to turn. All this was done successfully.

We were supposed never to tie up to navigational buoys but I must admit when they were disused ones and I was fortunate enough to spot them when visibility was poor, I always did, as it saved running my engines all the time and ensured my keeping correct position.

After tying up I settled down on the bridge to keep watch for any emergency that might arise, though, with the fog, there was nothing to be seen. One came, however, after about six hours. We had, for some time, heard the fighters racing overhead on their return journey but the fog was as thick as ever . . . Then suddenly! There was a big thud, followed by another within a few yards from us; we could actually see the disturbed water.

The alarm was sounded. At first we thought an enemy plane was after us. Then we noticed our decks and clothes were covered in petrol and it dawned on us that a fighter pilot had discarded his extra fuel tank, nearly hitting us in the process. The results would have been disastrous if we had been hit. All fires and cigarettes were immediately put out until the petrol had been dispersed.

On 11th June we saw an unidentified plane which came down in the sea off the Essex coast. We reported this together with a description and it later transpired that we had seen one of the first flying bombs. The weather was very bad that day and we had a particularly long day at sea. When we finally returned to base I collapsed and was sent to the RAF hospital in Blackpool to recuperate for a month. I returned to ASR duties for a further month before being transferred back to ferrying in September 1944.

So ended my varied experiences on active Air Sea Rescue. I wouldn't have missed a day of them. The very nature of the duties brought their own reward and I had the satisfaction of lasting out through the busy period.

AIR SEA RESCUE Part II
Ferrying Experiences

There was a limited number of ferry masters and crews and I was fortunate to be among them during the quieter periods. Headquarters were at Calshot and movements had to be made of high speed launches and RAF pinnaces to any part of the British Isles. In war time this was not quite as easy as it may sound. Among the tasks we had to cope with were:

1. *Navigation:* To have a head full of theory was not enough. Allowances had to be made for weather, tides, types of craft and the coxswain at the helm. When a small craft is travelling at speed, especially in a big cross or quarter sea, there is always the tendency to turn into it. A good coxswain allowed for this but I often found it necessary to allow from two to four degrees to adjust their average error.

2. *Routing:* We had to be clear how to obtain and carry out these instructions. They were issued by the naval authorities. The RAF only issued us with sailing orders.

3. *Signals and Communications.*

4. *Coding (for signals).*

5. *Stores Procedure:* Some of the launches were worth over £30,000. We had to take them on our charge before sailing, together with all equipment and hand over at our destination. This was no simple task.

6. *Method of challenge and reply at sea*

7. *Knowing what action to take in an emergency.*

Occasionally I was able to see the family while I was on duty. My ferrying duties often took me down the south coast and on one occasion I reached Poole harbour from Ramsgate and spent the night at home before going on. Next day we could not leave because of a gale so I was home again. We set off next morning but the port engine failed and we had to return—another couple of days at home! Then a serious defect showed up in the hull and caused further delays. In all I had a fortnight at home due to these problems. If I had tried to arrange such a convenient programme it could never have happened better. My friends at headquarters never allowed me to forget my good luck!

MY ROAD TO CANTERBURY

During my three years in the RAF I ferried many launches and pinnaces to and from many ports around the British Isles. Only a few of these journeys can be mentioned here.

CALSHOT TO BARRY

This happened to be my first long trip. It was in the middle of winter, just before Christmas 1942, when I sailed from Calshot in an Air Sea Rescue pinnace. My cruising speed was only twelve knots though I could do eighteen knots.

Unfortunately, like myself, my crew were inexperienced at sea, though my coxswain, Sergeant Farrow, had enjoyed three years on a marine section in inland waters. Fortunately, they were all keen and had no idea of the rough times ahead.

My coxswain proved to be a chain smoker and in really rough weather when the wheelhouse had to be closed up to keep out as much water as possible (they always leaked), the atmosphere became thick. Also, the three 250 h.p. engines were run on diesel oil which had a heavy sickly smell and this, mixed with the smoke, had an unsettling influence on my internal organs.

We called in at Dartmouth and Plymouth but on the next lap, to Newlyn, the weather deteriorated and by 13.00 hours a gale was on. Still we kept on our course and all went well until we were about five miles from the Lizard, which is a bad spot in a south-westerly gale. Without any warning one of our engines ceased to function. My fitter couldn't do anything about it so I decided to carry on with the remaining two, reducing speed to seven knots (I couldn't have done more than nine knots) owing to the big sea.

"Fire, fire," was the next shock! This time from my lookout who had sighted smoke pouring out of an engine ventilator. Throttles were closed down and my coxswain's face was more red than ever; his cigarette was almost hanging from his lower lip with his mouth wide open, wondering what was going wrong next.

It was the starboard engine this time. My fitter was so sea-sick I had almost to push him into the engine room and stay with him until the heavy smoke had dispersed.

This left us with one engine, so I decided to turn back and have a following sea to Falmouth, about fourteen miles away. As I write, I can see the expression change on my coxswain's face as I gave the order. He almost smiled with relief and by some miraculous movement he sucked his hanging cigarette into its correct position.

All this alteration, of course, entailed making chart references and plotting new courses, which, with the material at my disposal, was well nigh impossible owing to the acute movement of the launch and water breaking in on the chart, making it sticky and blurred. Still, I managed somehow and we reached Falmouth safely.

After a two days' delay we were away again, calling at Newlyn before proceeding to Appledore. It was very difficult entering the latter as there was still a strong south-westerly wind blowing, which caused a nasty race across the bar. Although it is a delightful spot, this was such a handicap to the place that I avoided it on all my later trips up the Bristol Channel. We arrived safely at Barry after another five hours' sailing.

CORNWALL TO AYR

We were ferrying a pinnace from Calshot. All went well as far as Padstow in Cornwall when bad weather set in and held us up for a week. I considered it up to me to try and make up for lost time as soon as the weather improved and informed my crew accordingly.

At last such a morning arrived; the wind had blown itself out, the sea had lost its fierceness, and only a big swell remained, with a smooth surface. Unfortunately, the weather report was bad and the gale was expected to return within twelve hours, so I only arranged to sail to Milford.

We sailed at 8 a.m. and by mid-day the sun was shining brightly from a clear sky. Although it was winter, the indications were favourable for a fine night. This seemed a chance too good to miss, so as we approached St Govern's lightship (twenty miles from Milford), I sent the following message, "If weather report favourable request permission to proceed on passage to Ayr. ETA 11.30."

We were soon abeam of Milford (six miles off) but no reply to my request had been received, so I continued on my course. At about 8 p.m. the following message came through, "Proceed to Holyhead for onward routing to Liverpool".

This was a puzzle to be solved, I was not bound for Liverpool, so I replied "We are Pinnace No. . . . bound for Dumbarton, request permission to proceed direct to Ayr. ETA 11.30 hrs. 12/3rd."

By 9.p.m. we were at our nearest position to Holyhead (ten miles). No further message had been received so I took another chance and pushed on. The weather was still perfect and I knew it wouldn't last for long, so the opportunity seemed too good to miss. At 11.10 p.m. the following message was received, "Permission granted, weather favourable."

It was up to us now. I had worked out a rota for the crew with four hours on and four hours off. As the night was still clear I had planned to rest for two hours from midnight, leaving instructions with my coxswain that if he hadn't seen the Hen and Chicken light by 1.30 a.m. (the extreme south position on the Isle of Man), he was to rouse me. This he did within an hour as we had run into thick fog.

I was naturally keen to spot the Hen and Chicken light so as to correct my course for the next eighty miles up to the comparatively narrow water between Northern Ireland and Corsewall Point.

After running slow for about forty minutes we sighted the light very faintly through the fog. Actually this meant we were much nearer the rocks than we should have been but the risk had been worth while because now I knew my position and I could increase my speed, as there was no chance of hitting land for five hours.

At dawn the fog was very thick and, to make matters worse, my coxswain was sure we were too far north but fortunately I stuck to my course and we picked up the land to starboard before 10 a.m. and passed Corsewall Point. The rest was easy and to round the trip off nicely the gale started to return and the wind was blowing quite hard as we entered the little Scottish harbour of Ayr about 11.30 a.m., after a trip of over 320 miles in a slow RAF pinnace in twenty-seven and a half hours. It was a record for ferrying and I believe we held it for the rest of the war.

THE GLASGOW HSL SHIPMENT FROM TEWKESBURY

Until 1944 reserve RAF craft, including HSLs, were stored up the Tewkesbury and Gloucester Canal. This is a very old waterway and, like most others in the country, it was in a dilapidated condition. The depths were uncertain and, to my own knowledge, at least a dozen craft suffered underwater damage while under way. I learnt through unpleasant experience of two spots which had to be avoided. No doubt there were others which I had been fortunate enough to miss.

This particular trip started from Saul (about thirteen miles up from Sharpness), a tiny Gloucestershire village, as peaceful a spot as you could wish to find, noted for its plums in summer and its cold and damp in winter! Unfortunately, in this case it was the latter, being late November.

The HSL we were collecting had been in the canal for months with little or no attention and the quarters were damp and dirty. It was surprising how quickly an experienced ferry crew would clean up and dry out a launch, making it ready for sailing. Every man knew what his job was and he had to do it. Apart from the cleaning and drying there were stores to take on board, food to be bought, meals to be prepared, engine and wireless equipment to be tested, fuel and water tanks filled, also sailing orders, routing instructions and signals to be obtained from Avonmouth Naval Authority about twenty miles away.

On this occasion all the above was carried out and we were actually under way within twenty-four hours of our arrival. We had seven days to reach Glasgow.

First Day: The first afternoon we went down the canal to Sharpness and proceeded down the Bristol Channel as far as Barry. There, more stores were taken aboard, which I had ordered by phone before leaving Saul.

Second Day—Barry to Milford Haven: Weather had deteriorated during the night and before we had reached Milford the wind had amost reached gale force, but there was worse to come.

Third Day: North-westerly gale—the worst conditions we could have for going up the Irish Sea. It so happened that three naval MLs were also northward bound and the four of us left about the same time, 08.00 hours, though not in company with one another. We raced them all to the Bishop Rocks, where conditions were so bad that I turned back and found the others had done likewise.

Fourth Day: The same experience as on the previous day.

Fifth Day: Weather as bad as ever but I had made up my mind to reach Fishguard which was only some twenty-five miles round the corner from the Bishop Rocks. All our gear was stowed securely and I gave the crew a pep talk before sailing. Fortunately the MLs also intended to have a try as they too were in a hurry.

We started off as usual, soon getting ahead of the MLs but as we approached the Bishop Lighthouse we again felt the full force of the north-westerly gale and I had to slow down speed to about twelve knots. It is an unpleasant spot in bad weather. There is a stretch of over five miles of rugged rocks running out in ridges of from six to ten miles from St David's Head. It was a wonderful sight to see the big waves smashing right over them and then re-forming and rolling on to the distant shores—though we were in too uncomfortable a position to enjoy the scene to the full. I had steered 8° to port to allow for the wind and tide, so as to be kept from being swept right on to them.

Our sixty-three foot launch seemed a small and insignificant thing against the might of the storm. Still, I had no intention of turning back. I had already had sufficient experience with power boat HSLs to know they would stand up to more than the crew would, so long as they were carefully and properly handled.

I went twelve miles north of the Bishops before altering course to starboard to go up the Pembrokeshire coast to Fishguard. This took me well north of a long reef north of the rocks and also put the sea on my port quarter instead of abeam. It took extra time but it was a wise move.

It was impossible for us to give a thought to food or drink. Every member of the crew had to stick to his post and hold tight as sometimes when we mounted an extra large wave, we would almost drop down the other side, and we had to watch that they didn't turn us round. It was very difficult to steer with the sea on our quarter; the waves wanted to pick us up on their curl and throw us towards the rocky coast fourteen miles away.

However, we reached Fishguard. It was an expereince none of the crew would forget. Everyone of them had been wonderful. They were one of the best bunch of boys I ever had and each was as thrilled as I was that we had made another step of our journey and that we still had a chance of winning through to Glasgow in time—especially when they heard the MLs had returned to Milford!

Sixth Day: The gale had been blowing at force eleven all night. We had been bumping about on our moorings in the harbour just like a cork. As the dawn rose we could see the Atlantic waves smashing right over the harbour wall. It was a wonderful sight but my heart began to sink. We had no more spare time in hand for the rest of the trip, so if we delayed sailing a day we would miss our shipment from Glasgow and all our previous efforts would have been wasted. Then I realised, here was a really big sea and if we could only get clear of the harbour safely and proceed with care, we could safely ride the storm so I phoned naval control at Milford Haven and told them I wanted to proceed to Holyhead.

Their first reply was, "You can't possibly do it, all sailing has been cancelled—even the Irish mail boat will not be leaving."

Fortunately, they knew me and evidently it-stood me in good stead for I told them I could make it if I went slow on two engines instead of three and would thus ride the storm.

A good many eyes were watching us as we left the harbour. Gradually we got clear of the dangerous coast. My coxswain stuck to the wheel and I never took my hands off the controls. Neither of us spoke for over half an hour, by which time we were three miles off the harbour entrance and, as I had anticipated, the waves were evening out and were so large that we could ride them comparatively easily. It was like going over hills and into the valleys beyond. We had to keep a careful watch for short waves, which were extras and reduce speed for them, as they were the most dangerous type to hit.

"We're through," was all I could say to my coxswain when we were three miles clear of the land and I well remember his equally short reply "Yes, sir," but there was a depth of feeling behind it.

There was a red conical buoy half way across Cardigan Bay, used by the submarines. I knew none was at sea on this particular morning so I had taken a course to cross its position, though there was little chance of our spotting it. I was steering 8° to port to allow for wind and tide and I only had to be one degree out to miss spotting the buoy. However, when we were ten minutes from the estimated time of reaching it, I kept a special lookout and in a few minutes, much to our amazement spotted the red marker bobbing up over the crest of a large wave almost dead ahead.

It will be difficult for anyone to realise the relief and surprise that was ours. To know our course was correct and that we were making way against the storm was a great uplift to my crew who began to sing.

During the remainder of the trip we only had ten minutes of serious anxiety. I had decided to go inside Bardsey Island, as it would give us about twenty minutes comparative shelter, during which time speed could be increased and we could all enjoy a hot drink and a snack to eat (it was November and very cold). This action was to teach me a lesson which only experience can. We did well until we had rounded the island and were proceeding on a north-westerly course, once again meeting the gale almost head on. We expected this but we certainly did not anticipate the sudden danger that loomed up ahead of us in the form of the worst tidal race I have ever experienced.

It was like a wall of water pushed up into the air, coming straight at us. There was only time for me to sound the alarm to make sure that all the crew stayed put and held fast. The coxswain was instructed to keep on course, meeting the waves head on, while I controlled the engines. Only the lightness and manoeuvrability of the craft enabled us to survive.

We mounted the steep incline of the first wave at full throttle and just before reaching the summit I closed down on all engines. Hesitating on the top looking down, we could hear the sound of the suction of the water waiting to envelope us. We turned down into the steep dip before facing the next wave when I again applied full throttle to reach the summit of the next wave. The effect of three 500hp engines responding immediately from the controls enabled us to mount the giant waves without being spun around.

This action lasted for at least ten minutes, although it seemed an hour, then suddenly we were through and the normal waves from the gale were as nothing compared to what we had been through. It was unfortunate that there was no reference to this on our chart; no doubt it was the strong spring tide that was running at the same time as the gale which caused this unusual disturbance. We arrived at Holyhead soon after 4 p.m. tired, bruised and hungry, otherwise all right.

Seventh Day: Only one more day to reach our destination in time. The gale had subsided. We sailed at 7 a.m. an hour and a half before dawn with the intention of reaching Glasgow the same day (210 miles).

We hardly knew ourselves proceeding along at twenty-seven knots on a smooth sea, with relays of hot drinks and sandwiches coming up from the galley. The crew seemed determined to make up for what they had to go without on the previous day.

We sighted the Isle of Man before dawn and all proceeded well until we were approaching the Mull of Galloway, a little after mid-day. An aircraft kept circling us. We took no notice at first, thinking the pilot was greeting us as they often did, then after one turn he slightly flapped his wings.

Now for an aircraft to circle us anti-clockwise, followed by wing flapping, was the signal that an aircraft was in distress. When I told my coxswain he laughed and reminded me that we were in the Irish Sea not the south-east coast. However, I decided to follow if the pilot returned and repeated his signal. This he did, and I set course towards the rocky coast ten miles away.

Fifteen minutes later we spotted a small object bobbing up and down on the water. It proved to be an inflated dinghy containing five wet and shaken airmen. They were an Anson crew on their first or second training flight! Their sergeant-pilot instructor was all right but the rest were badly shaken. However, they were soon aboard and receiving proper ASR attention.

Nearby the plane was still afloat through with only the tail above the water. I decided to try and beach the plane before proceeding.

We were only a mile from the shore. I picked on a small sandy beach with a ridge of rocks running out on either side. Towing a partly submerged plane is a slow and awkward business.

As we approached the shore, I had to have soundings taken continually and watch out for uncharted rocks. For the final few hundred yards we ceased to tow and instead went astern of the plane and pushed it with our bow slowly towards the beach. This gave us more water astern for our propellors. At fifty yards off we stopped. Then the aircrews' inflated dinghy was used to get seven men ashore with a long line and they gradually pulled the plane in until it touched bottom. It was then made fast and, being high tide, it would within a couple of hours be high and dry on the beach for the salvage party to deal with. The sergeant pilot remained with the plane and the remainder of my crew on shore returned on board. Without further delay, we proceeded on passage, having already signalled that I intended dropping the rescued crew at the little fishing village of Port Patrick, giving them my ETA so that an ambulance would be there to pick them up.

Just as we were leaving we sighted another launch (ASR) which had been sent to help. However, I could not stop for them as we had already been delayed over two hours and Glasgow was still a long way off (eighty-five miles).

Port Patrick is a delightful little harbour. The entrance through high rocks is so narrow that if you didn't know of its existence you would never find it. However, we got in safely and said goodbye to the aircrew, leaving them in the care of the villagers who had all turned out to wlecome us. An ambulance was on its way and due at any moment.

Having disposed of that load off my mind, I was greeted by another—fog was coming down fast. It would soon be dark and we still had nearly eighty miles to go. Within the next half hour visibility closed down to less than half a mile.

Under fog conditions it was not easy to find Little Cumbrae, the entrance approach to the Clyde. Navigational lighting was quite good on the north-west coast, though the lights on some shipping were very dim and were not easy to pick out in fog, so the next three hours was a very anxious time. For me, it was much worse than the gale on the previous days.

As luck would have it, visibility improved enough for me to spot Ailsa Craig when passing within half a mile and again later on when we were abeam of Holy Island, so that I knew I was on my correct course.

It was pitch dark before we reached the Clyde and the fog had come down again, so I had to steer by compass course from buoy to buoy and keep a constant lookout for shipping.

We reached Dumbarton safely and found that all other shipping had been stopped by the fog and we were in time for the special shipment on the following day.

Both the naval authorities and HQCC were good enough to send me an encouraging message on our safe arrival. It would never have been possible but for the excellent crew I had with me at the time.

THE NEW HSL THAT MADE WATER

It was during a hot spell of summer weather that I arrived, complete with crew, at a boat yard up the Thames near Hampton to collect an HSL to be delivered to Blyth. One of the first instructions I gave my coxswain was to have the decks swilled and to repeat the drill two or three times daily while the heat wave continued. This was, of course, to prevent the heat from opening up the seams and causing leaks.

We were soon under way and enjoying the delightful scenery of the Thames. It was a bank holiday, so many war workers had taken off their overalls and were basking in the sun on either bank of the river, or pretty girls were relaxing in a punt, which was, in most cases, being pushed along by their father or younger brother, though a few of them were fortunate and had their boys home on leave. They made the picture a really happy one.

War seemed a long way off and our loud 500 h.p. engines, though only two of them were ticking over at their slowest speed, seemed out of place. Our big wash caused the biggest disturbance. Those boating had to sit up and hold tight and those sitting at the water's edge on the bank had to move back to avoid getting wet.

It was a happy sight and the cheers we received seemed strange, yet encouraging, for we were usually on duty far from the sight and interest of the crowds, most of whom had little or no idea as to the nature of our duties.

We made fast at Westminster Pier, under the shadow of Big Ben. I had soon discovered on my Thames trips that this was the best spot to berth. It was so central and convenient to stores and communications. I always took the precaution of booking a berth in advance, otherwise the small naval craft had a habit of taking up all the available berths.

It was here that I conducted a group of Members of Parliament, including A. P. Herbert over our HSL and told them something of our work. I managed to interest them in the importance of giving ASR captains some distinctive badge to signify the work we did, as it was impossible for our naval friends, with whom we worked at close quarters, to distinguish us from any other ground staff of the RAF who were without some badge to indicate their duties. A. P. Herbert went so far as to have the question raised in the House but, of course, the Air Ministry had it over-ruled.

Sailing orders were soon obtained from the Port of London Authority and we sailed as near to high water as possible, both for depth of water under Tower Bridge (where the foundations of the original Tower Bridge are a danger to shipping near low water), also to have the tide with us down to Southend.

Saturday or Sunday were the best days for this trip as there was only a little traffic at weekends and practically no tugs trailing strings of barges behind them.

On this occasion it was a Wednesday so we had to proceed with extra care. I never knew when a tug with its string of barges would cut across our bows, however, all went well down to Southend pier where I had to land for final sailing orders and we proceeded the same afternoon for Yarmouth.

There I found time to contact my friends, Mr and Mrs Palmer who owned a good class store in the town, and the Rev and Mrs J. M. Todd. On my south bound trips the latter on numerous occasions welcomed me and helped me cope with washing my clothes!

We sailed early on the following morning for Blyth; it was a long trip but we had plenty of time in which to do it. However, it was not to be. A strong north-easterly wind had sprung up during the night and there was a short sharp sea for us to pound our way through. Just the conditions in which to pick out the weak spots in a launch.

Within less than an hour after leaving Yarmouth, a message came up from my wireless operator that he could hear water splashing up against the deck of his cabin. I noted the time and position and stopped to investigate. There was over a foot of water in our centre and forward bilges. They would have to be emptied before proceeding further. So for an hour we worked on the pumps, while another HSL which I had signalled came and stood by in case of need.

The pumps were quite unsuitable and inconvenient to use, being situated on the upper deck and when lifted, pulled the water up and invariably into the face, or over the chest and arms of those who were working them. To make matters worse we were rolling badly in a short sharp sea; all hands had to hold tight to avoid falling overboard, and to put up with occasional spray as waves lapped the decks. After an hour of this my coxswain was muttering all sorts of uncomplimentary things about boat builders, not forgetting the designer of the pumps he was using with the crew.

The water had been reduced by half; not enough, as it was still coming in, but I decided to proceed at slow speed and make for Grimsby. On arrival, there happened to be a Squadron Leader Scott from 17 Group on a visit to the ASR unit. He came aboard and saw with what we had contended and thought I would be unwise to proceed.

However the next day was fine, and under such conditions I knew the hull was all right so I sailed for Blyth and we had a very pleasant trip. On arriving arrangements were made for slipping for under-water inspection, after which I sent in a full report to HQCC.

It so happened that it was patched up and remained at Blyth for months, before it was decided that it should be returned to the boat builders, and I was once again sent with my crew to Blyth to have the pleasure of taking it all the way back to where I had originally collected it!

The trip was uneventful until reaching Southend where I was warned of fog and told to watch for a signal on passing Tilbury. Fortunately the fog was so thick when we were abeam of Tilbury that the naval station ashore was not visible. If it had been we should have been stopped and told to stand by until the fog lifted. Curiously we did not have to keep W/T listening watch while proceeding up and down the Thames, above Southend. I had reduced speed to a minimum and was keeping well over to starboard so that now and again a glimpse of the bank was possible and this was my warning to keep out a bit.

We only saw an odd tug now and again through the damp dark gloom and one vessel, about 3,000 tons, going hard astern without sounding the recognised and required three blasts. However by putting on a burst of speed we shot away to port and missed a collision. The vessel had either touched bottom with her bow, or nearly done so, for she was right off the deep channel at a narrow bend in the river where a long ridge ran out from the northern bank.

It was a ticklish job finding the correct arch to go through under the main London bridges, also I was afraid of craft coming down the river, as we couldn't see right through them. However, we were proceeding very slowly and making a good noise on our navigation horn and we eventually arrived safely at Westminster Pier.

On contacting my friends at the Port of London Authority they informed me we were the only movement up the Thames from Southend. They had been unable to warn us at Tilbury as they hadn't seen us and as a final gesture they added that the RAF had done well to get through.

Next day it was clearer and we proceeded to our destination at Hampton. On arriving I received instructions to attend an enquiry to be held between HQCC and representatives of the firm of boat builders concerned.

I had found from previous experience that some of the civilian firms contracting to the RAF were not averse to trying to pass the responsibility for defects in boat or engine construction on to the poor RAF captains and crew dereliction of duty. This is what happened in this case. It was actually suggested that it was a put up job on our part! They even said that the launch had never made water! Their reason for this deduction being that they had found dry sawdust in the bilges. Also if we had swilled the decks regularly during hot weather everything would have been all right.

It is easy to note from this that they had no sound case and were even contradicting themselves.

Fortunately, I had an answer to each of their accusations. A squadron leader from Group had vouched for the excessive water in our bilges when we entered Grimsby after only a few hours at sea in rough weather.

It was later admitted that for approximately six months the launch had been at a mooring awaiting an engine part before handing over to the RAF. Not once had the decks been washed down, when in the contract they had to do so each day.

While this enquiry was on I submitted that the bilge pumps were quite unsuitable and I was again criticised by the boat builders in no uncertain terms, who considered them both adequate and suitable. That being so, I asked if we might have a demonstration.

My request was supported by Wing Commander Sweet from HQCC and my critic fell into the trap for he seemed pleased to carry out the demonstration. Now to appreciate this incident to the full it must be known that he had his best suit on for the occasion as a probable cost running into four figures was in question. The water in the bilges was none too clean but he had asked for it and he was going to get it.

Up we all went on deck, the cap was taken off one of the four pumps and the demonstrator put his hands round the handle of the pump ready to lift with all his weight. It was then obvious to me that he had never worked one before, having probably originally passed them for us from a report and plan or sample in his office. In the meantime we had all stepped ashore where we could have a better view of the proceedings. When he lifted with all his might, up came the water with force out of the pump on either side of the draw shaft, hitting the man in the face and chest, covering his shirt and suit with greasy bilge water.

My luck was in, I had won my case, for all I had to say was, "Gentlemen, you can imagine the difficulties my crew had in trying to work four such pumps in rough weather." While the unlucky man left us to change his clothes I was taken out for a good lunch with my senior officers and so ended another interesting episode.

FIRST SHIPMENT FROM LONDON DOCKS

Nearly all RAF craft for shipment overseas were shipped from west coast ports until 1944. Then as shipping returned to London Docks after the air raids had eased up, it was decided to despatch a few RAF craft from these docks. I arrived with the first new power boat HSL for this purpose. Fortunately, I went to my usual berth at Westminster instead of the docks and found there was a week's delay before shipment. My crew had no objection to this with free lodging in the heart of London and plenty of time off for a few days.

My next discovery was that they hadn't any experienced RAF personnel to handle the lifting arrangements, including the assembly of the cradle. It so happened we had helped the Glasgow team on previous occasions and therefore knew the procedure of carrying out the whole movement. So HQCC asked me to remain with my crew and take responsibility for the shipment. Unfortunately, it did not stop at that. Soon after an order came through for me to collect another HSL from above Hampton and it had to be done within the next few days.

The chief difficulty to be dealt with was how was I, with only one crew to ship one launch and collect another on the same day. It required careful planning and this is how it worked out.

Early one morning all personal gear was removed on to the landing stage at Westminster together with most of the ferry kit. One of the crew was left in charge with permission to purchase food stores ready for our return in the evening. The piermaster agreed to keep an eye on our equipment.

This left a crew of eight and myself. We then sailed down the Thames to Princes Dock and berthed alongside the quay astern of the vessel on which the launch was to be shipped. Here I left my coxswain in charge with one fitter and three men to start preparing everything for lifting the following morning. Two of them had their gear with them and were to remain as boat watch for the night. The coxswain and the other two men had to meet me at Westminster Pier in the evening, to load our gear on the other HSL on which they were to sleep for the night.

I then left with the remaining three men, comprising one wireless operator, one fitter and one deck hand and proceeded to the boat yard above Hampton. On arriving, the HSL had to be examined and checked and by moving fast we were ready to sail by two o'clock. The river pilot, who we always had with us as far as Westminster, was at the wheel, my wireless operator stood in as a deck hand and I was free to help as well.

We hadn't proceeded for more than a few miles before we ran into fog. The pilot cheered me up by saying it would soon be too thick to move and we would be stuck with no food or sleeping gear and at a distance of nine miles from the other three members of the crew who would soon be shivering on top of our pile of gear at Westminster! Somehow or other we just had to get there.

Soon, as predicted, the fog closed in and we could only see a boat length ahead of us and we made fast to a cadet training ship. From there I phoned my stranded coxswain at Westminster who told me conditions were just as bad there. However, I told him to hold on and await further orders. I then tackled the pilot who had been on the river nearly all his life and knew every inch of it. So I asked him if he could direct me by hand signals from the bow if I took over the controls and the wheel. It was a new idea for him and he expressed willingness to try—though he was certain we should only make two or three miles at the most. That didn't concern me, all I wanted to do was to keep moving.

So with a deck hand on the port side and another on the starboard with a handful of fendoffs each, we cast off. I was ticking over at slowest speed on one engine, with another running in case we had to go hard astern, and the experiment worked.

Every bridge we passed under safely, I called to the pilot, "Well done, let's try one more." It took us two hours to do the last seven miles, and I seldom saw a thing as we passed except the arches of the bridges under which we went. It was a curious sensation moving as though we were blindfolded, suddenly making a sharp turn to port or to starboard without my even seeing what we were avoiding.

By the time we were within a mile of Westminster Bridge I could see through the fog that my pilot was really excited. This was something he had never done before and he would be able to talk about it to his family and friends for the rest of his life! It would stand out as one of his great achievements. He deserved this uplift, he had done well. Soon his message came back to me to watch out for Westminster Bridge. Its supports are very wide and the tide races past them. They would certainly be nasty things to hit. However, we got through safely. We started up our third engine for manoeuvring and turning round into the tide, and I felt my way to starboard until at last we spotted the MLs lined up along the landing stage of the pier. A berth had been kept free for us ahead of them and we slipped quietly into it, receiving a big welcome from the navy and my own coxswain and men who no longer had visions of sleeping all night on top of the ferry gear.

The next day all went well with lifting the first HSL and the day after we said goodbye to London as we sailed down the Thames on another trip.

DUMBARTON TO TERNEUZEN (HOLLAND). Dec/Jan. 1944/45

Dumbarton on the Clyde is at the best of times a cold, damp place to visit and our marine craft base was about the worst spot in it. Only just a few feet above water level, two thirds of the ground being covered in thick mud and water, so that it was impossible to move about without getting shoes dirty and feet wet!

This was the spot where we arrived on a cold, wet December morning to collect Pinnace 1329, which had to be ferried to Holland. As the ferry kit was unpacked there was not only the mud and slush to contend with but also a fine Scottish rain, which ensured our blankets, sleeping bags and personal gear being well and truly damp by the time it was on board. Even if those conditions didn't ensure it, the conditions on the pinnace did. It had been lying unattended on a mooring for months and was in a damp and disgraceful condition. It took the crew a full day to get it reasonably clean.

The trip through the canal from the Clyde to Firth of Forth—Bowling to Grangemouth—was an interesting one. We did the trip in two hops, the first from Bowling to the village of Kirkintilloch, taking six hours thirty-five minutes, a distance of seventeen miles and about sixteen lock gates to go through. The following day we proceeded to Grangemouth, a distance of twenty miles, and this took nine and a half hours and included a two and a half hour wait at the end of the canal for the tide to rise enough for us to proceed down the Carron River to Grangemouth docks. There were about seventeen lock gates at the eastern end of the canal.

The trip through the canal was hard work. The locks were very small, only allowing us two or three feet to play with in length and beam. This meant very careful handling so as not to hit the hull on either side when entering the locks and stopping before the bow collided with the gate ahead of the lock. When there was a strong crosswind blowing, we had to enter the lock gates with enough speed so as not to be blown on to the heavy swingpost of the gate and then to stop within our own length. This meant going astern on at least two engines and had to be done without any swing round of the stern.

Apart from one member of the crew whom I kept in the galley, all the crew shared the strenuous work of opening and closing the lock gates which exhausted them. The men had to go ashore at the approach to each gate, run ahead to open the gate, one at the bow, another astern, with lines to throw up to the wall above for making fast before the water was let in or out. The remaining two members of the crew stood on the port and starboard decks with fendoffs ready in case we touched the sides.

I always took the wheel and controls and had my coxswain on the bow so he could signal me if necessary. When there was a strong wind blowing and we entered the gates with a good way on us, his face was a picture—full of anxiety until he felt the pull of the engines going astern slowing us up. From that moment he was too busy to worry, throwing lines and warning me by hand signal that he was sure the bow would ram the gate ahead. On this trip we found a bicycle; most useful, so that one of the men could go ahead of us to warn the control man at the electric or hand bridges which had to be opened for us to pass.

On the following morning we sailed for Methil, a small harbour north of the Forth. There was a strong north-east wind blowing but we were reasonably protected until we passed the Forth bridge, after which for the remaining fifteen miles we had a rough passage.

Whenever we went under the Forth Bridge if there was a new member of the crew who hadn't been under before, one or more of the others would take him on for a packet of cigarettes that a train would cross while we were within sight and so far as I can remember they won every time.

The following day we sailed before dawn for Blyth, but being December and very uncertain weather, my early sailing was chiefly to take advantage of high water at mid-day when I would be abeam of Berwick and could take shelter if the weather was too bad. Berwick harbour is very small, three quarters of a mile up the Tweed, and can only be entered with safety two hours either side of high water. Within an hour of leaving Methil I knew we were in for a bad time and that we should do well to reach Berwick. The north easterly had increased to gale force and by the time we turned on to a few degrees east of a southerly course a very big sea was running on our port side.

It was on such occasions that a little forethought proved helpful. We were only in a sixty foot pinnace cruising at twelve knots and under such conditions Blyth was far too long a distance to run. If we had sailed later we would have been too late to shelter at Berwick, but having sailed early it was full high water when we were six miles off the harbour, so I altered course for the entrance. Visibility was poor and there was no buoy to mark the position when we altered course for the shore, so I was glad when having run nearly five miles, we sighted the church spire in the distance. Almost at the same time we saw the large waves crashing over the sea-wall at the entrance to the River Tweed.

It looked a tough proposition to enter under such conditions as the entrance channel was so narrow and the heavy sea was running right up and breaking over the bank on the port hand. No pilot was out to meet us; in fine weather they were frequently trying to insist that a pilot was necessary! This was an unnecessary cost which we had to meet.

I signalled ashore that I was entering and took over the wheel myself. This was officially against orders, but I was responsible for the safety of both the launch and the crew and in practice if the coxswain remained at the wheel, he had to take instructions from me and at such time there was neither time to give nor take instructions.

Tricky handling in a rough sea was an exhilarating experience. On this occasion I slowed down a quarter of a mile from the entrance and took note of the waves and their course across the bar. We approached at slow speed waiting for an extra large wave to pass us, when it came I put on a burst of speed and followed it as fast as we could go before another wave could catch us up. We just raced along the narrow entrance, one big wave washing along the high sea wall on our starboard side and another and another coming up astern of us. All this time the crew was absolutely silent, watching the wave astern in case it should catch us up and turn us round into the sea wall, but by the time it reached us we were too far up and it had lost its fierce momentum. We were safe!

The coxswain took the wheel again and everyone was busy preparing lines and fendoffs ready to go alongside. Berwick was the cleanest spot we visited on this coast and we always enjoyed our nights there, for however much the wind blew we had such good shelter in the inner harbour that it didn't disturb us.

Next day we reached Blyth in rough weather and the following day Hartlepool. The weather remained bad and made each trip uncomfortable. Hartlepool to Grimsby is a good day's run in a pinnace. We left Hartlepool in a fine drizzle with a strong east wind. Visibility was down to a few hundred yards but, apart from the discomfort of pounding and cold, all went well until we were within ten miles of Flamborough Head. There is often a nasty sea running off this headland and though we were still a good distance from it, I could tell we were in for a nasty time as the wind had increased to gale force. I decided to make for Bridlington, a pleasant little harbour just a few miles round Flamborough Head.

Our official course was six miles out from the headland but I took a chance and cut the corner as I had heard from a fisherman that the tidal race was not so bad inshore, which proved to be correct; it also reduced our distance to Bridlington by nearly three miles. It was a wonderful sight seeing the waves smash against the north-east harbour wall sending the spray right over the harbour like fine rain. We entered without trouble and found a good berth. The only difficulty being that the harbour dried out at low water. This was most inconvenient when living aboard, also it limited the times for sailing. Apart from this, it was always looked upon as one of our favourite spots on the east coast.

The gale continued for a few days, so I was able to go by bus to Hornsea for a day. It was the home of my childhood and the place where my brother was born. We moved from there to Bournemouth in 1908 when I was four. Though this was my first visit since then, I was able to recognise from a distance the Congregational church where my father had been minister. One Sunday morning my father was away and the pulpit was occupied by a stranger; he was about to announce the first hymn when I stood up on the seat and shouted at the top of my voice, "No daddy—so Freddy go home!"

Having a good look round the church, I recalled the fancy clothing that I had been dressed in, white buckskin shoes, velvet shorts and tunics adorned with large diamante buttons and a fancy lace collar. The old home which I went to see looked just the same and the tennis courts were still on the opposite side of the road where I had spent hours picking up the balls. Three to four years old must be our happiest years, no trouble beyond castor oil; there was Jock the dog to play with, steam engines and trains in the play room at the top of the house, which were equally enjoyed by my father. I still remember the startled look on his face when he caught something alight from the steam engine and how he pounced on the flames to put them out.

Bournemouth had developed from a few fishing cottages into one of our largest and most beautiful holiday resorts in less than a century. But Hornsea, with its coast-line braving the easterly gales, was unchanged with the passing of the thirty-eight years except for signs of age and decay. I pondered on the rise and fall of towns and likewise that of business enterprises. Both are so often dependent not only on position but also on the vision and drive of those at the head. The afternoon was spent in the company of a dear friend of my mother, Mrs Askew, and her daughter. They both remembered me and I greatly enjoyed this link with the past.

Evening soon came and I was back in my little cabin slipping into my narrow sleeping bag for the night. We reached Grimsby on 23rd December, 1944. My crew very much hoped to spend Christmas in Yarmouth, but at 6 a.m. on the 24th the launch was isolated by a blanket of fog. You couldn't see the bow from the stern.

I have never, not even in London, seen such a complete black out. It was hopeless to attempt sailing so I had a meeting with the crew and told them if it lifted during the day or the following night we would sail, so as to give them their Christmas day in Yarmouth. Night came and it was no better and much to their dismay it was no better on Christmas morning. So there was nothing for it but to make the best of it.

I gave them two alternatives, either to go ashore for the day, or to stay on board. Six of us chose the latter and we planned the best Christmas dinner possible under the circumstances, having previously made a few special food purchases from various naval stores and saved up for such an occasion. The menu was good: soup, roast pork, pudding, mince pies, cheese, nuts and a double ration of rum!

We decorated my cabin, found a tablecloth and by the time the whistle went for lunch we had forgotten about the fog. We all had discarded our tunics and wore sweaters so we were a small happy party with no ranks dividing us. The spirit of Christmas was among us as we forgot the fog and the journey ahead. That evening when the shore party returned they all wished they had remained with us.

The following morning there was slight visibility up to 500 yards in places so at 8.30 with Skipper Scottie on the bridge of Pinnace 1336 following close astern of us, we sailed for Yarmouth. Scottie was a happy go lucky fellow, quite content to follow.

On our early morning sailings, he just donned his duffle coat over his pyjamas, plus hat and shoes, so as to look the part when leaving harbour, once outside, down he went to his cabin again for another sleep before his breakfast was brought to him. This was a fairly safe procedure for him under reasonable conditions, for all his coxswain had to do was to follow the leader.

It was hard going from Grimsby to the boom defence, a distance of about eight miles. The fog kept closing down so I had to rely entirely on compass courses; this is not so easy in closed waters with cross tides running and it was with relief we sighted close to starboard the Boom Examination Vessel signalling to us that it was all clear to proceed.

We hadn't been running for more than ten minutes after leaving the boom when suddenly the fog lifted and we were beneath blue skies in bright December sunshine; the sea was flat calm. The crew was soon singing and I heard the rattle of dishes below as the breakfast things were being washed up and the cook was busy preparing our lunch.

I pictured Scottie, asleep astern of us, while I was kept busy keeping a careful check on our courses, for we never went in a straight line from port to port. From Grimsby to Yarmouth the distance was only ninety-five miles and we had to alter course over twenty times, to follow the route as laid down by the Naval Routing Authority.

Just after mid-day while half the crew was at lunch, I had to sound the call "all hands on deck" (excepting fitters and wireless operator) for a few miles ahead a black wall of fog came into view. Signalling Scottie to note his position in case we were separated, I revved up the engine to full speed hoping to reach the north-east Burnham black conical buoy before being enveloped.

We sighted the buoy when the fog bank was just beyond it, standing like a wall out of the sea. We won the race, but with only two minutes to spare. I stopped my engines within fifty yards of the buoy, in the hope that Scottie would reach me in time. Just when he was within hailing distance the wall of fog enveloped us. To be plunged from bright sunshine into semi-darkness with the decks and rigging dripping with moisture within a matter of minutes and visibility beyond ten yards completely blotted out was no pleasant experience. The crew had to work in pairs as look-outs, one fore and the other aft, changing teams each half hour.

Scottie was completely lost and instead of hoping to see him, my desire became the reverse, for there was danger of us colliding and sinking one or the other—or both. There was no safe anchorage nearby. We were on the main east coast shipping route, so if we stayed where we were there would be the constant danger of being rammed. Therefore, there was nothing for it but to move on and to hope to reach Sheringham anchorage, a distance of approximately twenty-five miles.

In this short distance we had to alter course seven times, each leg being marked by a buoy, none of which, much to my relief was seen, for the only way to have seen them would have been to ram them. Then there were the constant listening and peering into the darkness for signs of other shipping, but we neither saw nor heard a thing for over two hours, except that of our own engines, and the wash of the water as the bow cut its way through the smooth even sea. At 14.20 hours, according to my reckoning, we were within a mile of Sheringham anchorage. Our next problem was to find out if this was actually so.

I took soundings and proceeded at low revs on two engines. Within a few minutes a bell was heard slightly to port; we altered course, closed down both engines and there looming up alongside was the bow of a large tanker. I went ahead slow on one engine almost feeling my way, keeping a few yards away from the tanker, until, when about midships, a voice hailed us from above. "Is this Sheringham anchorage," I asked. "Yes, you are three miles from the shore," he replied and added as an afterthought, "There are so many vessels at anchor that you could almost walk ashore over them."

All the same I wasn't risking spending a night or more among this enlarged company so I altered course for the shore. At 14.40 hours, according to the distance run and soundings taken we were within half a mile of the shore, not having seen or heard another thing since leaving the tanker. Down went the anchor, we were safe, for no large vessel would anchor so close inshore. After arranging a rota with the crew for keeping a constant watch throughout the night, my next duty was to send a signal to naval control giving them my position and intention.

My duties for the day were over. All I had to do was to wash and relax. My cook presented me with a fine supper and I settled down to writing my usual letter home, wondering when it would be posted.

During the night I was roused, as the fog had lifted in patches, and we could see a light ashore. In the stillness we heard a train in the distance and also the small waves as they turned over on the beach. The blanket was soon upon us again, but next morning, we felt the suspicion of a breeze. First we could see the bow from the stern, then within ten minutes, vision was up to half a mile. Off went a signal indicating our departure, which I hoped Scottie would pick up—he did. Then, with our anchor lifted, course was set and we went ahead at 1,800 revs on three engines.

Not having any idea where Scottie was, I kept a double watch on the look-out for him. Away to port I saw some of the many vessels on the move which had been using the anchorage. We were on a course to take us outside a wreck which was about five miles off the next headland. As we approached this position we spotted away to starboard a small object on a course to intercept us. Ten minutes later we met. It was 1336 and what a welcome we gave one another.

On being separated the previous day, Scottie, not having planned his course, steered one straight course of a little over twenty miles—hoping for the best and then on another 90° to starboard. He must have passed close to

(17) Elizabeth Riceman opening the new store at Canterbury watched by father and brothers David (left) and Jonathan (right).

(18) The Mayor and Mayoress of Canterbury with Fred and Betty Riceman outside the Rooftop Restaurant on Opening Day.

Photos by Ben May

(19 & 20) Two of the first window displays at the Canterbury store.

(21) *Opposite* An early special promotion, *Spring-a-long with Ricemans*. Note the mounted pilgrim, which has become the store's motif. Photos by Ben May

(22)   The morning after—sifting through the debris of the author's office.   Photo by Douglas Weaver

(23)   *Opposite* The disastrous fire of Spring 1963.   Photo by *Kentish Gazette*

(24)   *The Best of British* promotion. E. C. Redhead, M.P., Minister of State (Overseas) at the Board of Trade, and the author listening to Sir Leslie Thomas, M.P. for Canterbury.
Photo by Entwistle Photographic Services

(25) A presentation in 1963 to the author and his wife by Mrs. V. O. Merrell, hat buyer, on behalf of the senior staff at Canterbury.

Photo by Douglas Weaver

(26) Father Christmas lit up at night.

Photo by Ben May

(27 & 28) The Whitefriars development.

(29) *Overleaf* The main store at Canterbury.   Photos by *Kentish Gazette*

sandbanks and wrecks but his luck was in until by his soundings he knew he was near the shore. Actually, his bow just touched bottom but by going astern he got clear. Later on when the fog lifted a little he could see people on the beach and he had thoughts of going ashore for the evening!

But to return to our trip. We proceeded to Yarmouth arriving at 12.35 on Wednesday, 27th December. Here we were delayed with centre engine trouble, followed by more fog. We sailed from Yarmouth for Felixstowe on the last day of 1944 so I was now in waters well known to me.

Soon after arriving I made enquiries about my next route to Ostend. All previous sailings had been via Ramsgate; this was a long way round and would take two days. So I sailed up to Harwich to see the naval control to try and obtain permission to take a route almost direct across the North Sea in one hop. After much talking the naval officer in charge agreed to my request provided I accompanied an ML which was also bound for Ostend. In the meantime there was some unexpected excitement brewing. The new year was at hand and everyone was hoping it would be the last of the war.

Before giving my crew shore leave for New Year's eve I reminded them not to let themselves or me down by getting drunk and that all hands were to be on board and below deck by midnight. I turned in about eleven o'clock and was aroused on the stroke of midnight by pandemonium let loose from all quarters of the harbour, in which there were about thirty small naval and RAF craft.

On going on deck I found they were all vying with one another to see who could make the most noise. This was all right until someone started shooting off Very lights and soon the sky over the harbour was lit up with shooting colours—what a target for an enemy plane! Then another crazy crew started firing off rounds on a machine gun. This was getting beyond a joke so I quickly dressed and was up on deck again. I hadn't far to look for trouble. My crew was still below deck but not so on 1336 alongside where there was real cause for alarm with the men all drunk, including Scottie. He and another big fellow had long heavy crowbars and they were holding them with two hands and crashing them on their large ventilators and the derrick. Probably they thought they were in a brass band! Another was trying to fire a Very pistol with the cartridge pointing at their feet instead of the sky.

There was nothing for it but for me to intervene to avoid serious trouble. Jumping on board, I grabbed Scottie by the collar and hauled him across on to my pinnace and down into my cabin to sober him up. He pulled himself together and after a few minutes we went across to 1336 and his crew piped down. In the meantime excitement had increased among the navy, but in the end the noise died down of its own accord. The next morning, fortunately for all, the fog was so thick that all sailings were cancelled, but on 2nd January, 1945 we sailed for Ostend, in company with ML466 and Pinnace 1336. The fog was still thick, visibility being from a hundred yards to half a mile. It was cold and inclined to drizzle, not ideal conditions for a pleasant trip.

As was my habit I had prepared the various courses to be taken before sailing, together with distance to be run. I gave a copy to the captain of the ML and asked him if he agreed on them, which he did. Therefore, on sailing, though I was following the ML, I was checking his courses. I could never be satisfied with follow the leader without knowing where I was. The distance was just over ninety-nine miles but after the first hour we were nearly two miles off course. I didn't want to tell a member of the senior service in the lead that he was off course but in the end I called him up and tactfully gave him my estimated position, hoping we would check it with his. This he must have done for a few moments later he altered course. This same process occurred at intervals for the remainder of the trip. Visibility did not improve and when we were running abeam of the French coast on the last thirty miles, there was only a narrow swept channel on both sides of which there were mines and uncharted wrecks. I therefore repeated my signals from time to time. I don't know whether the ML's compass was out or if our friend in the lead hadn't done much navigating, but whichever it was, it gave me one of the most unpleasant trips I had experienced in comparatively calm water. However, we were off Ostend at dusk but there was so much shipping that we were delayed for an hour. When we entered the harbour it was pitch dark and we narrowly missed hitting a large wreck just inside the entrance which had not been properly marked. We had not received instructions where to make fast, but we found a berth as near the entrance as possible so as to have a quick getaway the following morning.

During the evening, Scottie and I had a look round the battered town. The shops were well stocked and we managed to buy a bottle of good perfume to take home with us. We had an evening meal out and it must have been months before Scottie fully recovered from the shock he received when he looked at the bill. For me, it was almost worth the price just to see his face and to hear his muttering.

A lot of German planes passed over during the evening but no bombs fell in our vicinity. The next morning we proceeded on our own to Terneuzen, which is a small town up the Scheldt on the bank to starboard a few miles from Antwerp. The fog had lifted, we only had nearly forty-two miles to go, so apart from enemy interference, which had been extensive earlier in the week, we were in for a pleasant trip. My only anxiety was to keep to the swept channel as the E-boats were busy most nights spreading mines and traps for large and small craft.

After an eight mile run on our first course we had for the rest of the trip to alter course every four to six miles each leg marked by a buoy, so I didn't anticipate any difficulty. We did not find the first two buoys and it was only after completing the third leg that we saw a buoy marking the channel. They were not pleasant waters in which to run adrift.

All the way up to the mouth of the Scheldt, the majority of the buoys were missing, so it was with great relief that I sighted the broad expanse of water at the mouth of this waterway. Here again I had received strict instructions to keep to the given courses all the way up to Terneuzen. There was a large number of big cargo vessels with the signal hoisted for pilot wanted and as soon as they saw us passing them they started up astern of us little knowing this to be our first trip up the Scheldt. Fortunately we found our way up without any difficulty. On arriving Scottie and I were kept busy arranging to hand over our launches on the following morning to the RAF base and then back to England for the next trip.

The officers of the local unit invited Scottie and me to dinner at their mess that evening, Wednesday, 3rd January, 1945, and they did us well. It was a grand building, staffed by Dutch waiters, who only a few weeks previously had been serving their Nazi rulers. We felt rather embarrassed after such a good feed, to find the local Dutch population in such poor straits, as they were so short of all the simple necessities of life. Just across the water from us the enemy were launching flying bombs. We could see them leave the ground and rise to a given height and then set out over our heads for England.

On the morning after our arrival we had handed our launches over, duly checked, packed and loaded all our kit on to a couple of lorries, said our farewells and were off over the bumpy roads, which for miles ran along the banks of canals. The enemy had destroyed all the lock gates—putting this method of transportation out of action. One could well understand the chaos this caused the Dutch people as their narrow roads were quite unsuited to cope with normal demands, let alone the demands of war. On arriving at the embarkation office at Ostend after much chasing around and talking I managed to get my crew on board a large landing craft bound for England. It was a bad night for sailing, raining, bad visibility and a strong south-west wind, so I knew what to expect once we were under way.

Though only a little over 200 miles to Tilbury we had to spend sixty-six hours aboard. It seemed like a week for there was nothing to do but talk, sleep and sit, if you could find a seat! To make matters worse, the food supply was quite inadequate for the large numbers of men on board.

All of us were feeling the worse for wear, as the ship groped its way up to Tilbury. Scottie and I knew we would have to work fast to get away from the docks the same evening, so it was a race to see who could tell the best story to secure transport for the removal of our ferry kit which weighed about one and a half tons. The idea was to secure any kind of vehicle which would take the gear and run up to a London railway terminus. Being Saturday, apart from the embarkation officers, the place was practically deserted.

Incidentally, there were no Customs officials to make us pay for our small purchases on the continent. The boys who had escaped from Arnhem had landed a few days previously and had to pay quite a big sum between them; it seemed unfair that we should get away with it, but the officials had to have their Saturdays off.

After much talking and phoning, I managed to secure what appeared to be the only truck available, an open Bedford. Scottie was not so fortunate but I managed to get his gear on to my truck.

It was freezing hard, but a few members of both crews volunteered to ride up to town on top of the kit and the remainder went by train. Having stowed our kit safely at Waterloo, we gave our crews a leave pass until Monday morning, when we were due to return to Calshot to report for the next trip.

THE SOS IN THE IRISH SEA

Those of us who were on rescue work did not often have to send out messages for help for ourselves. Only once did I have to do so.

It was early in December 1944. We had arrived at Dumbarton, Glasgow to collect a pinnace which had to reach Birkenhead docks by a given date for shipment. The distance was only about 220 miles but this is a long way when gales and storms are at their worst and it took us a week to reach Douglas in the Isle of Man. Here I was welcomed with the news that in spite of the delay I would still be in time for the Birkenhead shipment.

Next morning the weather report was that the gale would increase in force during the day, still from the north-west. As the big sea would be astern of me I was all for sailing, especially as it was a short run and we should reach the entrance to Liverpool by mid-day and so escape the threatened deterioration in weather. So we sailed at 8.30 a.m. Once we were clear of the shelter of the island we found an enormous sea following us on our port quarter making our progress swift and comparatively smooth. We were nearly half way across to Birkenhead and I was feeling pleased that I had sailed, when without any warning we swung hard to port and the crest of a big wave hit us before there was time to realise what had happened.

The coxswain shouted to me that the steering had gone. I immediately closed down on all engines and revved on the port engine to try to correct the turn to port, but no action of the engines had any effect on our course, we just went on turning to port. So I had to stop engines. On examining the steering gear a breakdown on a lower pinion was found and nothing could be done about it at sea. Being a pinnace we had no auxiliary steering so we were at the mercy of the gale, now increasing in force, until help came.

A German submarine had been reported in the vicinity so I had to abide strictly to the rules and only send out a coded message. This was not easy, for we were being thrown all over the place. My immediate job was to help my wireless operator code a message. He was being very sick but I admired the way he stuck to his job, especially as he knew he was likely to have to put up with it for hours.

We sent out the following message: "Steering completely unserviceable at 11.50 hours position 14 miles on 364° true from western light vessel, drifting. Immediate towing assistance required." The message was received in Liverpool at 12.09 hours.

The following message was sent by Liverpool to Destroyer 195 and ourselves at 12.35 hours: "Proceed to assist Pinnace 1354 in difficulty in position . . ." That message received at 13.08 hours and put new heart into my crew. It would be dark soon after 4 p.m. and they had visions of drifting helplessly all night and being smashed to pieces on the rocky coast some thirty miles away. We were all soaked with salt water, most of us had lost our breakfast and it was hopeless to try and eat under such conditions.

I kept them busy so as to have their minds occupied. We tried various ways to head into the wind with poor results. Everything below deck was secured as firmly as possible. Then at 13.35 we sighted a speck on the horizon. Good old navy. I even heard some of my boys begin to sing. It was a good thing they didn't realise what was still to come. The destroyer was within signalling distance at 13.45 hours.

I tried to persuade the captain to tow us to Liverpool but he didn't fancy the entrance in such a bad storm. So we had to go back all the thirty miles we had come. Even this was not going to be easy. It would mean going into the teeth of the gale which as the weather report had indicated was blowing harder than ever.

The first thing was to have the tow rope fixed properly. We had to keep two to three hundred yards away from the destroyer for fear of being thrown against her. They shot small lines at us; when we caught one we pulled it in and the heavier line was attached to it and eventually the tow rope. Several attempts were made as the waves were picking us up and throwing us away, they were also breaking over the destroyer and soaking the crew on deck. One rope nearly fouled the destroyer's propellors, until at last all was well.

The operation took over an hour and a half and, as we set off for Douglas, pitch darkness was upon us, we couldn't even see across our decks. We had six hours under tow, an endless experience under such conditions. Our forward mast had come adrift. It was pouring with rain, the gale was at its height. None of us had any food in us.

We were carrying no lights (except the destroyer which carried a shaded direction stern light) and we proceeded at five knots. Almost every big wave we hit seemed to curl over our bow, roll along the deck, and break again over the wheel house, dripping through the hatch cover down our necks. We aboard the pinnace were past caring about submarines and we all gathered in the wheelhouse (except one who had to take to his bunk).

We hadn't been under way for more than ten minutes before the destroyer called us up by Aldis lamp) asking whether there was anything we were wanting. What a question to ask us! If we had, what chance was there of our getting it. It was a kind thought on their part but they had forgotten that to us, even to reply "No thanks" entailed my poor wireless operator being held up with head and shoulders above deck to receive the full force of a couple of waves as they broke over us! In the end I had to request that no further messages be sent unless really essential.

My job was to keep the spirits of my boys up. I started off telling them we should soon sight Douglas lighthouse and in the meantime that we should feel relief at not being left adrift all night. Gradually one by one they settled down in a corner, or sitting on the wheelbeam deck leaving two or three on either side of me on the look-out. The occasion called for song and we sang for over three hours. The store-keeper found a bag of currants and these gave us something to nibble occasionally.

Then a cheer went up, a pin prick of a light could be seen ahead to starboard. Land ahead but it would take another three hours to reach it.

More songs and an occasional snore and eventually the destroyer dropped anchor in the sheltered waters just off Douglas. A launch was standing by to tow us into harbour where we arrived a little after midnight.

While I was ashore sending off signals, my crew was busy lighting stoves to dry out our cabins and having a quick whisk round to clear up as much as possible. Meanwhile the galley boys had a hot meal on the go. At 01.00 hours we were all sitting down to it, our clothes having dried on us.

The following morning, on close inspection, it was found that repairs had to be effected in Liverpool, so HQ sent another pinnace to tow us across. We eventually reached Liverpool having survived five hours anchored in dense fog en route.

THE FLOATING MINE INCIDENT

It was quite a frequent occurrence for us to sight loose floating objects including mines when on both rescue and ferry duties.

Curiously enough, though I ran long distances off the normal swept channels (shipping was confined to swept channels except naval and ASR craft on duty) I never saw a mine in unswept waters.

Originally we had instructions to shoot up floating mines or to report them. Then for some unknown reason we were instructed not to signal their position while at sea but to report their whereabouts on returning to harbour.

The incident that stands out in my mind was while on a trip to Newlyn. About an hour before dark we were in the main swept channel about twenty miles from the Lizard. We sighted an object only about fifteen yards from our bows, in fact the wash lifted it as it shot away from our bows. I immediately slowed down and signalled engine room to disengage two engines, and at the same time turning helm hard to starboard and cruising slowly round the object before stopping.

114

The crew by this time was all on deck. None of us had ever seen an object quite like it before, however, we all voted it as being a mine. I was ferrying and had no ammunition on board. I knew this to be a busy channel and some ships were bound to be up and down during the night. What was I to do? Well, I took a chance and coded a message giving the position of object and time sighted and gave it to my wireless operator to send to Plymouth. We proceeded on our journey. Twenty minutes later we sighted a couple of minesweepers so I eased down speed and as we passed signalled them a copy of the message I had already sent to Plymouth. Their captain thanked me and we proceeded on our way, forgetting about the incident.

A few weeks later when I called in at Newlyn there was a sealed official note from the Captain of Minesweepers, Plymouth, Dartmouth and Falmouth. I at once thought I was being reprimanded for signalling about a supposed mine against orders but actually the signal read as follows:

Subject : MINE
1. The commendable initiative of RAF Rescue Launch 2714 in closing the minesweeping vessels, to report the mine sighted off St Anthony on the 26th February 1944 is much appreciated.
2. Such co-operation is of great value to the war effort and possibly saved a casualty either to one of HM Ships or a Merchant Vessel.

This brings the story of some of my war-time experiences to an end. There were others, plenty of them, but the few I have told serve as illustrations of the general picture. There is just one closing reference that must not be omitted and that concerns the crews I had. As is to be found in every walk of life, the personality of each one contributed in a greater or lesser degree to our efforts. Over a period of three years I naturally had many different crews. I had, however, two special crews for quite a time. To have lived together for months on end in the confined space of a pinnace or HSL, to have shared the discomforts, risks and thrills provided a link between us that I shall always remember. It would have been so easy to tire of one another's company when thrown together in such circumstances, but never once did I have to break up a quarrel. The greater the difficulties the more they stuck together.

If, in some small measure, I was able to give increased confidence to our boys in the air and to help some who came down, I have to thank my crews who stuck to me through thick and thin and who never once lost heart or complained when taken on hazardous trips.

These ordinary men, who did their duty faithfully without thought of praise or reward, returned to their families and so long as their war-time spirit lasts the sun will never set on this land we love so dearly.

So when the armistice had been signed I knew my duty was done and I had no desire to spend months with nothing to do. I was fortunate to obtain my release and to be home two days after hostilities ceased.

CHAPTER THIRTEEN

RETURNING TO CIVILIAN LIFE

Like many others, I returned ready to carry on where I had left off three years earlier—but this was not to be. The thrill and excitement had gone out of business which had become automatic with almost everything controlled by coupons. If a business was purchased, it was often more because of its coupon value (buying power) than its profitability.

Purchase tax was something quite new to me, with all its variations and unexplainable lines of demarkation. Those who had kept our retail services going during the war years, and in particular department stores, had become used to the new pattern of trading. They could do nothing else but just jog along with it which they had done, very profitably.

Naturally, I had read about these things, and seen some of them when on leave but it was quite different to have to work with these hampering restrictions. Why advertise? Why promote? Why improve your business? The real issue was to get coupons and stock.

No, there was no chance of picking up work just where I had left off. Perhaps I had changed too. Three years of excitement at sea, of cold and heat, of storm and calm. Yes, perhaps I was different, and it might take some time to settle down.

None of these things, however, occurred to me when I hurried to the store on the first morning after my arrival home. I was soon to discover other changes. Another generation of the Beale family was now ready and eager to enter the family store just as I had anticipated earlier. One of them had actually been there most of the time I had been away, and there were others returning from the forces in the near future. It did not require much imagination to realise the problems that this would create. Our dream castle, which had seemed so secure, began to topple and then fall down around us.

My wife shared the disappointment with me but what could we do? Before the war we had kept our two small boats, a 17ft open Brooks launch and a 36ft cruiser, in Poole harbour. Now our home had its own wide frontage on to Christchurch harbour and we had planned when the war was over to have our own slipway from our private beach and our own moorings. It was not money that had taken me back to Bournemouth some fifteen years earlier and money alone would not compensate us for leaving now. However, it gradually dawned on us there was no other way out. We should have to make a start elsewhere.

It meant, in a way, starting all over again, and at a time when I felt least equipped to do so. Of course, the discussions that took place were frequent and difficult—and just as distressing to the Beale family as to us. We were treated with every consideration including the offer of financial help for our possible intention of starting on our own, then or at a later date. They did everything they could to help me find another suitable appointment.

A year passed before I left, and during that time I visited a number of old fashioned businesses ready for development but none seemed just right. During this period a city gentleman, complete with frock coat, came to see me at the request of Charles Clore (later Sir Charles); at that time I had never heard of him! The purpose of the visit was to find out if I would consider becoming the managing director of a store in Reading which Charles Clore was acquiring. My first reactions were entirely against it. However correspondence followed until eventually Charles Clore himself came down. Although I still had no thoughts of accepting his invitation to join him, I found him an interesting personality to talk to. A few points of the conversation remain with me.

We were walking through Bealesons' fashion showrooms, when he suddenly turned to me and said, "This is a popular priced store." I agreed. "Well," he added, "my store, Heelas of Reading, is a high class store. What do you know about that class of business?"

I told him once you understood the principles of distribution, if you had discernment and good taste, you could tune in your management to suit the business you were operating. It was felt that the position of the Bealesons store was best suited to the medium class trade but if I was in control of a high class business, I was confident that I could run it equally successfully.

Then we had a few words in my office, when it was obvious he was trying to weigh me up. He did not miss a thing; everything he said was with a special purpose and it helped me to realise the importance of finding out all one could about a person before entrusting him with responsibility. Was I happily married? How long had I been married? How many children had we? When he mentioned that he would like to meet my wife, I replied, "Certainly, if she is at home." After telephoning we drove out to have tea at Mudeford.

Again, it was obvious he wanted to see our home setting and if we were a happy and contented family. What wisdom he showed—how many in his position would have gone to so much trouble? Before we parted, he again asked if I would reconsider my decision, but at that stage I still had not changed my mind. He asked me to visit the store and meet the retiring managing director, Charles Hayes so after about a week, my wife and I drove to Reading, and spent the better part of a day with Mr Hayes in the store.

The store's potential impressed me as soon as we entered the front door. An imposing frontage, the position was right, the high class trading excellent, the area it covered should justify a large increase in turnover and there was an excellent team of buyers and senior staff. Everything had been standing still for many years. The interior was out of date, and it seemed to have just gone to sleep. However, it had not lost its note of quality and style.

We liked Mr Hayes immediately and he must have reciprocated, for it was rather pathetic the extent to which he tried to persuade us, there and then, to come to terms with Charles Clore. If only I would do so, he promised me support on the board, or in any way I wanted. He was, in fact, really past helping with any up to date ideas, but knowing his goodwill would be helpful in the town and with customers and staff I told him that, should I come, he must promise never to interfere, but support my proposals, plans and general management, even if he did not always agree with them. He readily gave this assurance. Later he proved a good companion and friend. Away from business we were soon calling him "Uncle Charlie".

As we were getting into the car my wife said, "Well, you won't think of going to that old fashioned place in spite of Mr Hayes being so charming, will you?"

When I told her it was an opportunity almost too good to miss, she was amazed and wondered whatever I expected to do with the place. However, she would not mind moving to Reading if we decided to go there. When Charles Clore contacted me again I agreed to meet him at his London office. It was an illuminating occasion.

His legal adviser, Leonard Sainer, was present to note down the terms agreed. Incidentally, I took immediately to Leonard Sainer who proved a good friend to us all the time we were in Reading, and I cannot remember any discord between us.

Charles Clore was looking at me and started the conversation, "What do you think of the store?"

"Good, but out of date."

"Can you make a success of it?"

"Yes, on my terms."

"What are they?"

"That I should be appointed managing director."

"Agreed."

"That I receive a salary plus bonus and share arrangements."

What I asked for was considerable, but fair for what I felt I could do for the business. Again he agreed without hesitation. I can think of no one else in this country in like circumstances who would have agreed so readily to these terms. However he was prepared to be, what he may have felt, generous, if by so doing he would get the person he wanted.

"Anything else?" he asked.

"Yes, just one more condition—the most important item of all. I will only come if you can give me your word that neither you, nor any other member of the board will interfere with my management. If you want this store brought up to date, I must have a perfectly free hand, and I can assure you that I will not let you down."

This was the only point on which he hesitated. His eyes seemed to penetrate mine. Dead silence. Mr Sainer did not say a word. Then a question was thrown at me, "Will you always listen to what we have to say?"

"Of course, sir, so long as I get the last word."

Another silence and a futher searching look at me. Then he just said, "Agreed" and left the details to Mr Sainer to include in the legal form. During the following three years, we had our disagreements, but he never once went back on the promises he made.

My wife and I had a busy time ahead of us. Apart from making my rough plans of Heelas, we had to sell our lovely home and find another, say goodbye to our friends in Bournemouth, and in particular, at Bealesons. It must have been a relief to the Beale family to know that everything had planned out this way and we left, I know, with their good wishes and interest in the new responsibilities that lay ahead.

CHAPTER FOURTEEN

HEELAS OF READING

To take over the mangement of a business that is ready for re-organisation offers scope but presents its own problems. There was much to do planning step by step, each contributing to the final picture.

A minor incident soon put the conditions of my appointment to the test. For years the business had revolved around Charles Hayes. If he had been a woman, he would, I suppose have been looked upon as a prima donna. As it was, the staff, especially those of long standing in the store, were always at his beck and call. Of his ability which he had used to good advantage in his younger days, there was no question, but he had settled down with age, and was out of touch. He had an office about 12ft by 7ft on the ground floor, surrounded by a glass partition, from which he could see all that was going on.

On the second floor there was a large, expensively panelled, well furnished board room, which was hardly ever used, as the business for some years had not held board meetings, except for the annual formal ones.

The ground floor was soon to be replanned and refixtured and every square foot was needed for selling, so I told Charles Hayes that I was sorry but his little office would have to go, but I would give him another, more comfortable, and I would use the board room. The shock this caused was almost unbelievable; it was the only time he went to Charles Clore about me. A special board meeting was called, but there was nothing they could do, except to voice their objections. Every change distressed Charles Hayes for a time, but once he saw the results brought in more sales, he was as pleased as anyone.

Apart from this minor move my time was mostly taken up with getting to know the buyers and to find out what help they needed to do more business. Some of the older ones were not able to take kindly to change. The linen buyer in particular was a stubborn man, but he knew how to buy! However, even he forged ahead, once he accepted that change had come, especially when he realised it could result in an increased salary and bonus!

Gradually the picture emerged, mostly in my own mind, of what the final results would be:
1. The name for quality and style must be held at all costs.
2. Existing buyers and management team would have to be reviewed.
3. Existing premises to be altered, so as to give the maximum selling space.
4. Planning a sales programme to ensure that the store would be constantly in the news.

TO RETAIN OUR GOOD NAME FOR QUALITY AND GOOD STYLE

It usually takes years to build up a good name, but it can be lost in a few months once inferior merchandise is introduced, or the setting or services allowed to deteriorate. However good the remaining exclusive stock may be, down will go the sales, once the store's name for featuring only the best had been lost, and when it has gone, it is seldom, if ever, regained. Quite a few stores have found this out to their cost. While we were dealing with these problems some of my business friends told me we would never get the crowds into the store and still retain the high level of trading which had been enjoyed for so many years. Some of the buyers of long standing were not backward in supporting this theory. However, I was satisfied that, with care, these fears could all be proved wrong.

REVIEW OF BUYERS AND MANAGEMENT TEAM

This did not prove as difficult as some might expect. It was fortunate that the majority of those already there formed, on the whole, a splendid team. Some had settled down and were just ticking over; others had given up the struggle to obtain the support which enabled them to show progress. My plans were to treble the turnover in three to four years. With this in mind, existing buyers were not permitted to continue buying for departments in which they were not really qualified. Some had the number of departments they controlled reduced.

This meant taking on new people to buy for these sections, which in most cases, were being poorly run, and also for new departments. The services of some excellent new buyers were obtained, who liked the challenge our expansion programme offered, and incidentally, their coming helped to reawaken our existing buyers and put them on their mettle. I have never had a better team of buyers or managers of service departments—for they were equally good—despatch, removals, storage, funerals, maintenance and counting house. They welcomed the introduction of new management. My predecessor certainly knew how to pick his team—the success we achieved would never have been possible without the ability and support that they were able to give during these coming years, when the store made such surprising progress.

Although I was heavily occupied while at Heelas of Reading in planning and executing the reorganisation programme, I still made time to travel to compare methods of trading with those of other successful retailers. In this respect my trips to America and Canada paid good dividends and I continued to make regular visits. My practice was to meet the heads of progressive department stores, exchange ideas with them and in the evenings fill my notebook with points I had noted, suggestions and ideas for future action. I seldom actually copied any of these but I am satisfied that by observing the wider interests in store life it helped me to have a better approach to my own problems.

During my first visit to New York after the war, I had an appointment with the principal of one of the main stores. His secretary welcomed me, asking if I would wait just a few minutes, as he had two visitors from Scotland with him. I happened to say, "I expect they have come over with some of their lovely knitwear," and she said, "I think they have." Shortly afterwards they came out of the office with glum faces and I said to them, "Didn't you get an order?" They replied, "Not this time." I wished them well elsewhere and went in. The principal was a charming man and gave me a wonderful reception. I asked him "Didn't you like my Scottish friends' knitwear? I think it is very good."

He said, "It is, but I couldn't buy it because it was not presented properly, I want the best knitwear they have, properly wrapped and boxed, and easy to sell." So, that was a lesson not only for my Scottish friends, but for me. Half the battle in selling is to find the right goods at the right price and to see that they are properly presented. I never forgot this.

OBTAINING EXTRA SELLING SPACE

It did not take long to discover how much space was being wasted in this vast area of buildings, erected at different times, with different levels and ceiling heights, divided in most cases by thick walls, some having special entrances from narrow outside passages. Some was used for living-in accommodation for staff, furniture storage and some sub-let for office use. Like many other old buildings being used by department stores, there were a number of open wells in the selling floors. These were filled in. They served no useful purpose, caused unnecessary draughts and were the cheapest way of obtaining extra floor space.

Charles Hayes and some of the older buyers were horrified. Criticisms also came from further afield but with the support of the Fire Brigade, our licence to do the work was granted. Once this was done, it was quite apparent that the ground floor had been greatly improved; instead of those old fashioned holes, with questionable daylight from high above, they now had a ceiling with modern illumination; the upper floors had new carpets, fixtures and the departments were sectionalised making a surprising improvement—much to everyone's satisfaction especially when the sales increased.

STAFF LIVING-IN ACCOMMODATION

This was out of date but, again, there was strong opposition especially from senior buyers, some of whom had lived there for years, when they heard that I was contemplating withdrawing this facility.

At that time small houses were difficult to buy in or around the town, but there were larger ones at comparatively low prices.

Warren Towers was one which caught my eye. It was only a few doors from Charles Hayes' home and stood out majestically on Caversham Heights, a grand view with a large garden and a healthy spot in which to live. It was purchased; suitable alterations were carried out, turning rooms into flatlets. No-one wanted to go on living in the store, so more space was added where we most needed it.

When we moved from Bournemouth my wife and I had also found a lovely house on Caversham Heights. The house had previously been owned by the Huntley and Palmer family.

ALL STORAGE IN THE MAIN BUILDING HAD TO GO

This took about eighteen months before it was completed. One large piano store on the ground floor was not discovered for some months after my arrival, though it was on one side of the ground floor about half way between the front and rear of the premises. No one, except the removal manager and one or two of his men seemed to know it existed. It had its own special entrance from outside and did not show up on the old plans. However, there was a big kink in the middle of the store, which I thought must be an open space and that I might at least get a building permit to erect a temporary passage through from the front to the rear. It was only then that the piano room was discovered; needless to say, although some of the pianos had been there for years, they were soon removed to our main warehouse.

Now we were ready to carry out the necessary building work, but this was at a time when we were still living under post-war restrictions. Retail distribution was frowned upon by some politicians, indeed, it was frankly hinted that our level of trading was an expensive luxury. But if £40,000 or more was to be spent on building alterations and minor extensions, very good reasons would have to be found to justify the necessary permits.

However, our numerous applications for building licences were passed one by one, so the various reasons given must have been sound. One factor helped; we owned a building which had little value to us, situated on the other side of the road at the rear of the store. It was self contained and happened to be just what the local authorities wanted, especially as it was in the centre of the town. It was agreed to vacate it provided permission was obtained to adapt part of our main store to give us alternative space. The licence which followed covered a large proportion of our overall requirements.

There was one other useless space that we turned to, a large storage section and stockroom cellar under the front of the store. At first our architect said it would be impossible to open it up; the foundations could not be disturbed, and also, in part, there was insufficient head room. These difficulties were overcome, and eventually the area housed our men's ready to wear department and a barbers' shop.

THE STORE'S NEW LOOK

It did not take long to decide where to position departments as additional space became available. To give extensive details would not make interesting reading, so at this point I will only make general reference to the expansion of a few departments and the introduction of some of the new trading sections.

It was during this period that I first began to see the advantage of separating departments and to give special and suitable layouts and colour treatment to each. It was the nature of the building that probably encouraged me to look at it in this way. Many store principals frowned upon what we were doing, both at this time and since, but I have not changed my views.

In a good class of store you can make shopping easier and more interesting if important departments are treated as speciality shops and given an individual outlook. This does not, of course, mean you are unable to see one section from another—there must be a through look—but this can be done without detracting from the individuality created in each department—particularly when fixtures, carpets and colour schemes are treated differently.

I have seen other stores, particularly in America, with just open spaces with different types of merchandise assembled side by side, with little or no relevance to each other. Frequently such items as men's shirts would be next to say ladies' hosiery or men's clothing next to fashions. In one store in Australia there was an Elizabeth Arden section next to the hardware. When I told Miss Arden she was horrified and took appropriate action.

With little or no difference between departments in the fixturing, floor covering and general decoration the value of stock promoted is reduced and it is just asking for greater competition from speciality shops, the best of whom pay special attention to environment.

It was at this time also that I began to take advantage of self selection in the selling of shoes, even in our high level of trading. We made sure that a selection of all the leading makes stocked were on view, so that it was not just left to sales staff to introduce what styles they thought most suitable for a customer, but the latter also had the opportunity of making an independent choice. This has since become common practice. Incidentally, the increased sales were far in excess of the average department stores at that time. Each of the fashion departments also had special treatment. These are the really profitable sections of a store—they should have privileged treatment and they were given this at Heelas!

With the new look of the store in mind, the demand for good fixtures was a factor that caused me considerable concern. Realising the high cost of having them made and the urgency of our needs, I was naturally looking for alternative methods of acquiring them. My luck was in! I happened to notice an announcement that Peter Robinson, Oxford Street, London, were ceasing to trade so all their fixtures had to be disposed of before Christmas Eve. An immediate telephone call confirmed that they had not been sold and there were only a few days left for them to deal with the matter as they were handing over the premises to the purchaser. I visited them the following day and a few minutes indicated to me that most of the fixtures would be ideal for our requirements. The quality was first class, and there were glass counters, wall fittings, display units, movable cash units and general store fittings. It was obvious to me that Peter Robinson were in a fix; some other stores had shown an interest but they were all too busy before Christmas. We had a large removal business that was idle at this period and therefore I had no problem in sending vans to move the stock and our warehouse could accommodate the purchase without any difficulty. So, without any delay I told the representative that I would give them £5,000; he was horrified, and said they would not consider it. So I said, "Go and offer it to your directors." He did, and he was back within a few minutes saying they would take £5,000 provided the fixtures were out by Christmas Eve. I suppose this was one of the best purchases of its type I have made, and it was only the circumstances that made this possible.

Incidentally, after Christmas, having found out some of the other stores that had indicated an interest, at a later period I contacted them and by selling them a few single items, I obtained more than half the total cost I paid. This must have saved us many thousands of pounds as our new floor space was opened up for trading. When I mentioned this to Mr Clore on his next Saturday visit, he said he thought we had done well!

At the same time we planned to attract crowds, particularly on Saturdays, so in some sections we separated the lower priced ranges from the higher. This applied especially to fashions. One successful experiment which caused comment was the large second floor in one of the front buildings of which only a small section was used at the time of my arrival—and that for the Times Book Club. The vacant space being large and light was turned into a dress fabric floor, moving the stock from what had been a small department on the ground floor. There were some who said fabrics must be on the ground floor; this may be an advantage in popular price selling, however, our emphasis was on the best, so that more space which could be added to the environment and display, the more selection offered, and the better it would be. We could then make more use of the services allied to dress making, with a competent adviser and paper pattern service. Having a carpeted floor and being free from the crowds that went through the ground floor on busy days also proved a great advantage. The results surprised us all, for the turnover rose from a little over £25,000 per annum to approximately £100,000. Its contribution to the new life and goodwill of the store was considerable.

Once again, this points to the truth that it is not just where you position departments, but the chief contribution to success is rather the standard of value, stock selection and general background. This makes the shopping public talk, and there is no better form of advertising. All departments in the store were given improved trading facilities, more space if they required it and more stock selection. Special attention was given to the weakest departments, and a few which had not previously been operated.

Digressing for a moment, a suggestion box had been installed, but, as in most stores, little use was made of it, so far as producing profitable ideas. However, it is worth having even for only one good idea every year. At Heelas I remember one such contribution. It came from one of our removal men, who had for some years been studying, as a hobby, the life and destructive work of the death watch beetle and how best to dispose of it. Realising the damage they were causing in so many churches and old buildings, and also that treatment in most cases had been neglected during the war years, he was sure that, if he was given equipment, he could offer a good service, which would be profitable to the store.

So, up he came to see me, never thinking that I would accept his proposals. However, his knowledge was so sound, his enthusiasm so real, and he appeared to have the ability to put his ideas into practice, I agreed to promote him and put him in charge of developing this new service.

It meant, to start with, one large van and training a team of six men. From the month the van was put on the road, it was fully booked up and within a year there were three vans with their crews working independently. They soon were not only dealing with the death watch beetle but cleaning buildings and carrying out other work, either themselves or sometimes sub-contracting.

It proved a profitable investment, a good advertisement for the store, and operated satisfactorily alongside our removal and funeral service which were by far the best in the area, together with our floral service, another new introduction.

THE FOUNDING OF THE INDEPENDENT STORES ASSOCIATION

It soon became apparent to me that, if we were to be competitive with the most progressive retail groups and at the same time obtain information of the changing market scene, we would have to plan to interchange ideas with other independent stores. With this in mind and knowing most of these businesses around the country a few of whom were members of the BMC (British Merchandising Club) which later became ADS (Associated Department Stores), I contacted them for their views regarding the advantages of an association of our own.

A draft programme was drawn up indicating the aims of the association and after discussing in considerable detail with John Beale of Bournemouth we thought it would be best first to influence one of the larger independent stores to obtain their support. If this was forthcoming we agreed to share the cost of inviting a dozen store chiefs to a dinner at the Savoy. We chose Gerald Bentall of Kingston, and I agreed to meet him and his brother, Rowan, with whom I had already discussed improvements that we had made at Heelas. After interesting discussions at Kingston over lunch, Bentalls agreed to support the idea and gave much personal help to see that it was launched in a way that would provide the facilities we all knew were needed in the quickly changing post-war retail department stores.

So John Beale and I provided the dinner at the Savoy which was a most enjoyable and satisfactory occasion and the founder members agreed to exchange information under any heading that would be of mutual advantage. Roger Day was appointed secretary and particular assistance was given by the late Gerald Bentall. Later the Independent Stores Association amalgamated with the Associated Department Stores and formed the Associated Independent Stores.

GENERAL PROMOTION

However hard we worked under all the previous headings, the store would never make the progress Charles Clore hoped for unless we were constantly in the news. This we managed by one means or another. Our buyers went near and far to obtain the best merchandise, and whenever they visited centres like Paris, we turned this to good account. We constantly had leading personalities visiting the store—this too was news. Our evening Dinner Fashion Parades, held at least twice a year, became an outstanding social occasion (evening dress essential!). They were always filled to capacity.

So the image grew and Charles Clore paid me the questionable compliment of telling me I was a good showman, even if I was not such a good merchant! I was never certain why he underlined the latter, because I always considered I paid as much attention to merchandise, as I did to promotion. Perhaps, in this case, he thought I spent too much time on the former. I still think, however, that the dual policy of promotion and gaining the best supplies, running side by side, was right.

The Christmas trading season, as usual, received all the support we could give. Few stores put on better attractions. One, featuring Christmas through the ages, attacted so much national publicity that coach loads of visitors came long distances for day trips to see it. I still have a folder of illustrations of this unusual seasonal and educational display which took ten to fifteen minutes to see properly. The following is the wording on an invitation which was widely distributed:

CHRISTMAS THROUGH THE AGES

An ambitious presentation tracing the origin of every custom and legend associated with the modern conception of Christmas.

Elaborately presented with modern theatrical technique and occupying an area of 3,500 square feet. Historical accuracy in architecture and costume provide a panorama of pageantry and splendour covering a period of nearly 2,000 years. Each scene peopled with beautifully executed "Mary Nicoll" figures.
  The True Spirit of Christmas portrayed in a Unique Fashion.

Some of the questions which are answered by
Christmas Through the Ages.
Where did Boxing Day get its name?
Why does Father Christmas have a Reindeer Sleigh?
When did the first Christmas Card appear?
What was the Kissing Bough?
Why does Father Christmas come down the Chimney?
Why do we hang mistletoe at Christmas?
Why do we hang stockings at Christmas?
What was the first Christmas Carol?
Who was St Nicholas?
Who was Good King Wenceslas?
Who were the Waits?
Why do we burn logs at Christmas?
Why do we use Holly Evergreens?
When did we first have Christmas trees?
What was the origin of Christmas Puddings?

* * *

We made a résumé of our Christmas plans:

1. *Attraction:* "Christmas through the Ages". Fourteen scenes giving a walk through of approximately 300 yards and illustrating the origin of the customs which make up the modern Christmas.

Opening Date: 23rd October, 1948.

Historical accuracy from point of view of dates, costume, etc., to interest schools and churches. Theatrical effects and lighting to give each scene maximum dramatic value and popular appeal.

Admission charge 6d children and adults. Blocks of twenty-five tickets to schools, etc., for 10/- (50p). Entertainments Tax avoided by presence of lecturer (retired school teacher) putting attraction in live entertainment classification.

HEELAS OF READING

2. *Father Christmas:* Placed at end of walk through attraction. Will sell tickets for 2/6d (12½p) and 5/- (25p), parcels obtainable from fairy assistant. (Believed visitors will be more ready, psychologically, to spend money on presents after seeing a good show than they would if confronted by large inclusive admission charge.)

3. Souvenir booklets of attraction produced in style of kiddies painting book, selling price 6d (2½p).

We planned the arrival of Father Christmas on a grand scale too, complete with band and coach and four. No store could have had bigger crowds. Photographs show the main street in front of the store crowded and all traffic stopped.

Charles Clore lived only a few miles from the store and he was home on Saturdays, so I had the pleasure of welcoming him most Saturday mornings. I was unable to fix any other engagements for those mornings, and it was also our busiest day of the week. With a quickly expanding business, like many other managing directors, much as I appreciated seeing my chairman, I must admit I often wished it could have been on a different day. This does not mean that I did not welcome his visits; of course he was entitled to know what was going on, and he certainly knew how to look for results.

I learned a lot from his visits, as from our first meeting I realised he was both an unusual and a remarkable man. As he had to give so much thought to the development of his assets, it left him insufficient time to appreciate the value of the people who were contributing to his success. Anyway, who am I to judge? His outstanding achievements since we parted at least confirm my first assessment of him when we met in Bournemouth.

MY ROAD TO CANTERBURY

DIRECTORS' MEETINGS

These were straightforward and to the point as we had covered most of the business on Saturday mornings. However, I still had to make my official report on the progress to date, and of our future plans, which of course went into our official records. Mr Clore never made these occasions difficult for me.

DISHONESTY

I do not think that Mr Clore had any idea of the extent of the difficulties that had to be contended with under this heading, though, of course, he was given reports on the worst of them. We did seem to have more than our fair share, probably arising from the lax management over past years, and also from the vast expansion programme we had initiated. There were a large number of small incidents detected, a couple of more serious cases are worth detailing.

A deputy buyer
During the first few months at the store, I could not understand the reason for one department showing such a low gross profit over the previous two or three years' trading. I told the buyer that this must be as a result of not running his department efficiently, not recording the correct selling prices on his invoices, not showing his full reductions—or dishonesty.

When I mentioned the latter, he was horrified. Never in the whole of his business career had he ever been spoken to like that, or ever accused of being dishonest. When I pointed out to him that I was not referring to him personally, it made matters no better. He could not understand that as the manager of his large and expensively operated department he was responsible for knowing what went on; he could not account for being a few per cent below the expected gross profit, which he admitted he, himself, had anticipated.

The culprit was discovered purely by accident. There was a comparatively small amount of money missing, and it was connected with a sale carried out by the deputy buyer. I had him in my office, remembering that this was the department where a few thousand pounds were missing over each of the past few years and my questions were phrased accordingly, in the hope of drawing him out. This fortunately proved to be the case—he lost his temper with me when he indicated I was suggesting he was dishonest. This, I had not actually done—I had only put the idea into his mind, and to cut a long story short I told him if he would tell me the full details of what he had done over the past three years I would not prosecute.

Under this condition, rather to my surprise he agreed that it was true he had either been taking goods or money or sold at reduced price to effect a sale and gain commission, costing the department £2,000 to £4,000 a year. He was of course immediately dismissed and no action taken. A point for other managements to note was that he went straight to a competitor and was given a senior appointment, without them asking us for a reference!

A dishonest driver

Prior to the Christmas trading, all members of staff were asked to co-operate by having any parcels they took from the premises checked, so as to make it difficult for anyone to take unauthorised parcels off the premises. The first evening this was carried out, a driver was stopped and he took offence and demanded to see me. He was in such a temper when he came to my office, that it became obvious to me he had something to hide, and this was his sub-conscious reaction. I therefore, explained to him the purpose of us initiating this ruling, and that I knew he would be anxious to help catch anyone who was dishonest, and therefore, no honest person could possible object to what we were doing. He changed his tune so suddenly that it made me even more suspicious—however, I let him go thinking that all was well.

I then contacted our despatch manager and informed him that if at any time a parcel was found on a van which was not recorded on the delivery sheet to say nothing, but just let me know. About a fortnight passed when I received the information that a large parcel was on the van driven by this man and no record had been made. Was he to take it off? I said, "Certainly not, all I want to know is if it is not on the van when he returns." When the van returned some time after closing, the parcel was missing. I was given this information at home and immediately telephoned the police. They took action and it was about midnight when the telephone rang again; it was the police asking me to go to a certain address. It was a nice house, beautifully furnished, a charming wife with a young child asleep in a cot. The driver was, however, missing and this was about 12.30 a.m. The inspector asked me if any of the things in the house could have come from the store. As I looked around I said, "Practically everything."

Eventually it came out that although he had received money from his wife to pay for everything they had for their new home, he had stolen most of it and on that particular evening he was in the process of furnishing a friend's house! He went to jail for a year. Incidentally, he told me he bore me no malice—he had taken a risk and had to pay for it.

There is one other incident representing another type of dishonesty, which we sometimes have to contend with in department stores. In this instance, it occurred when I was walking in the direction of the store from the railway station, having just returned from London. It was about 8 p.m. when suddenly I heard an electric burglar alarm signal coming from the store, so I immediately ran at the double to find out what was happening.

En route I passed two policemen who accompanied me. I let them into the store through a rear entrance and they immediately said to me, "How can you find anyone in an enormous building like this? Where can we start as there are so many hiding places?"

Realising that the highest valued items were in the fur department, I said we would go there. It so happened that this department was next to the shoe salon which had a long stockroom behind where it would be most likely that an intruder would hide. On arriving one of the policemen said, "I can't see anyone, sir."

I replied in a sharp voice, "I can, he is just round the corner." At that the chap must have taken fright and knocked a shoe box down, revealing his position, whereupon he was taken by the police to the station for questioning. He had no shoes on and it was evident that he had been going through the fur stock with the intention of stealing. Indeed, he may have already helped himself from the other departments. He was not a member of our staff but had been with us for a fortnight demonstrating a mechanical model exhibit.

His excuse was that he had nowhere to stay, so he hid himself at closing time until everyone had gone and slept in a bed he had made underneath the demonstration table. He had been there for three nights and it would have been easy to have arranged to take goods to a considerable value off the premises. Although he admitted that he had no right to have hidden there or to have been going through the fur stock, or indeed, to have been on the premises at all without permission, nevertheless, the court was sympathetic and he only received a caution.

A SUCCESSFUL TRAINEE WHO INHERITED £10,000

We had a young man in our maintenance department who was showing excellent promise being most enthusiastic and interested in his work. It was quite evident that he could make steady progress and eventually gain an executive appointment but £10,000 came between him and success!

One day he came to see me in my office to hand in his resignation. On telling him that we would be very sorry to lose him and enquiring where he was going, I was almost stunned to receive his reply, "Nowhere special," after which he went on to explain that he had just received a legacy of £10,000 and naturally he was going to enjoy himself. No amount of persuasion on my part could change his mind so he left, and we had no connection with him for about a year, when once again he asked to see me.

He came into my office—a very different man to that of a year ago. Though he wore an expensive suit, it had suffered from wear far more than one of mine would have done over a longer period. He looked disillusioned, weary and dispirited and seemed to have lost his zest and interest in life. I asked, "Have you learned your lesson? Do you want to come back to us?"

His reply was unexpected, "I don't want to work again but I shall have to, as all my money has gone."

I asked him, "What has happened to all the friends you had?"

"They've gone too," he said. If he had returned to me as he had been before he left I would certainly have given him another chance, but I was not prepared to take the risk for it was evident that he was a changed personality. I never saw him again.

When we entered our third year of trading practically all our building expansion was completed and within a further few months it would all have been in use. Therefore, I was most optimistic about the future progress of the store. We had already increased the turnover to approximately one and a quarter million, and we would quickly reach two million. This would have been a satisfactory return on the floor area that would shortly be in use. I mention this, so as to indicate more clearly the shock that was to come to me when I was requested by Charles Clore to attend a special directors' meeting.

Although I was managing director, I had no idea of the nature of the business to be finalised but on finding also in attendance the managing director of another large group of stores, I realised at once that the time had come when Charles Clore was going to realise his improved assets, which had been brought about by the progress we had made. It appeared to me that those concerned had never considered that I would be disappointed; indeed, in their light they were most complimentary to me and indicated that, so far as status and salary were concerned, I should, in both cases, enhance my position. However I realised it would mean lowering the level of trading standards which we had fought to maintain and after the three years' hard work, I felt I just could not be a party to this.

My successor was appointed and I agreed to stay for three months to enable him to gain whatever information he wanted from me, so that the change could be effected to the best advantage of the company. We were, whilst working together, made joint managing directors, and Charles Clore surprised me by indicating that my successor was a man who could give one hundred per cent effort to the business—against my smaller percentage! However, his stay with the company was of shorter duration than mine—about one year—when it became apparent that his change of trading policy was a failure. The business was then sold to the John Lewis Partnership.

Though I had stayed purposely to be of help to him, during the whole of this period, he never once asked me a question about policy, buying, selling, staff, promotions, or what I would suggest for the future profit of the business; he just was not interested in anything that I had done. His mind was already made up that he was going to lower the standard of trading to bring it into line with some other business where, no doubt, he had had that type of experience. There was one occasion, however, when he came to me as he was in trouble! He pointed out that as I was the senior managing director, it was my responsibility to deal with the problem. We had a member of the staff in our workshop who, if he was not a member of the Communist Party was definitely one of their sympathisers, for although I was not so interested in his politics, I was concerned that for some time he had been causing unnecessary trouble, which made it difficult for some of the men who worked with him, and in particular for the workshop management.

He was being watched and in due course, if he did not mend his ways, I was satisfied that he would eventually overstep the mark and would be dismissed, but I had told the personnel controller that he must be very sure of his ground before doing so. My successor to be must have fallen out with him the first time they met—and actually hit him! Now it was left to me to deal with the results, for with an incident of this nature, and a man of this sort, the union concerned was quickly brought in. A strike throughout the town by the engineering side was threatened and this would have involved some thousands of men.

It took me nearly a fortnight of sometimes humiliating, as well as exacting discussions to solve the problem in such a way as to avoid strike action being taken. However, after resolving it satisfactorily, my successor was then landed with this man for some time to come until, I believe, the whole of this profitable side of our company was closed down.

One lesson I learnt from this change of management was that it is much harder to raise the quality standard of trading than to lower it and when the latter takes place it does not take long to change the overall trading standard which only major upheaval can correct. The actions he took cannnot have contributed to increased turnover, and must have lowered the trading profits. However, there was so much value in the various properties owned by our company that it must have been on this basis that they effected, what I assumed, was a satisfactory sale to the John Lewis Partnership, who since then have taken full advantage of the scope the valuable site offered them and the name which over a long period had built up a large following of valuable shoppers.

Before closing this chapter which covered some of the most exciting developments with which I have been connected and from which I learnt so much, it is fitting that I make reference to the advantage I had of finding outstanding talent in most sections of the store which had not been fully used. Without mentioning names, I soon realised that if they were given adequate space and proper facilities for up to date presentation and a careful guide to their buying programme, I was really half way to turning a business that was run down but quietly ticking over, into a successful enterprise.

It was unusual to find at hand buyers who understood quality and service with a knowledge of the best markets from whom they could obtain their supplies. Fortunately, I was quick to recognise this and the speedy improvement in their trading performance ensured that I received not only their loyalty but full support in all that I was aiming to do. No store can really progress without this standard of support but none could enjoy a higher one than I had. It was a sad day when I had to say goodbye to the staff, increased in number by over 50% and who were among the happiest and most loyal group that I could have wished for.

CHAPTER FIFTEEN

MY FAITH AND MY WORK

At this point in the story when I had finished with working for others and was about to start on my own, it is appropriate to record the enormous influence of my faith on my business career and indeed on my whole life.

It happened while in my teens. At school religious teaching had not gripped me nor had attending church twice on Sunday. Indeed, like most others the sermons bored me although the music and singing did at times inspire me. It was only when I was thrust into store life at the bottom of the ladder that I gave a thought about God. Fortunately, I had an enquiring mind, so I was soon asking myself questions as "Is there anything in the church and its message? Are there spiritual sources of power and guidance that a raw recruit like myself could draw on? What about the Bible and its message—is it really the Word of God?" These and many other questions kept me thinking and I knew I would never know the answers as they were relevant to me unless I put them to the test in my own life. So I made a secret pact with myself.

I would for a period of two years give the church a chance. I would attend church regularly I would put what I could into the services; I would try to learn from all that was said and sung; I would enter into the life of the church and help in whatever way I could. So I found myself working behind the scenes for any functions where an energetic lad could help. Welcoming people as they entered church on Sundays, talking to men and women who I knew possessed a faith that was real.

I was invited to give a talk and I chose the life of Sir George Williams. This was a story that had always fascinated me for he had entered store life when conditions were at their worst, long hours, little, if any, freedom, "living in" under conditions which only the strongest characters could survive without being affected. However, he had the ability and the will to succeed and knowing the conditions under which many young men were thrust into he made up his mind that once he had succeeded in business he would do something to alleviate their hardship. The story is one which any young man or woman leaving school or university today would profit by. His integrity and intelligent application to his work enabled him to rise to the top and Messrs Hitchcock in the city became Hitchcock Williams, a well known department store at the end of the last century. Then he was ready for his life's objective—to help boys and young men—and he founded the Young Men's

Christian Association, the YMCA. It is a great story and preparing this talk certainly helped me.

During this period there was an entire change in my attitude to life. The difficulties that I had dreaded became a challenge. A purpose in life began to take shape. One of the special advantages that I enjoyed as a member of the Richmond Hill Congregational Church in Bournemouth was that it was among the strongest Non-Conformist churches in the country. It has been said it contributed as much to the speedy growth of Bournemouth as any other factor. Its minister, Rev Dr J. D. Jones, PhD, MA, CH, whose ministry lasted thirty-nine years, was one of the most effective preachers in the country. He had a world wide reputation and he was invited to preach the sermon at the opening of the League of Nations after the 1914-18 war. His gifts were such that if he had wanted to be prime minister that appointment would not have been beyond his ability to attain. Yet in spite of his outstanding gifts, his faith was sure and his greatest gift to express the deepest spiritual experiences supported by the highest levels of theological learning in such simple language that ordinary people of all ages could appreciate and understand. It was no wonder that the crowds flocked to all services, chairs down all aisles and an overflow outside on numerous occasions.

The church had the support of leaders from all walks of life and some of the most influential people from home and abroad would be found in the congregation each Sunday. I well remember Lloyd George as prime minister attending. All this was a tremendous advantage to me; it gave me the opportunity of getting to know a number of men and women whose experience of life was different but who all shared a real and vital faith. Fortunately, I made the most of this.

It was not only great preaching that influenced me. There were many men with humble backgrounds that equally impressed me. I think of one: he was far from successful in business and it was a wonder he made enough profit to live from his small furniture and funeral business. Yet he had a heart of gold. He was a lay preacher and it was he who persuaded me to take the necessary steps to become one. Sermon preparation never came easy to me, but when I found it was a means of helping others, it in turn strengthened my own faith.

After two years when my trial period was over I knew if I was going to get the best out of life both in business, home and all other activities I just had to take God into account. Taking the Bible and its message seriously, working hard for the church and putting my growing faith to the test all helped.

It was realised that there would be ups and downs; it would not be living life in a feather bed, but it gave my life meaning, always something to strive after. I was no longer on my own. The presence of Christ had become a reality for me. So I signed on the dotted line and became a committed Christian. This was the best action I have ever taken. I knew it was not a pass to a perfect life, but there is no doubt so far as I am concerned that it made the right aims and actions clear. This was the way I wanted to go, but like others, often failed. The New Testament message became real to me.

As I now look back on a long life with so many varied experiences, all too often I was facing dangers at sea, or disappointments and problems that anyone carrying responsibilities has to meet. Many a time when the circumstances might have tempted anyone to give in, it was then that the way forward became clear to me and I became able to press on knowing that all would be well. No wonder that I can look back and be thankful.

When after three years I left home for further business experience, this became the real testing time for me. No longer a crowded church and an inspiring service. Instead back to dull services similar to those I had experienced during my school days. This time, they didn't drive me away. I had gained something too valuable to lose. So I remained loyal in attendance. They proved to be opportunities when I was called to give more through my attitudes to worship and this was good for me. Being young I thought I would try and encourage some young men to come to church. With this in mind I launched the Gloucester Rugby Second Team. Any way, this interested me, and I knew they would give church a trial. I was to learn a lesson—you can take a horse to water, but you cannot make him drink! So I had to look for other means of introducing new life to the church.

I tried to enter the ministry and saw the principal of Bristol University but he could not consider my application unless I had a reasonable knowledge of Greek. This was not an encouraging start as I had proved such a poor student during my school days. However, I found a young Greek scholar who for a reasonable fee agreed to give me an hour's tuition twice a week. How I dreaded those evenings. They lasted about six months when she told me it was no use; I was just wasting my hard earned money. So that concluded my efforts to enter the ministry. This still left open continuing as a lay preacher which over the years has been a great help to me, and I hope, to some who have attended services at which I have preached.

Much could be written of the early experiences but I will mention just a few. One was at a village church in Gloucestershire which I was visiting on my bicycle for the first time. A nice looking building—I was outside about 6 p.m. for their 6.30 service. The doors were locked but about 6.15 p.m. a young girl arrived and asked, "Are you the preacher?" She handed me the key and left saying she couldn't stay and she thought the organist would not be coming. I opened up the church, examined the organ, put on the lights and waited about five minutes but on one arrived. We had to have a service. So I went ouside where there was a steady stream of people passing, probably going to the Church of England. Being young I had to persuade some of them to help me out and about twelve of them did so. Incidentally I had to play the organ as well as conduct the service, so I was popping backwards and forwards from the pulpit—it was quite an experience!

A particularly happy period was around the time we were married. I had returned to Bournemouth and was then responsible for arranging the preaching supplies for about twelve churches around Bournemouth. A series of special evening services was arranged with some of these churches and these proved a great success—particularly when it was found necessary to have chairs down the aisles! Revisiting one of these churches a few years ago a member of the congregation was able to tell me the theme of one of those services which had taken place about thirty-eight years ago!

Since coming to Kent I have been privileged to conduct and preach at over 350 services. This represented a considerable amount of hard work as it has never been easy for me to prepare a sermon. It certainly helped me and I hope in some small measure they may have been of help to others. There are a few services which are worthy of mention as they were out of the ordinary and looking back on them I am thankful for the inspiration we were able to share.

One was the large United Reformed Church in Rochester where I preached on a Saturday evening as the then chairman of the Kent Congregational Association. The theme was "New Life for our Churches". I endeavoured to make this a challenge to the large congregation, for the church was full to the front row and even the gallery was used.

Another was the United Reformed Church at Margate (before it had been reduced in size), when I was invited to preach to the members of the Shoe & Leather Trades Union Conference. This again was a packed church to the front row and a large proportion of those attending were men. I took as a theme "Why go to Church?" I felt this was an occasion to help them consider this all important exercise in life.

One other I remember was at Dover when I was invited to preach at a service for school leavers in Charlton Anglican Church. It was encouraging to have a packed church of young people and on this occasion I offered them "Four worthwhile anchors for life".

Another occasion I recall (because it caused me some trepidation in advance of the service) was at the church of which my wife and I have been members since soon after coming to Kent, Westgate URC. We were without a minister and I had been invited to take services on numerous occasions and this one in particular included the service of baptism. Fortunately, all went well; it was a lovely baby and I looked upon it as an unusual incident in the activities of a lay preacher.

Such experiences as these give one satisfaction and private treasured memories that little else in life can equal.

CHURCHES AROUND THE WORLD

When travelling, what an opportunity it was to find out how others expressed

139

their faith, their forms of worship and the influence their faith had on other lives. It has always been my practice when travelling abroad to visit churches and to join in their worship. On my many visits to the United States and Canada I have had the opportunity of hearing a number of their outstanding preachers, seeing the effect of a church service on those attending worship.

The Riverside Church, New York, founded in 1931 with the financial support of John D. Rockefeller and others attracted me with that eminent founder minister, Dr Harry Emerson Fosdick. It stands out majestically on Riverside Drive with some twenty-two floors rising above ground level with suitable accommodation for its seven days a week activities. The church itself seats over two thousand, full every Sunday morning for worship. For me it was always an inspiration to participate. It was on one of these visits when we were only just able to get a seat. In front of us was a man with a figure of a world champion wrestler, tall and broad with hands like dinner plates. From his clothing and voice he had probably come from the middle west. To him this service was the thrill of a lifetime; he showed it in his face and in the sincerity of his singing and before the end of the opening processional hymn I happened to note great tears were unreservedly running down his cheeks. This moved me as much as anything in that service. Faith can do that—it was an occasion I shall never forget.

On another occasion after attending meetings of the International Congregational Council at Hartford, Connecticut in 1953 I was invited to stay with Dr and Mrs John Bennett, the principal of Union Seminary, New York which was situated near and with a close link with Riverside Church. Before leaving he kindly gave me a copy of Dr Fosdick's autobiography *The Living of these Days*, a great book with a great story which if reprinted would, I am sure, attract wide circulation. Here is a short extract:

The Riverside Church
Meanwhile the most painstaking thought was being given to making the new building not only a fully equipped center for practical service to the community, but as beautiful a sanctuary for worship as we could construct. Early in the planning of the new church Mr Rockefeller, who was chairman of the building committee, said to me, a bit apprehensively, as I recall, that he supposed I wanted a spacious auditorium primarily fitted for preaching to large congregations. On the contrary, I answered, I wanted a sanctuary primarily fitted for worship. We had the unique opportunity to build all at once not only a center of social service but a cathedral, where one could preach to be sure, but where not the pulpit but the high altar would be central and where beauty of proportion and perspective, of symbolism and color would speak to the soul even when the voice of man was silent. To that end Mr Rockefeller, ably backed by Eugene C. Carder, one of the church's

ministers, devoted himself with unstinted care and labor.

The major inspiration for the new sanctuary came from Chartres Cathedral—the cloister windows were actually made in Chartres but one who studies in detail the church's inconography will see that it reflects the interests and judgements of the modern world as well as the cherished values of the ancient Christian heritage. Among the statues in the chancel screen Sir Joseph Lister and Louis Pasteur stand with Hippocrates and others around Christ the healer; Henry Drummond and Pestalozzi are in a group around Christ the teacher; Abraham Lincoln, Florence Nightingale and General William Booth, along with fifteen others, surround Christ the humanitarian. I suppose that I am responsible for the fact that the carvings which crown the pillars in the nave narrate the major events in the life of Jeremiah—to me the greatest of the Hebrew prophets—and Eugene Carder, I am sure, chose the six preachers whose figures stand out in niches on the nave's south wall: Chrysostom, Augustine, Savonarola, Latimer, John Wesley and Phillip Brooks.

The sculptures over the west portal attracted the most public comment, for there, with Christ triumphant above the doorway, was an arch covered with carved figures—a series representing scientists including Charles Darwin and Albert Einstein; another representing philosophers from Pythagoras to Ralph Waldo Emerson; representing religious leaders from Moses, Confucius, Buddha and Mohammed to John Milton, William Cary and David Livingstone. When Dr and Mrs Einstein landed in New York City on December 12, 1930 they visited the Riverside Church that very afternoon. The news that he was sculptured over the doorway of a Christian church had reached him in Germany, and he had been reported in the press as wanting "to see that oddity". He was a charming guest and I recall the feeling in his voice when, looking at that arch of the world's foremost scientists with himself the only one still living, he exclaimed, "That could not have happened anywhere except in America." He was impressed also by the "scholars'" window in the nave and when he saw in the stained glass Immanuel Kant carrying an umbrella, he said with a laugh, "I will have to be very careful for the rest of my life as to what I do and what I say."

In 1929 we began using the lower levels of our new edifice for the Church School and at last on October 5, 1930, we occupied the completed structure, dedicating it formally on February 8, 1931. That was a crowning day after a long wait. Looking forward to it I had written a hymn which was using at the dedicatory service:

> God of Grace and God of Glory
> On Thy people pour Thy power
> Crown Thine ancient Church's story

Bring her bud to glorious flower
Grant us wisdom, grant us courage
For the facing of this hour.

That was more than a hymn to me when we sang it that day—it was a very urgent personal prayer. For with all my hopeful enthusiasm about the new venture there was inevitably much humble and sometimes fearful apprehension. One day Dr Carder and I sat together on the foundation walls of the new edifice, which had just reached the street level and said to ourselves with anxious foreboding, "What a tragedy if all this turns out to be a flop." Moreover, even if it were not a "flop" the possibilities were dreadfully present that it might not be the kind of success the Master could approve.

Dr Fosdick enjoyed a long ministry at Riverside and exerted a remarkable influence throughout New York and beyond. He lived until well into his nineties.

There was the Congregational Cathedral in Los Angeles where I attended worship on one of my early visits to the USA. Two things struck me at the time, the first was while I was enjoying the early morning sun in the park adjoining the church, a pleasant woman approached me and said, "Good morning. Had you thought of going to Church?" As it happened I had, but her kindly action has always remained with me.

The other link with this church, apart from its packed congregations and wonderful music and singing, was that the church had five ministers, all under the ministerial leadership of Dr Fifield including one for radio and one for youth, who usually went in a body of a few hundred from the church to one of the beaches for their services.

On many occasions I have visited Toronto which is fortunate to have many fine churches. Those I visited had full congregations, including Timothy Eaton Memorial Church but especially St George's United Church where a long-standing friend of our family, Dr John Short, was the minister for about twenty years until his retirement. He had succeeded Dr J. D. Jones of Richmond Hill Congregational Church, Bournemouth. To follow such an outstanding man was no easy task. However, he was soon accepted as a splendid successor and the church continued to remain alive with chairs down the aisles most Sundays. His ministry continued through the war years until after about twenty years he and his wife Lee decided to move to Toronto where we have had the pleasure of keeping in touch with them and also worshipping at St George's during his ministry there. Now both he and his wife Lee live in happy retirement in their home in Toronto.

Similar inspiring services were enjoyed in Hartford, San Francisco, and Port Everglades.

There is a fresh inviting looking Baptist Church in New London, New

Hampshire. In 1967 the congregations were small, there was little life in the church. Then came the Rev Robert William Thurston and what a man! Full of life, great preacher, teacher, counsellor and friend. The church was soon packed on Sunday mornings with all sections of the community represented, our daughter Elizabeth among them. We are grateful to her for introducing us both to Bob Thurston and the church through which he served. He was awarded the honorary degree of Doctor of Divinity in June 1976 and never was this award more richly deserved.

A visit to Australia gave me the opportunity of visiting Trinity Church, Perth. This was quite a unique experience, for the church was full for the Sunday morning service, mostly with young people in the 17-30 age group. They gave me a wonderful welcome and one evening while I was there a large group of seventy or more took me on a ramble in the hills. This was a great experience, apart from enjoying their active company it showed the difference a live Christian faith can make on the lives of young people. Life was worthwhile and they had a purpose to pursue.

It was a wealthy church, owning a lot of valuable property in the centre of the city. I was glad to learn that they gave away the whole of their income from their assets and all the operating expenses of the church were provided by its members and friends. The Rev John Bryant was their minister and it so happened a year or so later he and his wife were staying with us when we had our staff party so they too had the opportunity of meeting them. Looking back I am grateful for happy and inspiring visits to other churches in Australia, New Zealand, Kenya and South Africa but I must not weary my readers. On all these visits I was at the same time trying to broaden my knowledge of changing trends in retail distribution so my time was fully occupied and I have always had the satisfaction of enjoying what I felt to be a balanced diet!

CHRISTIAN STANDARDS IN BUSINESS

There are some who think the two are incompatible. They would keep church and business interests entirely separate, yet this cannot be done. If a person's faith is real, it should influence the whole of life. This does not mean inflicting the basis of one's faith on others but it does set standards which must be upheld and in themselves can become the best introduction to the Christian way of life. This does not mean our actions are perfect but it does mean we know what is right and what is wrong. Incidentally, when any business sets its standards by the basic principles of the Christian way of life they can succeed. Integrity in business is an asset; it provides a basis of trust and confidence.

There are some ill-informed people who consider it to be dishonest to buy stocks of any quantity at half price or less: they speak without the knowledge of the principles of trading. So long as there is a willing seller and no unfair pressure is brought upon him, then this is quite fair trading; this is when courtesy and consideration can help.

What effect does the Christian attitude to life have upon those with whom he works, especially employees? Leaving out the salary and pay structure which anyway has to conform either to the minimum rates or higher, what attracts the standard of staff a particular business requires? It is generally recognised that any business that is generous and considerate to its employees attracts those best qualified to give good service.

I have always tried to show concern for the general welfare and happiness of those I have worked with, as have both my sons, and without doubt it is easier to do this in a family business. It is nothing to do with money; it is a case of knowing as many as possible by name, encouraging them when they have done well; a letter or small gift of fruit or flowers if they are ill, or if they have had a loss in the family, or have had the joy of the arrival of a baby. Many today are starving for recognition, they do not want to be listed as a number. They want to be a real person with a name, when this happens there is encouragement for the best qualities in human nature to be developed. This, too, is good for business, it promotes loyalty and goodwill, actions essential to the success of a store that promotes quality and good taste and service.

There are many ways in which a practical faith helps in business, one that I have been specially aware of is an experience of guidance. Not all who claim the Christian faith enjoy this.

There was a leading politician, recognised as a gifted scholar, who was questioned on television about his faith. Yes, he believed in God and based his faith on the results of years of intellectual theological reasonings. Then he was asked whether he had ever experienced spiritual guidance. He replied, "I have never been aware of either guidance or help from a source of power outside myself." Yes, he believed he had been given life for a purpose, he believed in worship, but he had not been aware of a guiding hand. He wasn't saying it didn't happen—he would have been wrong if he had.

As I look back on a full and interesting life I am thankful that I can record with conviction that there were times when I just did not know which way to go or what to do to overcome some seemingly impossible situation. Then the way was made clear to me. All I did was to be quick to be aware of this guidance from a power outside myself, put my best efforts into pursuing the way that was made clear to take. To anyone who is out to make the best of life and to whom the way is hard and at times, uncertain, I would say, don't ignore the spiritual resources which are available to all to receive. They are real and if sought after can give a new dimension and purpose in life.

It is difficult to express in words all that my faith was meant to me in my work and in my life, but I am certain of this. Though all my standards and actions have not been as good as I should have liked them to be, I know they have been much better because of my faith which was always prodding me.

MY FAITH AND MY WORK

My belief in God and my awareness of the presence of Christ in my life has never been paraded before others in business. However, without asking, I have often been approached by someone who was anxious to talk about a problem because they felt I had access to a source of power that they needed. I hope in some cases I was able to help but of this there is no doubt, to share in some of the richest experiences of life brings great satisfaction.

This is the missing link the world needs to discover; the Bible is to many old fashioned but that is because they have not studied it. Also, we must keep open our lines of communication that guide us, without which we soon lose our way. We may have had it good in material things but without the balancing influence of spiritual resources there is no safe and satisfying future for this world. The experiences for which I am most grateful are that I discovered this truth early in life. I have since shared it with my wife and I hope to some measure with our family. It has given us a worthwhile purpose, both in business and in life, and an inner strength to meet every challenge and disappointment as well as appreciation for success and happiness.

CHAPTER SIXTEEN

A SHORT INTERIM

Once again I found myself in a position of looking for another appointment, at a time when I had thought I had really found the right niche in which to stay. However this was not to be. No decisive action was taken during the first half of the three months I had agreed to stay on at Heelas, but during the second I did receive approaches from other stores and groups, including one from the West End, none of which seemed to be the answer.

Anxious to avoid further experiences of having to leave and set up a new home, through no fault of my own, I again considered starting a business of my own. While investigating what was available at that time, I was approached by Lewis Hay, a well known personality who lived in Southampton and whom I had known for some years as we were fellow members of the Twenty Club. This club was formed in 1897 by prominent members in the department store world. He had been in charge of Plummers of Southampton for some years before his official retirement, after which he acquired a store in Deal which operated under the name of Clarabut, later some shops in Herne Bay trading under the same name, and a store in Whitstable under the name of Spenceleys.

He had a strong and outstanding personality, was tall, energetic, and with thick white hair he looked much younger than a man in his eighties. A rich man, his home in Southampton was pleasant but quite unpretentious, and it was evident that he did not believe in spending money. His pet aversion was the Inland Revenue. It was said when he died that he was years in arrears but no action had been taken against him as it was known that his estate could bear the full sum owed plus interest. His accountant must have found him to be his most difficult client in this respect as he frequently said to me, "I do not believe in paying these people my hard-earned money—they can wait for it until I die." He had succeeded the hard way and he gave me the impression that he did not make the best use of his money, finding it difficult both to spend and to give. This, no doubt, caused quite a few people he knew or who worked for him to suffer unnecessarily.

He telephoned me one day in Reading and asked if I would be interested in his stores. I told him Kent did not appeal to me. He then asked me to call to see him at Southampton without committing myself in any way. He was an old man and I was welcome to have his businesses if I would like them.

Although he was such a likeable personality, I was wary of him, but glad to accept his invitation. He produced his accounts which showed a remarkable profit, considering he spent practically no time in the stores and carried little stock. His wages were kept to an absolute minimum. How he did this and also enjoyed such loyalty from his staff was a mystery—perhaps it was his winning smile and the fresh carnation he nearly always wore!

After doing his best to impress me with the tremendous scope these dilapidated little businesses offered, he said, "Well, there is no point in arguing, Riceman, I will give them to you."

I said, "You don't mean that!"

He replied, "I am wealthy, and I am an old man. I don't need the businesses or the money; all you have to do is go and take them over."

I told him he could not do business like that, and he knew I would not let him, but I would go and have a look at them and see him again. This I did, with my wife, on a cold rainy day in January. The town of Deal was empty and after Bournemouth and Reading, we both felt it would be impossible to come down to a little business in such a small town. Herne Bay was worse, being a long line of old fashioned shops under one name. What shocked us most were strings of shoes hanging outside the windows. There was no through-way from shop to shop and customers had to go out into the street from one to the next. (It took nearly two years to get some semblance of order and character into making the store a single unit and, it cost a considerable amount to carry out the necessary structural alterations.) Whitstable did not impress us either, though it was better than Herne Bay.

However, my wife suggested we should return when the sun was shining, just to make sure. Though I felt this was useless, I took her advice and we paid a second visit. This time we drove to Deal via Folkestone and perhaps it was due to the better shopping facilities at Folkestone that we were encouraged to look further into the proposals we were considering. Deal, on this brighter morning, was comparatively busy and having regard to the site of the store, it looked as though there was scope for considerable improvement. The same applied in the other towns.

So back I went to Southampton and again I was offered the businesses without payment. However, I said I would be interested to take the matter further on the basis of a fair valuation of the business if he would agree to agents acting for us—he could have Mr H. Beecroft and I would appoint Mr Dudley Edgar of William Houghton. When I saw the latter, who was also a friend, he told me that he thought there should be no difficulty in bringing the arrangements to a satisfactory conclusion, especially as Lewis Hay did not want to charge me anything at all. After the second meeting with Lewis Hay, there followed two months of the most difficult period of negotiating that I have ever had to contend with, and after my three months at Heelas were up, the agents had still not finalised anything. Lewis Hay still assured me there would be no difficulty and suggested I should go down and take over the stores at once, leaving it to the agents to complete the arrangements, which could be back-dated to the date I took over.

This, I reluctantly agreed to and so my wife and I settled in our new home, Felder House, Worth, situated some four miles from Deal, twenty from Herne Bay and twenty-three from Whitstable. It was originally built for Admiral Sir Reginald and Lady Henderson in 1907. Beautiful gardens covered some three acres and a further eight acres of meadow. This made some compensation for the drab and out of date little stores we were acquiring. Having a good home during the first years in Kent proved a great help in reminding us of better days in business which we had previously enjoyed.

A month passed during which time appropriate action was taken to commence reorganising the three stores. At the end of this period I was informed by Mr Edgar that he felt in this case it would be impossible to come to a satisfactory conclusion with Lewis Hay as he kept changing his mind and was not prepared to stand by the basis of the terms which had been originally agreed when the whole transaction was placed in the hands of the agents. Having acquired a new home and moved in, I was not prepared to accept this so I contacted Lewis Hay and asked him to call a meeting of our solicitors and agents in London. This he agreed to, and a most unusual procedure followed—quite unorthodox, and beyond the comprehension of the experts who were there to advise us. It started off by them confirming that no agreement was likely to be forthcoming, when I leaned across the table to Lewis Hay and said, "Don't you think we could settle this by ourselves, in another room, in five minutes?"

To the surprise of everyone present, he said, "Certainly we can," so out we went.

I asked him what was troubling him? His reply was "I don't want to pay you anything for collecting my hire purchase accounts."

"Well," I said, "You are giving me the business so I don't mind doing that for you, if it would give you special pleasure."

"Would you?" he said.

"Certainly, if you are prepared to sign an agreement here and now that everything else is in order."

"Well," he said, "We have nothing more to argue about." I then pointed out to him that our advisers would not want to conclude arrangements that afternoon but I did not see why he should not have an undertaking from me that I would not back out, to which I felt sure he was entitled. I must admit that I did not indicate that the same applied to him. So we returned to the room and I left it to Lewis Hay to make his announcement.

"Everything is settled, gentlemen," he said, "But we want an agreement now. Riceman has said he will sign this." The solicitors and agents said this was impossible. In the meantime I was whispering to Dudley Edgar telling him that we must draw up a legal document there and then, which I would sign, likewise Lewis Hay. He was quick to see the point and, although I am sure he had never done such a thing before or since, between us we recorded it on paper, finalising the terms of settlement. I signed this in the presence of my legal advisers and agent—likewise Lewis Hay, in spite of the protests of his solicitors. I was informed when I left that it was quite unnecessary to press the matter in this way. However those who told me so were proved wrong for the next morning Lewis Hay contacted his solicitors saying, "I am not going ahead with it"—but it was too late.

CHAPTER SEVENTEEN

THE KENT ADVENTURE—SPRING 1950

After years of striving to help others develop their stores successfully, now we were on our own. The write up in the trade press about "Three Stores in Kent" looked good but it was a different matter when they were closely examined. They were old fashioned, and nothing had been spent on them for years so the premises were badly in need of maintenance as well as bringing up to date.

No one can launch out into business on their own unless they can make an assessment of their financial requirements. It was under this heading that I shall always be grateful to Charles Clore who had a flair for the profitable handling of money. While at Reading I had come to know the manager of the chief branch of the Midland Bank in Threadneedle Street, S. J. B. Cull. He handled the store's banking accounts at Heelas of Reading. He was therefore fully acquainted with all my changes at the store and the effect they had on our trading results. I went to him with details of the companies we proposed to form. He must have thought I was capable of operating my own business and his advice ensured I made the best use of our limited financial resources.

The first few years were bound to be difficult and we would need all the financial help we could obtain. First we had to buy the three stores and their freehold, then we had to cover the cost of increased stocks if we were to achieve increased turnover and spend money on the premises before we thought of any expansion programme. After recording the capital requirements, Barry Cull agreed we would need a figure of around £60,000. The bank would help but we must first obtain all the security available.

Our parents were anxious to help though their resources in retirement were limited. It was a surprise to find my father, who had always been most careful with his savings, prepared to put them in a development which was entirely new to him for he had never been associated with any form of business. The detailed records have been destroyed but my father and mother loaned us approximately £16,000 which was a large part of their savings. My wife's parents gave us the deeds of their home as a £10,000 security with the bank. We had saved abut £15,000 and the bank accepted the deeds of our home as a further £8,000 security. So we had over half the £60,000 available in cash and security to cover the bank loan.

Fortunately, the Deal premises were in better condition than those at Herne

Bay and Whitstable and it was here I looked for a quick increase in turnover with minimum expenditure on the premises. Money just had to be spent at Herne Bay so as to make the most of an imposing 300ft frontage on a corner site. The buildings had to be opened up inside which was a costly alteration but it did give us the chance to go all out for increased turnover that with improved gross profit was our first objective during our first two years trading. This brought us an encouraging surprise. The improved trading results increased the value of our freehold properties. We were able to negotiate a sale of Deal and Whitstable freeholds at a figure that enabled us to cover all the developments and expansions of the stores for some years to come, leaving the Herne Bay freehold as security with the bank should we require any borrowing, though little was needed until the building extension at Deal was completed. As the stores' trading continued to expand it was not long before the value of our leasehold premises was as valuable as the original freeholds and we had enough reserve capital to acquire another small business in Maidstone.

Having dealt with the financial structure we were free to plan for the future but let me return to our opening years. The secretary of the three companies was Nigel Duncan, one of the able administrators that my predecessor had persuaded to work for him. He was just the person I needed as he was petrified of spending and therefore every financial undertaking whether it was improving the premises or expanding our stock, or advertising, received his critical scrutiny of all that was involved and he nearly always finished by telling me that we could not make profit on our first year's trading.

Lessons already learnt in the hard school of retailing.

Never before had I paid so much attention to the previous experiences that were likely to prove helpful and these were supported by advice from some of the wisest and most successful men in retail distribution. Nonetheless, there was still much to learn. Fortunately, I realised this which enabled me to avoid what might have proved to be many costly mistakes as I always checked up on the cost of ideas before acting on them.

Actions that contribute to success.

Though the stores were making a small profit it was evident that this would not continue unless further capital was injected. Very little money was spent on price tickets, indeed at the Herne Bay store they managed by painting prices on the backs of the lids of shoe boxes; after coming from a high class store with wonderful window displays it was quite a come down to see displays marked in this way.

After a review of all the staff and making additions where necessary the stock selection was taken in hand with more effective window and departmental displays, and then followed whatever temporary action could be taken to add more selling space. I embarked on a final attack on living-in accommodation on the store premises as I had done at other stores. I had always felt it better for staff to live off the premises to ensure security as well as in the interests of the staff themselves. This provided me with a new office and more selling space at Deal.

The public soon realised that something was happening and they began to take note of our more progressive trading policy. The first year's results were a little better than Nigel Duncan predicted but left much room for improvement. However I did not expect the position to be any different until the turnover was increased sufficiently to cover our increased trading costs.

The Deal development created unexpected problems largely due to the closely knit community who were not eager to encourage the expansion of a department store in their midst. The question of ancient lights with the adjoining bank premises proved an unexpected problem and the then manager, who was friendly with our neighbours on the other side, showed no indication of desiring to help us. However, plans were eventually completed which provided us with a considerable increase of space on our first and second floors in an expansion we were undertaking. The building, when completed, proved a great success and gave us an area that permitted most of the departments that one expects to be included in a modern store, although of course the space and selection was bound to be limited.

It was about this time that apart from my fairly regular trips to the United States and Canada I thought it would be a good idea to visit Australia and New Zealand and so planned an around the world trip to include these countries, covering around 30,000 miles in 107 hours' flying time—rather slower than what it would be today! Incidentally, I was one of the pioneer travellers on the first Qantas plane from Johannesburg to Perth, Australia. I had already stopped en route at Rome, Cairo, Khartoum, Entebbe and Johannesburg, where nothing eventful happened.

Not so across the Indian Ocean, where the first overnight stop was Mauritius. This proved to be an unfortunate night, as my hotel accommodation was infested with insects that not only crawled but made unpleasant noises. Fortunately, I am a good sleeper and by the time I awoke in the morning they had all gone and the sun was shining. I discovered a lovely bay for a refreshing swim, surrounded by a coral reef. In the afternoon a heavy thunder storm was at its height when we took off. Knowing we had a twelve hour flight ahead and that the old fashioned plane would be full of fuel, I had a few minutes with my imagination working overtime and I was not free from anxiety until we were above the clouds. Early the next morning we sighted far below us, what appeared to be a tiny rock. It was one of the Cocos Islands with a runway just large enough for us to use and built by our forces during the last war. It was a small flat coral island, not more than twenty feet above the sea. The islands had been settled by John Clunies Ross in 1827 and annexed by Britain in 1857.

I had still to learn the lesson that water in different parts of the world, unless you know it is safe to drink, can cause trouble. Being excessively hot I naturally satisfied my thirst and it was only after arriving in Perth I realised how unwise I had been. Curiously enough it affected my middle ear and caused me considerable trouble for the further twenty-nine days of travel I still had to complete. It was Captain Fremantle who hoisted the British flag at the mouth of the Swan River in 1829 and founded what is now the city of Perth, a beautiful centre. The department stores had great scope for expansion as the population was scheduled to increase steadily for some years to come.

There was one particular store that interested me. It had excellent premises, but I soon realised it was being badly operated. When I met the chairman and managing director I realised the cause. I believe he was a solicitor, but it was evident he had had no experience of life in a department store. The one floor which particularly interested me was the lower level, which had its own frontage on a street at the rear of the premises, offering scope as a magnet to draw additional shoppers.

Linens were one of the main departments, occupying a frontal position. There were beautiful long tables on which there were only a few items—one with sheets, another with pillow cases, etc. When I pointed out what wonderful space he had and why didn't he put more merchandise on display, his answer was that his purchases had been related to his sales in the previous year. This must have been a bad year, as there was practically nothing to sell! I thought this provided a wonderful opening for us as a famly to emigrate, so I asked him if he would like to come to an arrangement with me. He seemed quite interested and promised to let me know if he decided to take the matter further. As it happened, I heard nothing from him and eventually he sold to another store group—no doubt they made a fortune out of it.

From Perth I moved to Adelaide, spending some time in John Martin's store and Myers' Emporium. Then on to Sydney where I spent a few days, mostly with David Jones Department Store. Here I was to learn the importance of attracting postal business from shoppers who lived too far away to visit stores frequently in person.

Little did I realise when leaving Sydney for Wellington, New Zealand, that I was to have an adventurous take off in a seaplane. This was the only one operating at the time and it happened to be on a Friday evening. When I saw the crowd waiting at the small airport at the water's edge, I casually enquired if there were planes going to other resorts, I was told, "No, there is only one; it is for New Zealand." I remember saying, "They won't all get on, will they?" and the reply, "I expect they will squash us in"—and this is what happened. I had an outside seat on the port side by a porthole and it must have taken thirty minutes or more to accommodate all the passengers. The next problem was the luggage. The steward could not get it in the special enclosed storage space available. In the end it had to be lashed with ropes. This took some time. At last the engines were started and I thought that this was it—full of passengers and luggage. As we moved forward I expected to see daylight before me, but my porthole was under water and I thought that we must be a submarine! After what seemed like a few minutes we stopped, turned around and travelled under water again back to where we had started. This happened twice, and I kept wondering what was going to happen. The third time we were lucky, for daylight appeared instead of water and we gradually rose at the far end of the harbour leaving the Sydney beach and the life of a prosperous and expanding city behind us.

The trip was uneventful and arriving in Wellington I found that everything was closed down until Monday morning—even the hotel only had cold meals available. However, the Saturday newspaper was printed and one of the headlines, which I noted with interest, was, "Seaplane arrives safely from Sydney carrying its heaviest load ever"!

During the weekend I happened to spot someone I knew whom I had seen at the last meeting of the Twenty Club a month earlier. I have forgotten his name but will always remember the surprise of us both meeting like this at the other side of the world.

I learnt quite a lot from the small varied department stores in New Zealand. Two things stand out in my mind. One was a store that had been planned by an architect who probably was competent in planning the construction of the building but he had no idea how merchandise should be positioned and presented.

Although the owner of the business took great pride in his achievement it was obvious he was not going to get the best use out of his investment. The business had been started by his father and he had the advantage of capital and freehold premises but he obviously had a lot to learn.

Another store that impressed me in Auckland had quality, well supported by a remarkable and tasteful selection of fashions and fabrics. This demonstrated to me that if a person has taste, colour sense and can assess the likely public response to a changing fashion, and if all this is presented in the right setting he can soon achieve success.

I had an interesting trip from Wellington to Auckland travelling by bus calling at Napier en route where there was a serious earthquake in 1931, when hundreds of lives were lost. What had been an inland harbour was replaced overnight by land and the coastline had been entirely altered by the addition of 8,000 acres of new land. I soon asked if they were anticipating any more earthquakes and everybody seemed to be quite hopeful that this would not happen!

However, there is what they call a Geyser Valley that runs through Napier to Wairakei which must be one of the natural wonders of the world. I spent a day here examining the various underground disturbances that are quite remarkable. Everything works to a time schedule, to a second, and it is not likely to alter unless there is another earthquake. The crust of the earth is so comparatively thin that these large forces are moving not far below the surface; one section is named Boiling Cauldrons. Steam vents may start every hour or every ten hours, but each has a given time and is sign-posted accordingly. At the time I was there they were commencing to tap this steam to fuel a large power station.

On the journey home I called at Fiji, Honolulu and San Francisco where I spent two interesting days but by this time my ear was causing so much pain I had to get medical advice. They wanted to pierce it. I didn't like the idea so they said the best thing was for me to go straight home. I made the trip via New York and fortunately after some medical attention I was soon fit again.

It was about this time that the manager of the National Provincial Bank, next door to us at Deal, retired and I thought it would be neighbourly to welcome his successor, Mr Francis John. I found him to be a delightful person, and this courtesy call proved to be one of the most profitable actions that I had taken since we came to Kent. It happened soon after our friend Barry Cull retired from the Midland Bank in Threadneedle Street and his successor proved to be somebody quite different. Instead of being invited to lunch two or three times a year I was kept waiting for an interview and often left standing in his office like an errant school boy.

It so happened that the Canterbury dream was beginning to take shape and it was evident that there would be no helpful reaction from this source. So, after a pleasant chat with our new neighbour I asked him what he thought of our future in Kent and mentioned the Canterbury dream. His reaction was most encouraging. He thought it was a splendid idea, offered to give me his full personal support and was confident that the bank would be behind us if I was able eventually to carry through my dream. It was not long before our account was transferred to the National Provincial Bank.

Although Canterbury was looked upon as the ideal position in which to build the sort of store I always hoped to operate an opportunity occurred in Maidstone and it was thought to be a good idea to test the market there in a small way before any further developments were made elsewhere. Although the trading results improved, they did not warrant the time that was given to the branch and after two years it was sold providing additional capital which helped to swell our credit balance at the bank. We did learn two lessons:

1. Always go for a key position. For any retail operation it is worth paying more rent to be in a central position than to obtain an attractive rent in a secondary site for it could cost almost as much to operate the latter as the former.

2. As this Maidstone establishment was fifty miles away, it could not justify the time and costs required, both for management visits and the interchange

of stock. Only a large trading unit could have overcome this disadvantage.

Even though we were developing our trading from comparatively small beginnings, I was already on the lookout for any means to make us known beyond the borders of the south-east. With this in mind I advertised for someone who might be interested in helping me develop post order business; as a result Mr George King came to see me, and so commenced a long and happy association which has lasted thirty years rising to Group Company Secretary.

We could not afford large advertisements but we took regular weekly space in the national press including the *Daily Telegraph, Daily Mail, Daily Sketch, Daily Mirror* and others.

It was interesting how we searched for items of outstanding value that would appeal to postal shoppers. Two of these will always be remembered: one was glazed chintz and 54″ satin both of which we sold at 5/11d per yard in attractive colours—thousands of yards were sold throughout the country; the other was a big purchase of Clarks desert boots including large sizes for men and this was a very successful offer.

Small printed leaflets with other offers were enclosed with all orders despatched.

This mail order service was continued for a few years and although it did not contribute large profits it did enable us to make large purchases at very competitive prices and helped to establish our name as a retailer, both to suppliers and the general public.

A team of managers, buyers and senior staff had developed over the years. One hesitates to mention names but there were a few who were so closely associated with our speedy development that I must record their names to make this story complete. In addition to Mr King, mentioned above, there was Mr W. A. Dawson who came to me as a trainee buyer after leaving the army as a major; it was not long before he was appointed buyer of the travel goods section at Reading. His efforts proved most successful. He came to Kent with us and became manager, and later director of our Herne Bay store. Also he was associated with the group buying, and the early stages of planning for Canterbury.

Sidney Thomas our manager at Deal and Mrs D. A. Lee our accounts manager both came to Canterbury before retiring. Denis Hedges from the maintenance team at Reading chose to come to Kent and take charge of the building of our extensions, maintenance and new interior improvements. He loved his work and always felt he was part of the development that he was helping to build. When Canterbury was opened he continued in his same capacity until, unfortunately, he was taken seriously ill and was unable to return to work, though he continued to be interested in all that was happening.

There were many friends who helped with the buying but the most outstanding name was one who was proud to be called "one of the old school", Miss Matthews, our fashion buyer, careful and discerning in her views as well as in the care and presentation of everything she bought. She would never allow wastage under any heading, every pin was saved, every piece of tissue paper was ironed ready for re-use, and she knew how to buy at a discount so that the contribution to the progress of the business, with the support of her friend, Miss Brett, was considerable.

We were fortunate in the standard of staff in all sections of the business and some of our happiest occasions were on our annual party held in the gardens of our home at Felder House. In the early days, all the members of the family had to help prepare and serve the food, as we could not afford outside caterers. This was a big undertaking to provide a good meal and serve it for up to three hundred people. There was always fun and games and a concert if not a film in a large marquee. These occasions were not fully appreciated by the younger members of the family as these parties took place in school holidays and they really had to work hard! Nevetheless, it was an early initiation into the hard work that is always involved in the management of a family business and I suspect they enjoyed themselves, in spite of the efforts required beforehand.

Although we hoped to establish a similar trading standard for each of our three small stores it was found that Deal had a greater demand for the better quality ranges than Herne Bay and Whitstable though even in some sections there was an opportunity to trade up and we took full advantage of this. However, this meant that a group buying set-up could not be successfully established. This brought home to me the delicate division between group buying without individual stores influencing the selection and the older method of each establishment making its own selection.

This reduced the advantage of savings on large purchases and it soon became evident to me that only stores that were trading under similar conditions could successfully adopt a group buying set-up. We were situated between the two, too large to specialise in one level of merchandise and too small and with varying public demands to take advantage of central buying. We eventually adopted a flexible buying policy giving each store freedom of selection under supervision in most departments and sharing in bulk purchases where there was an attractive price advantage linked with this. The departments that benefited mostly from these were footwear, knitwear, some fashions on occasions, carpets, hardware and other household departments.

It was found that even though our overall turnover was not large we often had a buying advantage over larger stores as when we heard of a stock that was to be disposed of at an attractive discount we could see it and make an immediate decision as to whether to proceed with it. There was no reference back to headquarters and this resulted in many most attractive purchases which helped to establish us as being trading centres of unusual value. A few examples will give some indication of this.

Soon after arriving at Deal, I was at one of the blanket factories in Witney, when they had over a thousand blankets to be cleared before stocktaking, which was in the process of being finalised. This proved to be the best post-war blanket purchase I made, agreeing to purchase the whole stock at a surprisingly low price. There was some excitement when a large van drew up at the front entrance at Deal with this delivery but the question was where to put them? The event started in about four days' time but the stock had to be sorted, ticketed and priced, so eventually they were put inside the main entrance on one side of the store—taking up nearly half the area! However, it is interesting to note that while they were being ticketed shoppers took no interest in them—indeed, not a pair was sold until the commencement, a date which was supported with the large front window displaying tickets telling the full story and "Not more than three blankets to one customer". This was supported by suitable advertising, and to my relief on the opening day there was a queue for them right down the High Street and it was not long before the whole stock had been sold. This indicates how important presentation can be.

On another occasion, Mr Dawson went to see a large fire salvage stock of fully fashioned knitwear. He did not at first tell me about the results of his visit as they badly smelt of smoke, and he rightly felt that this would not enhance our fashion department. However, I asked him to show me the samples; the quality, colour and make was excellent so it was arranged that these samples should be taken to a cleaner to see if they could treat them and it was found that this could be done at a cost of a shilling each. Mr Dawson tried to buy the whole lot which went into quite a few thousand, but we were only able to obtain a little over half the quantity. Barkers of Kensington took the rest. We paid in the region of five shillings when the retail value of them when perfect was anything up to £5. We sold them at prices under £2. We could have sold many more than the few thousand we had obtained. I believe Barkers sold theirs in their sale complete with smoke odour for about 16/- (80p). Our shoppers were delighted and we received a splendid contribution to our much needed gross profit.

Footwear gave us many opportunities of large successful purchases and two outstanding ones come to mind. I was visiting our friends the Clark family at Street who were as considerate to me as owner of a small business as if I had been linked with a large store. On this particular occasion they had little to offer me but I never assumed that a factory of their size hadn't got something to clear. When they appeared to have offered me everything that was available which was not exciting I said something to the effect that surely they had a warehouse full of surplus stock and the clearance manager said, "Well, we have a large quantity of desert boots which we make for the American market but which are quite unsaleable in the UK. These have got to be cleared but they won't interest you."

I asked if I could see them. A pair was brought and it was the first time I had been introduced to what for many succeeding years proved to be an excellent seller and widely featured throughout the country.

On learning that they had to move the stock as they needed the storage space and that they had around five thousand pairs I said I would gladly take them at 2/6d per pair (12½p). He was rather shocked at the suggested price and went to his managing director but was back within minutes saying, "They're yours."

We fortunately had a top floor in our home which we used as a reserve store and we were able to put the boots there. This proved an introduction to the hard work involved in store life for the younger members of the family as they all had to be priced before distribution to our three stores and the family also had to handle the movement from the top floor to waiting vans on Boxing Day! I well remember the various methods which were adopted to save time and they were thrown down in bundles to be caught in blankets or sheets below. On the selling side, the public responded to them as quickly as I had done and they were sold at 19/11d per pair. Some might think this was profiteering but I never considered this to be the case. They were being offered at less than half the normal price after we had taken the risk of buying an enormous quantity; the public was delighted and so were we to see an overall financial improvement.

Incidentally, there was a good proportion of extra large sizes and at that time policemen with large feet in London, who had difficulty in obtaining boots, heard about our offer and we had many visitors and letters asking for them. The stock was cleared within months and when I tried to obtain a further delivery the following year we had to pay a lot more for them!

As we had to struggle to obtain supplies of the best known makes of shoes I had the pleasure of coming into contact with some of the most outstanding men in the footwear business and one of these was A. G. Ramsay who was at the time sales manager for Brevitt Shoes. He had invited me to a warehouse where he had a stock of high class shoe ranges to clear but they were all in AA (narrow) sizes. This gave me food for thought, the size range although limited was excellent in many ways, the quantity was large, running into four figures; how was I going to find enough women with narrow feet irrespective of the price to clear such a large quantity of a particular fitting.

However, as stocks were always short for extreme fittings, I thought it would be well worth while to take a chance. Tom Ramsay, as he is always known, didn't try to persuade me to make such a purchase and I finally asked him if I could have them at a very low price about 5/- per pair, (25p); he eventually agreed. They were highly priced shoes selling at about £5.19.11d (almost £6) and we offered them at considerably less than half price but the margin was so large that although we sold less than half the quantity in the first year we were able to cover both the cost of the purchase and the normal mark up, so for the following two years the remaining stock was on offer at sales and was greatly appreciated by the public enabling us to improve our turnover without any additional cost. This method of stock control is probably frowned upon by the majority of merchandise controllers but we were building a business from scratch, and I have never regretted doing this as we were able to increase our financial resources and at the same time enlarge our stock selection.

Arising from this and other meetings with Tom Ramsay I was able to assess his true value as a merchant and as a delightful person with the type of personality which I felt would be invaluable to a good class department store. Looking into the future, I invited him to change from his existing career in manufacturing and wholesale distribution of footwear, to that of taking charge of our footwear interests in our Canterbury store when it opened. This led to his becoming general manager, and then store director, and this proved a happy and profitable association.

Another large purchase was a salvage stock of carpets in the region of £50,000 at selling which we were able to offer to the public for £20,000; getting such a large stock in the 1950s was quite an undertaking. However, the quality and prices at which we were able to offer a wide selection was such that shoppers came from long distances to purchase, quite a number from the Canterbury area, some of whom were later involved in deciding whether we should be given an opening to establish a store in the city!

There is one other purchase with a story behind it. It was a few days before Christmas and before I left for London I was asked in the lingerie department whether I could possibly get a stock of housecoats for the sale, though it was hoped that quite a few could be sold before Christmas Eve. My luck was in, as I walked into a manufacturer who had at the back of his showroom a few hundred that he was prepared to let me have at a price I couldn't turn down. It was arranged that they would be packed in cartons during the day and I was due to catch the 5.40 p.m. train from Cannon Street. He promised to have them ready by 4.30 p.m. loaded in his van to take me to the station.

When I arrived back at the warehouse later that day he told me there was trouble at Cannon Street, the trains were running late and some not at all but I thought it was worthwhile having a go and we set off with me sitting in the front cab with the driver. When we approached the entrance to Cannon Street station the crowds were blocking all entrances and the driver said it would be quite impossible for us to gain entry. I said, "Come on, blow your hooter and I'll do some shouting." This he did and with me shouting "Gangway, gangway, please", the crowds opened up until we were able to back the vehicle on to the loading ramp. The driver though by this time was very disturbed. "We'll never get through the crowds and anyway the trains probably won't run." I told him to stay with the van and I would be back.

I worked my way through to the entrance of a platform where the stationmaster was standing and told him I had a priority delivery for Canterbury—"Well," he said, "This train has been standing here for over an hour and it has been full during this period. If you can get your goods on the train and it goes, splendid—but it's up to you!"

So I went on to the platform where I found a number of postal men loading Christmas parcels. They kindly lent me one of their trucks which I wheeled to the entrance where the stationmaster and ticket collectors helped divide the people for me to move through with me once again calling out "gangway, please, priority delivery" and it was not long before I was back with the van, had the cartons loaded, piled high on the truck and was setting off back to the train. This time the driver pulled the truck and I again called out my successful call of "priority delivery, gangway please". Once again the station staff helped and I was not even asked for a ticket! The Post Office staff kindly took my cartons into their coach and told me how sorry they were I could not go as a passenger but it was against the rules; however, they promised they would drop them all out at Canterbury for me. I started walking along the length of the train where every seat and corridor was jammed with people until I came to the front of the train where there was a small guard's van and five of the railway staff, supposedly drivers, who were arguing. There was one seat in the van which was occupied by a man in a bowler hat. I said to the men, "Hello, you're up against it, aren't you? What are your wives going to say when you don't turn up at home this evening?" This set them thinking so then I said, "Why don't you go slow as far as London Bridge from where I understand the signal system is normal." This was the gist of the conversation and they thought there was something in it and one said, "We certainly don't want to stay here all night so what about it?" So the senior one left to make an offer to the powers that be and when he came back, the driver was ready to go.

I went up to the man with the bowler hat and asked, "Where are you going?" and he replied, "Tunbridge Wells." I said "Oh, I'm sorry, you're on the wrong train, this is going to Canterbury and Dover" so he got up and left, and I sat down! The purchase was for the Deal store (Canterbury store not yet opened) and it was the quickest way of getting them to Deal.

When we arrived at Canterbury my son, David, met me and said, "You're five minutes late father." I told him I didn't think that was too bad in the circumstances and when he read the papers the following morning about passengers stranded until midnight and later, he agreed with me that my timekeeping wasn't too bad! The purchase proved a great success both before and after Christmas.

There were of course many other exciting trade purchases but the few referred to give some indication that we were able to enjoy our work and at the same time ensure the progress of our business. One further lesson that stands out in my mind arises from one of the large group of stores where instructions had been given that a fixed mark up of 25% was to be put on purchases in certain departments. The idea was to offer keen prices, but this did not always work, as was the case when the buyer representing this group went to purchase some surplus stock. As they could only make 25% the buyer agreed to pay considerably more than they need have done so that they could still get a price they felt would give them a more satisfactory return and offer the public the sort of reduction which they considered attractive. I was not bound by any fixed margins and so was able to buy at a much lower price and still sell at the same price as the larger store was doing! This brought home to me the importance of never trying to obtain the best value by a restriction on the margin between the price you purchase and the price you retail—this is what in the trade is termed mark up—but best value is always something that arises out of the keenest price one can purchase in an open market with goodwill.

The winter and summer sales were great occasions and months of hard work were applied to each. We knew we had to make a name for ourselves, not only for Deal and the other two stores we were operating, but also as a contribution towards the eventual opening in Canterbury. Every department had to participate and no reductions were permitted to be shown unless they were real. Once the public discovered that the values are worth examining, people talk and your reputation develops. When the sales finished, equal effort was made to introduce each season's fashion ranges supported by various promotions, some of which have already been mentioned, but a regular feature was, of course, the fashion parades, which were well attended. So, a business that was only doing a turnover at the three trading outlets of approximately £200,000 in 1952 reached half a million by 1962.

The trading policy for Canterbury was beginning to emerge from the development of our store at Deal. Since the extension to our premises had been completed we had more than doubled our trading area where we introduced a number of what some traders would have called unprofitable departments. This did actually happen in one or two cases but they added extra interest to the store as a centre to visit so there was a further increase in the shopping public from further afield.

An attractive restaurant was one service which had the usual problems. In fact, on one occasion, with sickness among the staff, there was no one to prepare the food, and the family had to step in and fill the gap, and I well remember my wife taking charge behind the scenes for a few days.

Hairdressing was another service that brought its usual problems but again it was a service that was greatly appreciated as was also the men's hairdressing section. A delicatessen on the ground floor proved another innovation that brought in as many individual purchasers as almost any other section in the store. Then there were radio, television and electrical goods, also toys, all of which helped to offer ranges that one would expect to find in a much larger store.

Our efforts on the buying and expansion side of store life would have been ineffective without a lively sales promotion programme. My previous experience stood me in good stead under this heading and once again I was introducing trading features that I knew the public enjoyed.

Among several well known personalities that drew the crowds and provided the sort of free publicity that is essentially the most effective was Kenneth Horne who was at the height of his broadcasting fame. He gave us much enjoyment at a special lunch we arranged for the press and trading personalities connected with the opening of our new television and electrical floor.

At the lunch our dining room at Felder House was full and Kenneth Horne was anxious to demonstrate what an expert he was on carving chicken (I don't know how many of them there were) but this certainly proved one of the most humorous meals among many that took place in our home which was part of our policy of developing friendly links with key manufacturers and the press during the years we were trying to establish our name.

Another visitor who brought the crowds was Norman Wisdom; he spent a few hours in the store. His mother who lived in Deal was a very good shopper and loved the store and as Norman Wisdom's home had been Deal it was comparatively easy to obtain his support whereas it might have been almost impossible to have him anywhere else in the country at the peak of his fame.

It was a great day for Deal, the store and our staff. He really was at his best, a natural humorist taking full advantage of testing our beds, with help from our willing staff and spending time in most departments turning even the dullest of corners into places of fun and laughter. We were grateful to him for supporting us at a time when we specially needed it, having completed our extensions we had to achieve a big increase in turnover to justify them. He helped us well on the way to do this.

We were particularly proud of our extended shoe department with an entirely new attractive layout and my wife's uncle and aunt, General Sir John and Lady Crocker, came for this opening. They were well received by a large crowd and Lady Crocker performed the opening ceremony; it was a happy occasion as she came as one of the family.

Full advantage was taken of peak trading periods and our Christmas attractions brought in large numbers, Father Christmas arriving either by sea, air, train or coach, the children and all the family turned out to welcome him.

Each year efforts were made to have a different Christmas attraction. The arrival of Father Christmas was always a crowd puller and I am sure some Deal residents will still remember the morning when Father Christmas arrived at Deal station to be met by 'Achmed' the camel who was patiently waiting with the zoo keeper in the station forecourt. We had recently completed the addition of a new second floor to the store and before turning it into a selling area it had been fitted out as a small zoo from Chipperfield's Circus. Achmed was the star attraction but all the exhibits proved popular—bears, monkeys, birds, a chimpanzee, a kangaroo and two pythons who escaped one night taking up their new quarters in a pile of carpets in the nearby department!

Well, Father Christmas for the occasion was one of the store's maintenance staff. Mr Cornes had no previous experience of camel riding and Achmed turned out to be a real handful! His kicking display as Mr Cornes tried to mount was like a comedy act and amused the crowd. Father Christmas eventually arrived at the store not quite his usual calm self. One year he came by sleigh but perhaps the most popular was his golden coach on more than one occasion, led over a route arranged with the police and headed by a well known band. The famous girl pipers led the procession one year and the Betteshanger Colliery Band also was recruited. These events were well advertised and attracted many people into the town centre, not only from the Deal area but also further afield.

Fortunately, the Deal store was now big enough to offer the essential facilities for the growing demands which arose prior to the opening of Canterbury. It became the HQ for senior staff as they joined us and looking back to the establishment of Canterbury it is hard to envisage how the Canterbury store could have been started without the framework of the Deal store. There was complete harmony between the existing staff and the Canterbury team as they gradually joined us and it was found that they were able to help one another in many ways. No trouble or friction arose which is a great tribute to all concerned.

It is sad to conclude this chapter with the end of the store which we as a family valued as it had developed so successfully in a comparatively short time. However, disasters do happen and one Sunday afternoon in the autumn of 1963 when we were having tea, the phone rang telling us that the Deal store was on fire. Our daughter, Elizabeth, was at home and we went down together and found that the whole of the premises was a mass of flames and there was nothing we could do. The site was completely gutted and it seemed as though all our efforts had been destroyed. However, we called all the staff together the next day in the local cinema which the management had kindly loaned to us and we promised that if we could we would continue trading in small establishments and to re-build if it became practicable. If employment was not available to them all we would do our best to accommodate them in Canterbury if they wished.

Several small shops were opened, particularly covering fashions and footwear departments as we sought to find ways and means to rebuild the store. We were encouraged by over 500 letters from local residents some pleading with us to do this. However, planning regulations were such that if we rebuilt we had to provide car parking facilities on site so our overall trading floor area would be reduced and there would also be a time lag of two years. At the end of this period it would be like starting again from scratch. This we

(30) The Furnishing Centre in Burgate.

(31) The store executives, 1983. Jeremy Akester, George King, Ted Phillips, Fred, Betty and David Riceman, David Thomas, Walter Kilb.

Photos by *Kentish Gazette*

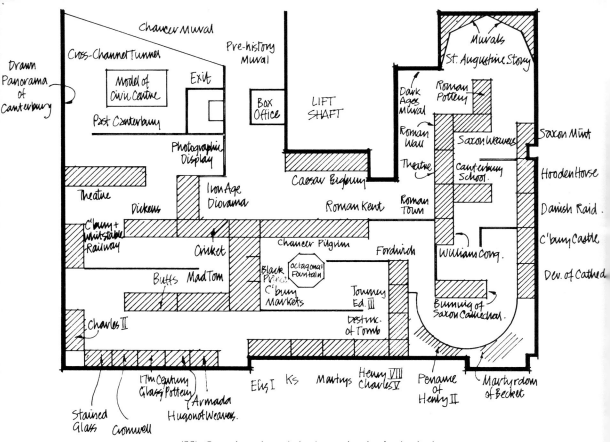

Drawn Panorama of Canterbury

Chaucer Mural

Cross-Channel Tunnel

Model of Civic Centre

Exit

Past Canterbury

Photographic Display

Pre-history Mural

Box Office

LIFT SHAFT

Murals

St. Augustine Story

Dark Ages Mural

Roman Pottery

Roman Wall

Theatre

Caesar Bigbury

Saxon Weavers

Canterbury School

Saxon Mint

Hooden House

Theatre

Dickens

Iron Age Diorama

Roman Kent

Roman Town

Danish Raid.

C'bury + Whitstable Railway

Cricket

Chaucer Pilgrim

Fordwich

Williams Cong.

C'bury Castle

Dev. of Cathed

Butts

Mad Tom

Black Prince

octagonal Fountain

C'bury Markets

Tourney Ed. III

Charles II

Destruc. of Tomb

Burning of Saxon Cathedral.

17th Century Glass Pottery

Armada

Stained Glass

Cromwell

Hugonot Weavers.

Eliz I

Ks

Martyrs

Henry VIII Charles V

Penance of Henry II

Martyrdom of Becket

(32) *Canterbury through the Ages*—the plan for the displays.

(33) The arrival of the Romans.

(34) The Canterbury to Whitstable Railway

(35) The Saxon Mint.

(36) Chaucer's Canterbury Pilgrims.

Canterbury through the Ages — continued

(37) Christopher Marlowe the playwright.

(38) The Buffs Regiment.

(39) The Murder of Beckett.

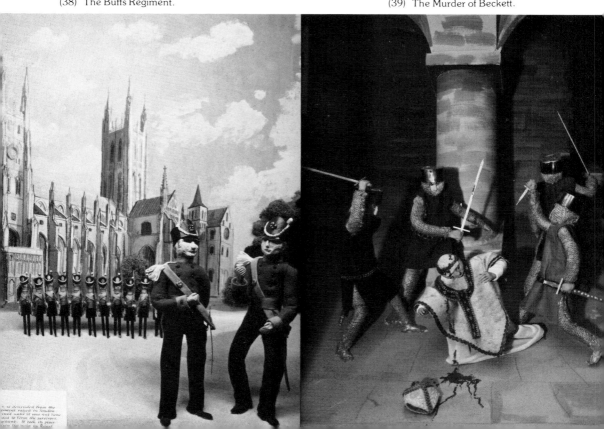

(40) *The Saxon Cathedral destroyed by fire.*

(41) *The Canterbury Martyrs.*

Throughout the history of the Church men and women have been
willing to die for their religious principles. Persecution was not been the
prerogative of a particular religious sect and today it should be borne in
mind that it would be very wrong to single out one faction for condemnation.
In the reign of Queen Mary I papal rule in the Church was restored, and
between 1555-58, 41 protestants, men and women of Canterbury, suffered
death by burning for heresy. The stake was set up in a field in sight

(42) The Roman Pottery Industry. *(44)* *Opposite* The Memorial Hall Library on its opening in 1972.

Photo by Colin Westwood

(43) King Charles II at Canterbury. *(45)* *Overleaf* Caroone House, a City of London development organised by the Congregational Memorial Hall Trust chaired by the author.

Photo by Colin Westwood

thought to be completely impracticable and with regret we had to cease trading in Deal. A number of the staff came to Canterbury and there was understanding by everyone linked with us, many of whom showed their distress at what had happened.

Incidentally a lesson for the future, for a week or so after the fire we received a letter from the insurance company's assessor telling us that they were not accepting the claim. This demonstrates how a firm can go into bankruptcy without having committed any management fault. In this instance the assessors refused the claim because we had fireworks on the premises which they claimed had not been properly dealt with. It so happened that on the Saturday before the Sunday fire I had been on my usual store round and had seen them unpacking the fireworks on the first floor and had told them to go and fetch the manager regarding the safe keeping of this inflammable stock. The staff were well aware of this and testified accordingly; as a result of this the claim was eventually accepted.

So a happy chapter in our trading life came to an abrupt and unfortunate conclusion although much of the life of Deal was transferred to Canterbury.

Trading at the Whitstable store progressed steadily and only a few items of outstanding interest occurred, one of which was in 1950 when a heavy north-east gale combined with spring tides broke through the sea defences along a wide stretch of the south-east coast which included Whitstable. The High Street was flooded and our store had water in it to a depth of up to three feet.

Fortunately we were fully covered by insurance. Incidentally, when reviewing this on acquiring the stores, I was asked if I would like to include flood cover. It was suggested it was omitted as there had never been a flood, and I remember saying, "There is always a first time. We will take cover." We were the only trading outlet in the town that had this advantage and likewise at Deal where the flood was not so serious.

On the day it happened I had gone to Bournemouth to visit my parents, one of whom was ill. An urgent telephone call came through in the evening from my wife explaining what had happened and that she had been to the store in my absence wading in water up to her knees, and was most distressed at the damage caused. I told her not to worry as it would give us the advantage of a sale, and I knew that we would be fully recompensed for any stock that had to be cleared, so that both the public and our store would benefit. We both did, the following week!

Small additions were made to our Whitstable property, by acquiring adjoining premises, and likewise at Herne Bay. In the Herne Bay and Whitstable stores, although money was spent on improvements, we were never able to create the same trading atmosphere as at Deal. We had the support of excellent staff and management, but the potential was limited and we therefore disposed of them both so as to concentrate all our efforts on Canterbury.

CHAPTER EIGHTEEN

A CITY OF LONDON DEVELOPMENT

I bring in here the story of my involvement with an important development in the City of London which started while we were in the early stages of planning the Canterbury store. It gives some indication of how business experience can benefit a good cause and, as so often happens, open up new avenues of experience which become useful in other ways.

After attending the May 1960 Assembly Meetings in London of the then Congregational Union of England and Wales at Westminster Chapel someone caught me by the arm and asked me if I could spare the time to attend one or two meetings a year as a governor of the Memorial Hall Trust. He was the late Bernard Honess who was both a governor and secretary of the Trust. All I knew about the Memorial Hall was that it was a Victorian building with a tower similar to the one grandfather, Frederick Sage, had on his beautiful home at Edmonton, North London.

I had occasionally visited Memorial Hall for autumn meetings or to make contact with friends whose office was in the building. It was a badly planned building with large but wasteful accommodation and greatly in need of modernisation. As a letting proposition it could never compete with a modern building. As so little work was envisaged I agreed to become a governor and was officially welcomed at a meeting on 27th April 1961, having little idea that I was about to undertake one of the most exacting business experiences of my life. Perhaps it is just as well that we cannot see into the future as we might be tempted to avoid some of the challenges that come our way from time to time.

Some two years passed. I attended the few meetings held and listened to the reports given by the members of the Board of Management. It was evident to me that the time had come when the Trust could not survive many more years unless a radical change took place. It had already had to borrow £25,900 from the Congregational Union and despite stringent economies carried out by Bernard Honess, the income was too small to undertake even essential maintenance. Also, looming in the background was the fact that competition for tenants prepared to pay large rents for modern accommodation was increasingly strong in the City. We could not compete with those owning newly built accommodation as investigation had proved that our premises were not suitable for modernisation. I came on the scene when it was beginning to be realised that the Memorial Hall, which housed the official headquarters of the denomination and other bodies of the church could not continue as a viable proposition in its present form.

Agents acting for the Trust were contacting developers who would look upon this sort of undertaking as most profitable to them, but the question of where the Trust came in was never made clear enough for us to come to an agreement. During my second year of membership, I offered to see if I could find someone who would give us a fair share of the equity.

I was eventually introduced to Sir Aynsley Bridgland, a successful developer in the City and elsewhere, and it so happened he lived at Sandwich Bay not two miles from my home. He intrigued me from our first meeting; a dynamic personality, sitting behind an impressive desk, ready to pounce on anyone who came within his reach. Fortunately, I saw beyond his fearsome exterior a man with outstanding ability and a heart of gold.

During the following year, we had many meetings, discussing proposals, mostly at his home at 6.30 on Saturday evenings. Gradually a plan evolved, whereby his company would provide the capital, give the Trust an interest in the profit rental and, at the same time, house our offices and library. We actually reached the stage where figures were being discussed and the appointment of an architect was being made, when I happened to learn that someone, acting on behalf of the then chairman and some of the executive, was approaching other developers in the City, with a view to obtaining more attractive terms. As soon as I heard this, I contacted the Trust's chairman to arrange a meeting. I told him that we certainly could not obtain better terms and if Sir Aynsley heard about it, he would have no further interest in us. He had given much of his time and support, not just for financial interest, but because as a young man in Australia he had attended a Congregational church and liked to feel that before his life ended, he could do something for the church which had been such a helpful influence on him in his early years.

Once I had made the position clear to Clement Hickling, the chairman, he saw the danger that was emerging and asked if I could possibly help. I immediately rang Sir Aynsley's secretary with a view to meeting him the following day. This was a most interesting meeting. On my arrival I realised Sir Aynsley knew what had been done behind his back and was ready to throw me out. Fortunately, I kept him from saying anything until we were behind closed doors. I pressed him to hear an important message I had to give him first. He must have known what I was about to do but was courteous enough to allow me to speak. I quickly apologised for the information I had only received the previous day and assured him the action had been taken by men who did not realise the underlying implications. He was good enough to accept my apology and assurance that it would not happen again. He told me that but for this visit, he would have communicated to the Trust on Monday morning that he was no longer interested in our affairs. However, now as far as he and I were concerned, the position was unchanged.

It was at this stage that Clement Hickling felt that as so much was involved, he could not continue as chairman with his failing eyesight. It was then that pressure was brought on me to succeed him. I knew what was involved and as it came at the same time as I was carryng out the development of our new store at Canterbury, I was not eager for this unexpected work. I had some idea of the possible years of negotiating that would have to take place. However, as there seemed no one else who was prepared to accept the responsibility and I had the assurance of the full support of the executive, I reluctantly agreed and became chairman on the 22nd July, 1963. My fellow members on the executive at that time were Rev G. R. Martin, Rev G. P. Smailes, Rev H. S. Stanley, Rev. L. T. Towers, F. J. Braybrooks, W. J. Cumber, C. C. Hickling, K. M. Kirby, R. F. Williams and B. Honess.

Although the work during the ensuing years was even in excess of anything I had anticipated, I must record that all of the governors, or members as they were subsequently styled, gave me their maximum support, which really made it posssible to carry out the extensive and delicate negotiations. The frequent meetings with Sir Aynsley continued and during this period I gained much useful information and will always be indebted to him for the sound advice he gave, advice which had obviously been used in the development of his own business empire.

At the time, building prices were rising so fast that our advisers were concerned that we would not achieve terms attractive enough to show a profitable income to the Trust. Sir Aynsley waved this theory on one side and assured me that if you had the right site to develop, providing the plans were suitable and the maximum use was being made of the site, then the more basic costs rose, the more one could charge and justify as rent. His theory remained sound until well after the period of our redevelopment had been completed. Without it, I could never have been as stubborn with our advisers as I was, thanks to the lessons I had learned from Sir Aynsley.

The time had come for appointing architects. A member of our executive committee, Ronald Williams, was an excellent young architect in his own right, as well as being a member of a prominent West End firm. I raised the question of his name with Sir Aynsley who, at that time, wished to appoint his own architect. However, after he had given the matter further thought, he came back agreeing to our suggestion.

All looked well for the future and then suddenly, Sir Aynsley died after a short illness, and with his passing all our plans with his firm were terminated.

After some months, his successor, Sir Cyril Black, MP, asked to see me and a meeting was arranged at his office, arising from which we felt there was little chance of his agreeing to a project similar to which Sir Aynsley had in mind. Nevertheless, he was anxious to prepare rough plans and a scheme, which we agreed to see. The results of his thinking were in line with the developers who had been on the scene before Sir Aynsley. They were willing to take over our freehold and give us approximately 9,000 sq. ft. of floor space for a peppercorn rent, and that was all. No share in the equity. I did not wait to discuss the outcome with my colleagues, knowing full well that their reaction would be the same as mine. The scheme was turned down without further consideration and we were back to square one.

It is surprising how a game of golf can help; not only one's health but also one's business interest. While playing, quite by accident, I raised the question of our problem to my opponent and he said, "Do you know Stuart Harvey of the Sun Life of Canada? All things being equal, they like to help churches." I knew the Sun Life of Canada but I did not know Stuart Harvey but naturally said I would like to be introduced to him. This took place at an early date and as no other scheme was in the offing, I made up my mind that this one had to be pursued.

Fortunately for us, Stuart Harvey had proved to be not only a delightful person, but one with outstanding ability. In the ensuing meetings we had to discuss methods of procedure before dealing with any specific ideas. He was given an entirely new proposal that neither he, nor as far as I know, any other insurance company had previously received. We wished to hold on to our freehold but they in turn naturally wanted to get all the advantages of a freehold even if they did not own it.

So the scheme evolved was (1) that the freehold would be leased to the Sun Life of Canada for one hundred and fifty years for a premium of £615,000 when it would once again be returned to the Trust. During the intervening period, buildings on the site could only be erected with the full approval of the Trust. (2) That the Trust would be provided with suitable premises of some 9,500 sq. ft. at a rent of £1 per annum with its own entrance and foundation stone incorporating the original one laid on the 10th May, 1872. (3) That the Sun Life would provide all the capital requirement and that our professional advisers would agree on the amounts involved, both in the operation and erection of the new building.

After interest based on $8\frac{1}{2}\%$ per annum had been met on the total amount advanced and all expenses covered, the remaining balance would be divided, payable six monthly, between the Trust and the Sun Life of Canada. Realising that a scheme of this nature would require the goodwill and backing of their head office, I paid the first of two visits to their principals in Montreal. There I was given a most courteous and friendly reception. I outlined the basis of the scheme being followed up by Stuart Harvey in London and we have since remained on most useful friendly terms which must have proved of value to proceedings as they emerged.

About this time it became obvious to me that we would not obtain planning permission for rebuilding unless we had possession of the whole of the freehold site which, incidentally, will eventually reach the new traffic circle replacing the present Ludgate Circus crossing. Unfortunately, the Trust had leased the end building to Fleetway Publications for a term of fifty years. Our secretary, Mr Honess, was confident that this could be re-purchased. I had serious doubts, for they had spent at least £50,000 on fitting it out as a catering centre for some of their staff.

In the circumstances, it was felt best that we should test the climate by writing to their chairman, Sir Cecil King. He sent me a courteous reply arranging a meeting with the managers concerned with their lease. I thought it best to invite them to lunch and booked a special window table at the Savoy, hoping to obtain their sympathetic support. As soon as we met, I realised they were prepared to accept a free lunch but not to give up the premises we had leased to them. They said they had spent a great deal on the premises since leasing them in 1950. However, I kept them off making any final decision, saying this would be better left to the end of the meal.

Then followed one of those amazing experiences which can happen in life and which one can put down to various reasons but I was convinced and still am, that it was guidance from a stronger power than myself. An unknown person walked up to our table from the other side of the restaurant and said, "Hello, Riceman, what are these men doing to you?" I replied to the effect that I represented a worthy charitable cause and it was essential to our continued existence that they help me. It was bound to inconvenience them but financially they would certainly not be out of pocket. He turned to them, knowing their names and said, "You had better look after my friend." I have never seen this man since, I have no idea who he was but his intervention made all the difference. I was able to say to them before they had finished their meal, "What would you charge for your lease and if you want to be as helpful as you can, why not fix it before the end of the meal?" They said they could not consider a sum less than £162,000. I thanked them for their offer to surrender the lease for this figure, which I accepted.

We all enjoyed the rest of the lunch and I came back to Bernard Honess and gave him one of the shocks of his life. However, the figure had to be agreed as the development could not take place without our being able to build over the whole site. No doubt planning permission would not have been obtained without it. Fortunately, the Sun Life saw the logic of my argument and did not query the price.

It never occurred to me that the scheme would not be finalised. At this stage, we had acquired the whole site on which to build and had found the source to cover our financial requirement. However, it was at this time that planning permission for city developments was not being freely granted. It was here that Bernard Honess made his best contribution to the overall development. He must have had a friend at court! He explained to the then Board of Trade the value of the work of the Trust, its valuable library and the help it had been to the city in providing accommodation during the war years. The outcome of his personal intervention was that an office development permit was granted, and we were free to apply for planning permission.

The following three years was a period of tough negotiating covering both the overall mutual principles involved, as well as the operation of the scheme and the details of the building plans.

Unfortunately, once again, a change of management raised problems which had to be overcome. Stuart Harvey was recalled to Canada and was succeeded by Derrick Marks. Fortunately, this soon resulted in a similar link of friendship as had existed with his predecessor. However, probably due to some head office directive, the details were no longer to be decided by him alone but in conjunction with Mr Norman Bowie, a principal of Jones, Lang, Wootton. This was when our real negotiating problems increased as both he and our professional advisers considered a scheme could not be viable unless we could cover all costs involved based on a rental of £2.25 per sq. ft. My estimation of a figure of between £5 to £7 per sq. ft. received a cold reception. However, the memory of Sir Aynsley still remained with me and I pressed on seeking my higher figure. It was only after an all day session that a figure of £2.75 was agreed. The professional advisers on both sides agreed that this figure ensured the scheme being a viable proposition. At last the way was clear to build.

Although normal problems were encountered in the erection of the building, these were overcome and it was completed in 1972 and will always remain a great credit to our late friend, architect and member of the Trust, Ronald Williams. His early and untimely death proved a great loss to us. With the proposed new Ludgate Circus scheme, the new building will eventually be in view to all the traffic to and from St Paul's, the City and the West End. Considerable study was made in selecting a suitable name for the new building which was incorporating Memorial Hall. Caroone House was eventually chosen, particularly because of its historical connection.

Now the time had arrived to obtain suitable tenants. It was obvious we would have no difficulty in letting the premises and we were able to provide excellent accommodation to the External Telecommunications Executive of the Post Office on terms in line with my previous estimates, namely £7.50 per sq. ft. with a rent review every fourteen years.

At last the day for the opening celebrations arrived. This was really in three parts. First the dedication of the foundation stone; secondly, the service of praise and dedication; and thirdly, the lunch at the Savoy for members of the Trust, their guests and all those who had been linked with the development.

The dedication of the foundation stone was suitably carried out by the late Rev Howard Stanley; Bernard Honess and I were privileged to uncover the stone.

The service was conducted by myself as chairman, prayer was offered by

Dr Huxtable, scripture reading by Mr K. M. Kirby, the vice-chairman, and the address by the Rev Howard Stanley. It was held in the hall which was full on this occasion with all those who had participated in one way or another in bringing about the development. They included representatives of the Sun Life of Canada, the Trust, professional advisers, the City, bank and press.

It was a moving occasion with references to the foundation of the library in 1831 and the building of the old Memorial Hall in 1872 to commemorate the faith of some 2,000 ministers who, for conscience sake, were ejected from their livings in 1662. In the old building, famous political figures met, the Congregational Union of England and Wales was formed there, as was the Labour Party, and the BBC used the large hall for broadcasting during World War Two.

The lunch, which was attended by about seventy including members of my family, was a happy occasion and again all those closely associated with the development were present. It was evident to all concerned that the efforts over the previous ten years had given us food for thought, indicating that if a scheme is worthwhile, every effort should be made to hold on and not be deflected or defeated by obstacles that are bound to arise. One will be left with the satisfaction of having participated in something which, although costly in effort, broadens one's horizons and enriches one's life. Anyone who undertakes a project of this size has to be prepared to give up a lot of valuable time. This development was no exception. It required years of work, hundreds of important letters, numerous meetings and for a period, almost weekly visits to London, not forgetting journeys to Montreal. But the effort was well worthwhile.

About this time it was evident that the Trust's secretary, Bernard Honess, would not be able to cope with all the extra work entailed with the development of the Trust's life and activities, so after discussing the matter with him it was agreed that he would stay on in an advisory capacity so long as his health permitted and I would look for a successor to him.

Fortunately, my quest was soon successful. I wrote to the Officers' Association, as a result of which I was put in touch with John Gowlett, who, as soon as we talked for a few minutes, I knew would be ideal for the appointment. He proved to be a most dedicated and intelligent person. He had previously been in welfare service in South Africa.

John Gowlett joined us on 1st December, 1974 since when he has given of his best to the work and interest of the Trust. Soon after his arrival I began to realise unexpected problems might arise. Previously, the Trust had limited resources to offer apart from the excellent library which still required its records to be brought up to date. On the financial side, the only concern had been that money loaned to the Trust would, in due course, be returned. There had not been, by any stretch of the imagination, the thought that there would be any enlarged financial resources available for other objects of a religious, literary or philanthropic nature. Now it was evident that there would be for the first time a substantial income that had every chance of increasing over the years. This occurred at the time the United Reformed Church came into being which left minority Congregational bodies still active outside the United Reformed Church.

With this in mind, I hoped it would be possible for the Trust to justify its continued independence and give the greatest possible service by endeavouring to meet an essential requirement in all the denominational bodies by introducing a housing scheme for ministers and their wives when they retired. This was the main reason that prompted John Gowlett to accept his appointment. It was realised that facilities on a limited scale were already operating but resources were not available to ensure everyone requiring this service being accommodated.

I outlined to the Council on the 2nd April, 1974 a scheme to meet this need. A house, or flat, chosen by a minister and situated in the area of his family and friends, approved by the Trust's surveyors as a sound investment, would be purchased by the Trust and become its property. The occupation of the property by the minister and his wife (widow) would be rent free. The idea was welcomed and the scheme, prepared by the members of the Council to give effect to my thoughts, was subsequently presented to the Annual General Meeting on the 24th May, 1974 and was approved by acclamation.

Briefly, the scheme evolved laid down that the occupiers would not pay rent or become a tenant but would be required to contribute according to a formula related to their means towards the general rates and maintenance of the property. The necessary details were worked out and legal documents prepared. It was my hope that the Trust would eventually agree, if so requested, to acquire all the existing properties owned by the church authorities on terms in accordance with those which applied under the scheme to ministers. This would give much needed capital to the denominations and, at the same time, ensure ministers and their wives looking forward to retirement to a home of their own choosing. This would not only help those in the active ministry but also those who were contemplating entering the ministry. It might well become a decisive fact in a man's decision to give his life to the service of the church if, looking ahead and having a sense of responsibility to his family, he was freed of unnecessary anxiety as to what would happen when he was unable to continue his ministry.

Unfortunately, this scheme, though launched, was not carried out to the extent I had anticipated. This was understandable as with the formation of three denominational churches grouping together the assets of the Trust could be claimed for other purposes. However, at the time of writing, about fifty houses have been purchased, and it is hoped that this will continue to be steadily increased. The assets of the Trust have been completely transformed as they are now free of debt and have a valuable income which is likely to increase and an overall asset exceeding £9 million.

I shall always be grateful for the ready assistance given by those closest to me during this venture. In particular, Mac Kirby, vice chairman, George Riebold, treasurer, the late Bernard Honess, secretary, his successor John Gowlett, the late Ronald Williams, the architect, as well as my friends, the members of the Trust, the executives of the Sun Life of Canada and our professional advisers for their services and friendship. All were individually essential in bringing this development to such a successful conclusion.

CHAPTER NINETEEN

A Canterbury Tale

Most stores developed by the present generation have had the good fortune of being established by fathers or grandfathers who are likely to have purchased the freehold thus giving today's store tremendous advantage in terms of rent. A store started from scratch without any of these advantages has high rents to meet and this is bound to have a wide effect on profitability; it can only become profitable if every advantage is taken of the trading facilities available and the adoption of the most suitable trading policy.

Before coming to Kent I had had the good fortune of having management experience at various trading levels; through this I had learned that it is often easier to operate a store at a lower price level in the right place than it is to develop a high class store where there is a greater risk. The latter has many advantages as there is less competition and it attracts the type of shopper who has more to spend, possesses good taste and in many cases is prepared to travel a long way to obtain service and be able to choose from a wide range of quality merchandise. However, there were financial restrictions to be met and it was quite impossible to think in terms of launching out at once in the type of trading which would have been my choice. We first had to establish a profitable business through which we might look further afield. This had already been successfully achieved through our smaller developments in Kent and after the first five years I began to look further afield for my real objective.

Canterbury had always seemed to me the only centre in which there was a possibility of shaping my dream. The questions were—when and how? In 1957 we were able to acquire a freehold site near the County Hotel and it had been hoped to obtain the necessary permits to erect a new building large enough to house our basic requirements. However, I was never happy with this as the frontage was limited and it would not have been large enough to house a furnishing section which at that time was looked upon as an intrinsic part of a department store. Fortunately, for us, the necessary permits were not forthcoming and eventually the site was sold; some lessons had been learnt and we were back to square one.

It was about this time that both our sons decided to enter retail distribution and, looking to the future, it was obvious that when their training away from home had been completed it would be in their interest if we could expand further on a basis which would give every opportunity for their continued progress over the years.

MY ROAD TO CANTERBURY

With this in mind, I paid frequent visits to Canterbury, talked with friends and agents there regarding any premises or sites for development that might be used for a department store. It was on one of these visits in the late 1950s that I happened to be in the office of Mr John Berry, a well known estate agent. He had no suitable properties on his books but just as I was leaving he said, "By the way, I've heard they are going to put up a row of shops opposite what is to be a new city bus station." At the time there was no road, only Simon Langton's Grammar School for Boys in its own grounds which was to be demolished.

I was quick to follow this up and he had a rough plan of what the city had in mind with a dual carriageway passing the front of these shops through which the main traffic would flow. With Mr Berry's consent I telephoned the town clerk and asked if the authorities would be interested in giving me an option on building a department store on the whole of this site with emphasis on quality. I have no record of the conversation that ensued but I well remember his startled reaction to Canterbury having a second department store within the city boundary; surely one was adequate for a population of 34,000.

I later learned that his view was shared by many other prominent citizens and further afield the idea of this development was not favoured. They were forming their judgement on the local population whereas I was forming mine on an immediate catchment area of a minimum of a quarter of a million, rising from further afield to over one million. The town clerk was helpful and suggested that if I really meant what I told him, would I please write officially to him stating my requirements and what sort of option was needed. This was done and I received a prompt reply giving me an option with adequate time for plans to be prepared and submitted to the authorities. The basis of the ground lease with the city would follow if and when plans were approved.

So, a start was actually made, but had I any idea of the problems and struggles that were to ensue I don't think that even such an optimistic person as myself would have attempted to go further, for Deal and the associate stores were now trading at a useful and profitable level. They were easy to operate, we had a happy staff and financially there would have been no problems. However, money and ease are not everything and the exciting challenge was accepted although rather reluctantly by my wife who felt it would be much better not to take on unnecessary risks.

As far as I understand, it is many years since a new family store has been built and opened on a new site where trading had not been carried out before. This was substantiated by leading advisers in the trade and in particular through the trade press. It had required the facilities of large groups to undertake this form of development so we proceeded knowing that unusual and complex difficulties would have to be faced up to and overcome.

Before plans were even prepared a trading policy was formed. It was to be based on a centre of interest and attraction having the marks of good taste, presentation, selection and service behind everything that was executed. It had to become a centre of international repute, it had to have adequate transport facilities, sea, rail and road and the position in question offered all these. There was easy access to the continent whence visitors could be expected in increasing numbers. As a city it had a reputation for attracting visitors from all parts of the world, Canterbury being one of the five main centres that were usually on their itinerary and if only our image was attractive and different we could well do trade far in excess of what a normal trader in the city could possibly expect. Our success would depend on this.

The site could not have been better and when the news became more widely known particularly in the trading world it was not surprising that there must have been others with far greater financial facilities than we had pressing for an opportunity to use the site to their own advantage. I was never informed the extent to which this happened but there must have been pressure behind the scenes as just before our building plans were ready for submitting to the Planning Committee and city authorities I received a letter from the town clerk withdrawing the option. Unfortunately, the actual letter was destroyed in the subsequent fire but I believe the reason given was that we were not prepared to build a twelve storey building. I replied appropriately to the town clerk but at the same time took a large file of correspondence that had been taking place between myself and his office to see the then chairman of the Planning Committee, Mr John Barrett.

After explaining to him what had happened and that I had spent a lot of time and money trying to produce suitable plans as promised, only to be told at a late date that I could not proceed further without even examining these plans appeared to me to be quite unfair and I was surprised that he and his committee permitted this. It was obvious that he was not fully aware of all that had taken place behind the scenes and therefore he was given my folder of correspondence to examine. I must have been with him for the better part of an hour without any discussion taking place and when he had finished reading, it was obvious to me he was concerned that this had happened. He agreed that I had a just complaint and he would take the matter up with those concerned and let me know if anything could be done about it. I was not present at any of the official discussions nor did I give any further information but from hearsay I gather that he had a battle over what had happened and stood firmly behind the importance of the city honouring its commitment unless conditions arose which altered the original intent. I understood that a vote had to be taken on the case he presented on our behalf and he won by a narrow margin. Anyway, I had a further letter, also burnt, telling me that I could submit plans but not twelve storeys. I could only build to a height of fifty-six feet and this presented serious unexpected problems as we needed a certain number of square feet overall in which to house the essential departments to be carried and also to justify the building costs.

Fortunately for us we had already appointed one of the leading London architects, Sir John Burnett Tate & Partners and our interests were to be looked after personally by their partner, Mr E. A. Blade. Our immediate problem was to revise the plans so as to give us the maximum floor space. Here, Mr Blade had a shock when I suggested to him that we would have to cut down our ceiling heights giving us lower heights on some floors than had ever been erected in a modern department store.

As a result of this we managed to include an additional floor and the roof top restaurant and offices were set back so as to cut down the visual height. However, we were optimistic enough to have the foundations and structure strong enough to take an additional floor above the present fifth floor (above ground) so for the opening we had, with the ground and lower ground floors, seven floors in which to operate and it is hoped that in the not too distant future we may receive permission to add another floor. This would make a tremendous difference to the store and I am still convinced that it would not in any way detract from the views of the cathedral.

Fortunately for us, our elder son, David, had originally intended to be an architect and had trained for two years before deciding to come into the business. That training was now to be invaluable and he was able at the young age of twenty-three to take over the detailed planning arrangements with our architects who were always appreciative of his intelligent help. In fact, Mr Blade told me after the opening that David was one of the few store executives that he had dealt with whom he could rely on for understanding and help both in the detailed work of planning and in its execution. This, of course, meant much to me.

At the same time, our younger son, Jonathan, started what must have been the most difficult part of his career, learning the detailed work of controlling, buying and selecting the right merchandise without which the store would never succeed.

After the architects had been given our ideas on the exterior look of the building we pursued with the consent of the local authority the possibility of building on the whole site which would not only cover the ground to be leased to us but also the corner now occupied by a public house. I had strong views on this and still feel that one building over the whole site would have been a far greater attraction. Numerous meetings were held with the brewers concerned and we offered to arrange suitable accommodation within our building, or even to operate the required facilities as part of the store's trading outlet. However, it was evident that this would be a protracted undertaking and we could not afford the delay to the erection of the main building, so we had to give up what might have proved a great help to the interests of the city and make the best use of the site. Plans were now submitted and with our architects' assistance were soon approved. Then started the period when the essential problems had to be faced and overcome.

INTERIOR PLANNING

We had to know what departments we were going to operate, the position and area that each would occupy and the way in which they would fit into the general decor of their floor. This was the undertaking that we had, at that time, to cope with. So, first, every department was listed on the most suitable floor and then fitted into the floor picture and each had to form part of the total. Owing to the time factor we could not build the major fittings ourselves so we called in the firm which was founded by my grandfather, Frederick Sage & Co who were incidentally the first main world shop fitters and in the last century installed the frontages of many leading stores including Harrods and Galeries Lafayette (Paris). At the same time he trained the numerous specialists who started their own shop fitting businesses during the early part of this century. I was naturally pleased that they still had the facilities to give us what we wanted at a fair price. Here again, David took over the details once it was agreed on the layout of the departments.

FINANCING

This, of course, would have frightened most families operating on their own. There were so many unknown factors to be dealt with and I sought the advice of anyone who was likely to be in a position to indicate some idea of unrecorded costs that would have to be met.

The cost of the building was easy to assess with the help of Mr Blade and it was evident that I would have to deal with this as a separate entity to that of other financial requirements. I, therefore, obtained an introduction to Mr Barry East, managing director of Town and City Properties Ltd.

Looking back on the visit I remember I had no doubt that I was making a good offer to someone who would be quick to assess the potential of the investment in which they were invited to participate. Once the introduction had been effected I realised I was speaking to a live dynamic person who would quickly assess whether something was worth consideration or not. He examined the plans, he asked me a number of pertinent questions as a result of which he soon had a picture of my objectives and how I intended to develop the store and my own confidence in its future success. Within half an hour he said, "Right, you can have the money," and a contract was signed on the basis of a ninety-nine year lease with three twenty-five year revision periods and the rent was computed on a reasonable basis. It was then I learnt that the cost of meeting the interest on the money as it was advanced would have to be met before the store opened and he would not entertain bridging finance nor any loans.

So, once again, I had to think in terms of the all-embracing capital required to cover general fittings and equipment, stock, expenses before opening, including advertising, costs which would have to be met before the store opened, trading loss for the first, and possibly, second year and hidden reserves to meet any unexpected emergency. If we had not included the latter the firm would not have survived.

Bridging finance was to be looked at under a separate heading so once again I was on the look out for an introduction to anyone who might help. With this in mind there were two objectives; on the one hand the structure of the firm, a new company in which the family would hold a controlling interest but others would be invited to invest up to forty or forty-five per cent of the total.

A few members of our family were glad to participate and a personal friend, Frank Benka, one of the most successful children's school outfitting manufacturers in the county whom I had known for many years, had always wanted to have an interest in a department store. I asked him if he would like an investment with a place on the board so that he would really feel he was associated with a lifelong ambition. He soon learned from his financial advisers that he should not entertain it but he went against their advice and was glad to share the risks that we were facing. I am sure he never regretted it because he retained a personal interest in all that we did until his untimely death in spring 1970.

We were still short by about £100,000 on the investment side and there was the bridging finance to be dealt with. Here again I was fortunate to be introduced to Mr McCartney Filgate of Lazards—one of the leading merchant banks in the City—and a basis satisfactory to both parties was arranged for advancing the money to cover these costs. So on the building side we could proceed. Having found my way into Lazards it was evident that they might be able to help me further and it was here that I was introduced to Mr E. W. Phillips, a director on their investment side. Before seeing him I had prepared an estimated sales list for all the departments for the first six months including the anticipated turnover over five years, with an estimated gross profit and expenses for each financial year. Preparing these figures before the building had been erected was an unusual exercise upon which I spent many hours and found most exciting as well as intriguing and it is gratifying to know that under each heading in the five year period I was not far off the mark.

Ted Phillips naturally required time to study the figures put before him and the proposal to advance £100,000 for a period after which it had to be repaid or could be invested in the company. The outcome was that they shared our confidence in the success of the venture and I will always be grateful for the personal interest he took in our affairs and still value the link of friendship that was established between us. Although we had many anxious hours in the first few years he never once queried our eventual success but at the same time was ready to advise and, if possible, help in any way he could. Arising from this we invited him to become a director of our parent company in June 1974 since when his advice has been greatly appreciated.

One of the wisest moves decided upon to cope with the problem of opening from scratch was the erection of a service building covering an area of some 22,000 square feet which we built on a freehold site we acquired within three minutes from the store. As our trading area in the main building was considerably less than we really required we could not afford to give any of it up to receiving and despatch and main storage. This all had to be done in this other building which incidentally was carried out by the building department we operated at that time. Here again, we were able to sell the freehold building when it was completed and add further capital to ease the overall financial burdens. The store could not have opened without it, as this was ready some months before we opened and there was therefore an address to which equipment, fittings and stock could be delivered, checked and if necessary, marked. We have since proved that a store does not have to have its main receiving and despatch department on its premises; they can operate equally successfully within easy reach of the main building.

There was much to be done before the Opening Day which was fixed for 17th September, 1962—our wedding anniversary!

Earlier in the year we were being informed that the building could not possibly be finished before Christmas. However, when the day arrived for the topping out ceremony we took advantage of this to instil into the workmen, with the help of suitable refreshments, how much we depended on them to get the store open. They, and all others concerned, surprised us with the efforts that they made and although we were not in a position to move in carpets, furniture, fittings or stock until a fortnight before the store was due to open, everything looked as though it had been ready for weeks at actual opening when, in fact, quite a number of departments were bare the day before.

During this period we had to contact suppliers and at the same time start interesting the shopping public near and far whom we expected to attract. I was invited to give a talk in London on the problems as well as the excitement of opening a new store which gained us some publicity in directions required and throughout all the arrangements prior to opening we had to think "big" under almost every heading.

Our displays were unusual and of a standard that compared favourably with the best in the country, carried out under the direction of Walter Kilb. The interior of each floor had to be colourful and arresting. The Rooftop Restaurant had to be exciting and introduce a new note into catering. The merchandise had to be in keeping with the policy laid down and this meant that, months before the opening, merchandise at home and overseas had to be studied at a level on which we had not previously been trading in Kent.

Behind the organisation that went on there was the engagement of staff.

This was a tremendous undertaking and again could not have been done if we had not been operating in Deal which became the centre for the engagement of the rank and file of our staff. Our senior staff were engaged mainly at Browns Hotel, Dover Street, London, where my wife and I used to go for a day or two at a time and interview buyers and senior staff by appointment. One exception to this was Walter Kilb who came to see us as a result of an advertisement in a German display magazine with the hope of attracting someone with flair and a slightly different image that would prove effective to a new store. We could not have picked anyone better than this young man who could hardly speak English but wanted to come here and, although he left us for a period, he liked the district and the store so much that he accepted an invitation to return to us.

Opening Day had arrived—Monday, 17th September, 1962. There was bustle on all floors from a very early hour; the builders were still working on stairways, shopfitters were either finishing departments or tidying them up to see us through the day, carpet layers were on the last lap, merchandise was still entering the premises from the service building. Fortunately, all the staff at every level had entered into the spirit of the occasion and worked as though they had been associated with the company for years. The weather was not kind to us and we feared that some rain forecast would keep the crowds away from the Official Opening at 2.30 p.m.

During the morning, friends of ours, associated with the store world began to arrive and encouraged us by their presence. They included representatives of the Beale family from Bournemouth, Rowan Bentall from Kingston, John Bedford from Debenhams and heads of other leading stores together with prominent local citizens. The Opening Ceremony was preceded with a spectacular procession through the city. The theme was "Canterbury through the Ages" supporting the exhibition in the store. This was planned and executed by Bill Dawson who as already mentioned had been on our management team since we came to Kent. The procession was led by a full brass band followed by about 250 volunteers all attired in suitable costume covering the long period of the life of Canterbury. There were also about forty horses which put the finishing touch to this historical spectacle.

In spite of the inclement weather the traffic was held up as a result of the crowds waiting to enter the store. The main doors were to be opened first and the usual satin tape was across the entrance. I had to say a few words with my family around me and I said:

> It has long been an ambition of mine to break away from tradition and to plan and build a new store with a difference, a store that would encourage the distribution of the best merchandise—both for the home and in the world of fashion. And with our existing stores in Kent, Canterbury seemed to be the obvious place for this new development. Here was a centre which could attract people from all directions, with

good public transport, car parks, a fitting setting and shopping centre. Here was a developing city, a beautiful city, a cathedral city, shortly to become a university city, population increasing, place in history secure and standing on the highway to and from the continent.

The youngest member of the family, our daughter Elizabeth, who had been allowed the day off from Benenden where she was still at school was to make the opening announcement and cut the tape. Although this was the first time she had spoken in public outside the school, she did this with charm and confidence—and the crowds surged in.

Our takings for the afternoon were satisfactory—not a large sum but we had made a start and the general reaction of the shopping public was encouraging. However, one of the other store chiefs who had been round the store told me that our layouts were not good; we would have to conform to the general pattern by opening up all floors and if we were to survive we would have to do this within six months. Fortunately, he was proved wrong as part of our policy was to give each department its own individual look at the same time making it possible to see through to the ends of each floor. This made access to all sections easy without in any way detracting from the individual emphasis placed on each group of merchandise and that practice in principle has been carried on up to the time of writing this story.

Closing time was announced over the tannoy. Preparations were in hand for the evening function with over a hundred guests joining us, included friends from near and far and many of the city's leading citizens. The catering was of the highest order and must have been one of the best meals offered for many a day—Scotch salmon, perfectly cooked, salads, meats, delectable sweets and cheeses all presented and served by the chef and his assistants in a perfect setting. Outwardly all was well but in the conversations that were taking place we overheard remarks to the effect that a store of this standing could not possibly survive for more than six months and that was the general view of many who were interested in the life of the local community. Fortunately for them and us, their assumption proved wrong.

One of our first mistakes proved to be that not sufficient planning had been done to deal with the enormous amount of dishes that had to be washed and preparation for the many early shoppers who were anxious to visit the Rooftop Restaurant for morning coffee. These were teething troubles which time and experience enabled us to put right.

Reference must be made to suitably stocking the store for autumn and Christmas trading. The question was frequently asked—how do you know how much to spend? As previously mentioned, turnover in all departments had been estimated for the first full year and prior to that for the first season, and this was again reviewed in the light of what we had to invest to provide a reasonable selection in all merchandise. The value of this was not affected by seasonal styling, therefore in most sections, other than fashions, the selection was far in excess of what we anticipated we would sell during the first few months and rather more than we expected in the fashions knowing that we would have to stand a loss on some of the stock during the first sale. This enabled us to have a selection comparable with an established store and encouraged greater turnover than would have been expected in the normal practice of limiting stock in relation to anticipated turnover.

Buyers were given detailed instructions and we were kept informed of the main suppliers and their terms from whom we made purchases. Quite a number of suppliers were glad of the opportunity to be associated with a venture of this sort as it was more than unusual and they were quick to realise the implications of promoting their name, particularly if a new product could be associated with it. We had a number of helpful instances under this heading. In most cases, suppliers agreed to wait for payment with normal discount following the first week of trading. This was a great help.

PROMOTIONS

The build-up of promoting the opening took us considerable time. This meant contact with local and national press. Our name had to be established in advance particularly as our trading policy was different to that which was being operated under our name at our existing smaller stores on the coast. The fact that this was a new venture and that staff at all levels had taken a risk in joining this venture offered scope to journalists and this was a great help. Our advertising policy, too, had to be established. The outstanding window displays helped considerably and went a long way to establishing our new image but they were almost too good and we had to modify these slightly as they were inclined to give the impression that we were expensive. This was not the case; our prices were higher but so too was the standard of the merchandise and could stand up to the keenest competition.

CANTERBURY THROUGH THE AGES

There was one promotion which required a lot of study and effort to prepare, namely the exhibition entitled "Canterbury through the Ages". This was the story of Canterbury and its historic background as far back as records exist up to the present time. It was illustrated by the use of colourful models, mural paintings, exhibits from local museums and many rare photographic records.

The exhibits were arranged in chronological order with captions giving the historical background to the items illustrated, ranging from the early Iron Age period circa 500 BC up to the present day. Interesting illustrations, mainly in model form, of the life of the city in Roman, Saxon and Norman times, the

A CANTERBURY TALE

Murder of Becket, Chaucer's Canterbury Pilgrims, the Spanish Armada threat were all included as were the more recent experiences through the blitz. Apart from the historical references there were numerous illustrations of outstanding activities in the city, such as its importance as an educational centre, the rise and decline of the weaving industry, the city's early sponsoring of railway transport and its special place as a home of English cricket.

The work was planned and carried out by local historians and artists, most of the latter from the staff and students of the Canterbury College of Art under the direction of Mr G. Maynard, ARCA, without whom we could never have completed the exhibition to such a high standard. We estimated that during the first twelve months it would attract well over 50,000 visitors and who can assess the value of that in turnover in a new store. Unfortunately, its life was cut short as it was one of the sections that was ruined by the fire—more of this later. We received nothing but commendation for the exhibition and I always remember Dr Hewlett Johnson (the Red Dean) who kindly came to congratulate us telling me that he had learnt more about the history of Canterbury in a little over twenty minutes in the store than throughout some thirty years of living in the city. In expressing his appreciation he recorded the following:

> I had heard of the exhibition and I know of the work of Mr Maynard, but when I saw the exhibition itself and the superb workmanship throughout I was greatly astonished. From the first scene to the last it was beautiful but also instructive. I personally left the long exhibition with a better knowledge of Canterbury and a greater love for the cathedral and a greater sense of responsibility for its preservation and its Christian mission.
>
> It is a splendid thought, too, that after deduction of costs the proceeds of this go to the assistance of some twenty-four charities, local and national, amongst which I am delighted to see The Friends of Canterbury Cathedral.

Dr Johnson also blessed for us the opening of "Helping Hands" an area in which collections were being made for national and local charities.

All went according to plan until the January sales and there was every indication that our estimates for turnover were on target. Then the unexpected happened, as it always will, and one had to provide for it when planning ahead. Fortunately we had done this. However the shock was considerable for we had the heaviest snow storm on Boxing Day for many years. This had a serious effect on our sale; the snow was with us until early March so our plans to attract shoppers from outside the city boundary suffered as access had become so difficult and our turnover was reduced to a low level.

Then the sun came out, the snow disappeared and we had one week of excellent trading. Visitors came from where we had expected. Orders for carpets and furniture were exceeding expectations and we were all set for a successful spring season. This was not to last. On Saturday, 23rd March, 1963, at about midnight when I was sound asleep I received a telephone call telling me that the store was on fire. I was soon in Canterbury together with my sons and manager, having seen the flames rising into the sky some distance before reaching the city. When gaining access to the premises everything was in chaos. The Fire Brigade had taken over and water was being poured on to the fifth floor where the fire had started just outside my office, in the restaurant kitchen. By the early hours of the morning all we had left was smoke, smell and dripping water on all floors and floods on the lower ground floor.

Letters and phone calls offering help started to pour in the next day, the most valuable of which came from the city council. Having lost all our management offices in the gutting of the fifth floor we were readily given permission to erect temporary offices on the car park at the rear of the store. The speed and genuine willingness of this gesture was so appreciated at this difficult time.

The insurance company was good enough to see me without delay and offered to advance a sum up to about £50,000 if this would help. Knowing that our immediate requirements were covered, I suggested that they wait for a few days and see what was likely to be involved—and this cost us dearly. Following the fire, an unknown person telephoned the police; I never knew exactly what the message was but it certainly was not complimentary and it gave the insurance company's assessor the right to withhold payment on our loss of stock and fittings until his examination was completed. He took nearly two years to complete this! The claim for damage to the building was accepted without any problem. I fear we were not well represented at an initial meeting with the insurers. It was an occasion when tact was required to establish a position on which reasonable terms might be negotiated, but our representative asked for conditions which were thought to be quite unreasonable and the two sides parted with views which were a long way apart. This was the opening of a never ending problem which arose from a lack of goodwill and co-operation which was essential to bring about a settlement. No immediate offer of cash was made and every obstacle was placed in the way of settling the claim. I was even told that it would be in the insurance company's interest if we went bankrupt as they then would not have to meet the claim; later it was realised that this probably would not have been the case, but it was another instance of the unpleasant conditions that were in existence at that time. So ensued a testing period during which we had to continue trading and find adequate capital to cover this knowing that the loss assessor could recommend that the insurance company should pay us nothing. This was quite beyond our understanding as we had suffered loss of stock, damage by fire, loss of trading potential and also considerable loss of fixtures and fittings. The total amount was just under £100,000 which I am sure in the normal course of events would have been met without delay.

After a period of nearly two years it was agreed that our claim should be put into arbitration, the arbitrator being E. J. R. Hickmott, a recognised expert on consequential loss. This was held in an office in Fleet Street attended by a counsel and legal advisers on both sides and I had five days of grilling when every effort was made to establish the case against us. The outcome, although not what we had wanted proved that we had received treatment that had not been fair; our claim was accepted in part and we received an award of something like £46,000.

The treatment we had received had not been what one would have expected in the normal way and might well have ruined the business at such an early stage in its life. It was a great day when the results of the fire had been put behind us and we were able to concentrate on the future of the company and all that needs to be said here is that the life established in the early stages now continued with new ideas evolving each year.

There were many outstanding features which gave us national and, in some cases, international publicity, that are worth mentioning. The first was a visit from representatives of the *Ambassador* magazine which was circulated throughout the western world. They planned to report on a number of successful department stores in the UK and chose us as their first. They promoted us under the title "A Canterbury Tale"—in and out of Ricemans and around Canterbury. This came at a time when we were badly in need of wider publicity and they provided us, free of charge, with eighteen pages, including advertisements which was also reprinted for additional private distribution. This was a tremendous boost to us and created considerable international interest and goodwill, as well as some jealous comments from leaders of other large department stores who thought that they should have been chosen first!

Most years after we had recovered from the effects of the fire we had numerous store promotions, often launched in September, prior to the busiest trading season of the year.

One promotion failed because it was too successful. For our first Open Shopping Evening admission was by ticket only and 10,000 tickets were issued. We arranged for free car parking in the multi-storey car park and the store itself was filled with unusual attractions, competitions, gifts, a tombola and fashion shows. The doors were to be opened from 7 until 9 p.m. We expected a good response, instead of which people descended on the city from all directions. Seldom, if ever, have the police stood on one side permitting cars to be parked on double yellow lines, in odd corners and for a time even the traffic was held up. The buses that we had laid on to transport shoppers from the main store to the furnishing centre found difficulty in getting through the traffic, so that full advantage was not taken of this. Instead of having to encourage visitors to enter we had to have control on the doors as every floor was so full it was almost impossible to enjoy the facilities that had been planned within. Indirectly, although many were naturally disappointed, it did indicate that a promotion widely launched could attract large crowds. At the next open evening the situation was reversed; we were so careful not to encourage too many to come that we did not have sufficient! This is how we learn.

"Now we are Five" was an excellent autumn promotion. We felt we were growing up and our main troubles were behind us, so all our efforts were made to achieve a successful autumn and Christmas trading period. There were many innovations which added interest to normal shopping and established a pattern of autumn promotions which in one form or another has been carried on most autumns since.

Another feature which enjoyed national publicity was "The Best of British" when the store was filled with British goods and we received tremendous support from the best suppliers. The news of what we were doing soon leaked out to other stores, particularly through the press who had prior knowledge of our arrangements, and these stores were soon featuring similar promotions. I wrote to the then Prime Minister, who wished us well and sent one of his colleagues, Mr E. C. Redhead, Minister of State (Overseas), to attend our opening dinner with two prominent manufacturers—Mr Myron Akerman of Chester Barrie and Mr Eric Hall, who has had a long and successful career in footwear—who were the guest speakers. Our MP for Canterbury, Sir Leslie Thomas and his wife and leading local citizens were also present together with representatives of local and national press. We also received a message from Edward Heath, then leader of the opposition:

> Warmest congratulations on your efforts and initiative in helping exports. As a Man of Kent representing Kent in Parliament, I think that the geography and history of Kent gives us special responsiblity in the overseas fields. Best of luck.

We also had a message from Douglas Jay, President of the Board of Trade:

> It is vital to our national prosperity that we maintain a steady increase in our overseas sales. I am therefore most pleased to note that Ricemans of Canterbury have shown enterprise in displaying a selection of the Best of British products and am confident that this promotion will enjoy the success it deserves.

The store was decked with flags, there were special windows and departmental displays and exciting advertising in the local and national press. I had always been keen on open evenings for the elderly and infirm, not only in Canterbury but in other stores, and found the staff pleased to support them. The purpose was not primarily to take money but to help many of those who needed special assistance when shopping, including the use of wheelchairs. Refreshments were provided free and there were special offers to save them money on their Christmas shopping. Few efforts made in the store brought us more satisfaction than the words of appreciation that we were given after these events.

Large premises had been vacant for a year or more in Burgate and we discussed the possibility of moving our furnishing departments from the main store, which would then be operated as an independent furnishing centre with about 12,000 sq. ft. of selling space. This opened in 1970. Apart from improving the area devoted to furnishings we gained space in the main store for urgent expansion of existing departments. This was a successful move and we were soon looking to expand the premises. Fortunately the first and second floors were about half the size of the ground floor and in 1974 we opened a 5,000 sq. ft. extension which allowed us greatly to improve our presentation. It was not long before we realised we needed an attraction that would encourage potential shoppers to walk round and we therefore opened a coffee room on the second floor. This certainly proved a draw. However, after a few years space was so urgently required for selling purposes that it was closed. We soon felt we had made a mistake and in 1979, while my wife and I were abroad, plans for a new catering unit were put into action and it was decided to call it "Freddies". I was glad about this as small catering units can encourage traffic flow in most stores, as this certainly has done.

About 1970 the city was planning to develop the Whitefriars site situated at the rear of the store. We felt most strongly at the time that it would be in the interests of the city and shopping public if this could be linked with our store and Marks & Spencer but the city council had other ideas. However, we asked if we could present alternative plans and this was agreed, providing they were submitted within a fortnight. Our architects, Sir John Burnett Tait & Partners, in conjunction with representatives of Marks & Spencer, produced an excellent plan that would have provided some shops, an extension of our store and of Marks & Spencer and additional car parking facilities on the top floors linked with a new bridge from the multi-storey car park.

Both Marks & Spencer and we were delighted with the proposal and went to the meeting hoping that it would prove acceptable. Unfortunately our plan was turned down. When the council's own plans for the development were executed they gave as a priority space for a supermarket and an extension to Marks & Spencer. They wanted small shops included in the project, and our requirements were never given the consideration that we had hoped for. However, we managed to secure the three first floor shop units which we opened in 1973, and with the help of the council built a new second floor extension over the Whitefriars development for an opening one year later.

Apart from providing two new restaurants (one for staff) the remaining space was devoted to an expansion of our fashion departments giving us a total area of 18,000 sq. ft. on one floor for this most important aspect of our business.

In 1979 we tried to turn back the clock and come to terms with the brewers who operated the public house adjoining the store. With the support of the city authorities and the help of Healey & Baker, London, plans were prepared to extend our store over the whole of this site, providing accommodation for the existing public house to operate in part of the ground and lower ground floors. Although negotiations reached an advanced stage they could not be concluded to our satisfaction and the cost involved was such that further delay might have prejudiced our success. With reluctance we withdrew, which was unfortunate after so much work had been put into it. However one learns from such experiences and we looked elsewhere for space.

By the late 1970s we had acquired space in Whitefriars on the ground floor when we took over the premises of a Do-it-Yourself shop and finally in 1982 after a very complicated and long period of negotiation we obtained the first floor trading area of International Stores which provided us with an additional 8,000 sq. ft. of selling space. This additional space, being directly underneath our main fashion floor, provided an excellent opportunity for the further development of our young fashion business. We therefore moved the Miss Selfridge shop to a much larger space in this new area and adjoining it we were able to re-establish our own Top of the 80s. The idea for this department originated out of a recent visit of mine to New York and although our first effort of introducing this to the second floor was successful, it was inadequate in space. The new facility has enabled us to make a much more exciting environment in which our emphasis on fashions for the young was expanded to cover co-ordinated accessories, with the additional advantage of a new stairway linking this floor with our main fashion floor above.

Thus by a roundabout way we have developed a close trading link with Marks & Spencer and it is interesting to note that the Whitefriars developments have given us the unusual advantage of turning our second floor into a major traffic flow area.

As the store developed we reviewed our leasehold interests particularly that of the main store. It became obvious that the value of our property had greatly increased since the opening of the store. This was at a time when Town & City Properties Ltd were re-trenching their activities and Mr East was no longer connected with the company. We thought it worthwhile seeing if they would sell their holding interest in our main building and after considerable negotiation we were able to acquire their underlease from them. The Prudential owned the head lease and they were left with an investment that was unattractive as we retained 75% of any rent review. Eventually they agreed to sell us this head lease so that we have escaped all payments of rent other than the nominal ground rent that was fixed for ninety-nine years in

1962. These actions naturally enhanced the assets of our company in spite of the prices we had to pay.

The personal note has always been a prominent desire of all members of our family and this obviously meets with general approval from staff at all levels who are encouraged to feel that the success of the store is to a large degree dependent on the personal contribution they are in a position to make. We have received over the years so many letters of appreciation coming from shoppers abroad as well as from various parts of this country which are the best encouragement we can get to pursue the policy which has created this goodwill and at the same time encourage those who have contributed towards it.

Over the years, like any business, we have had our fair share of complaints and the majority justified but many not. Without doubt the real problem area here is anything that works can go wrong. We try to deal fairly and often generously when rectifying a problem and we have found it to be one of the most effective ways to promote goodwill. One complaint that I should like to record here is a good example of an extraordinary tale of woe illustrating the time and trouble some customers go to in relating their problems to us:

The Umbrella
I purchased an umbrella of the automatic kind
And I'm the sort of fella who likes to have a bind
When things don't work as advertised, it just ain't good enough
I've done my bit by paying up, but it won't do its stuff.

It's lovely when it's raining and it opens like a treat,
One almost enjoys walking on the saturated street,
But when it stops I get really cross which produces a large frown
'Cause whilst it goes up easily, the bloody thing won't stay down.

Now this of course would be all right if we had perpetual hail,
Or if the winds were moderate instead of blowing a gale,
But as it is I'm petrified and permanently scared,
'Cause every time there's a gust of wind, I take off like a bird.

So search the skies on Saturday and watch me flying over,
Having cruised along o'er Watling Street all the windy way from Dover,
Make ready your apologies and say "We're sorry brother,
But drop in whilst you're passing and we'll change it for another."

The above poem was acknowledged and an offer made to replace, when the customer was able to call. The customer replied after a few days with:

191

MY ROAD TO CANTERBURY

I bought an umbrella of the automatic kind
And I'm the sort of fella who likes to have a bind
When things don't work as advertised—it really is a pain
So I mount my worthy warhorse and charge in to complain.

My brolly, as you know by now, would simply not stay down,
So it's been living in the spare room, lying on the eiderdown,
Until last night a friend decided she would like to stay,
Which meant my umbrella simply had to go away.

I thought, "Let's have just one more try as the thing has got to move"
So pushed it down the handle where it slotted in its groove,
I stood there flabbergasted, as it hadn't worked before,
Then opened it up and pushed it down to my wife's shouts of "encore".

I tried another dozen times to prove it wasn't a fluke
And everytime it folded up by way of quiet rebuke,
So I offer my apologies with a face that's very red,
The umbrella's in working order now and so's the spare room bed.

With the interest of our staff in mind we set out in 1974, when our second floor extension was completed, to install what we hoped would prove to be one of the best staff restaurants in the country, with subsidised meals and refreshments for staff at all levels. In October of that year when members of the then Independent Stores Association visited us for a two-day study and the welcome dinner was held in the staff restaurant it gave us considerable satisfaction to hear some say that the restaurant was one of the few in which such a function could be held. It was obvious that they were appreciative of what we had done.

The store being situated so near to Europe has encouraged continental shoppers to visit us, particularly from France, Belgium, Germany and Holland. At the same time more and more Americans like visiting Canterbury and many find their way to the store for some of their main purchases while on holiday in this country. They appreciate the easy access to all departments, the wide selection that can be obtained and, above all, the personal service.

SECURITY

Shoplifting and other dishonest practices have greatly increased in recent years. Stores have had to incur expenditure introducing deterrent measures not needed twenty-five years ago. What are the reasons?

Unfortunately the moral standards of our people have deteriorated with the lessening of home influence and religious life in the community. It is said that retailers encourage shoplifting by the open displays of goods but with ever increasing wage costs selling has to be more and more on a self-service basis. There are security methods available for specific items that make it difficult for anyone to remove them without being detected but the majority of items on sale cannot be made secure from theft. It is a serious problem for management.

Our rule is that everyone caught will be referred to the police, with rare exceptions where circumstances are such that it would be callous not to consider them. The courts are taking a more serious view of cases but all too often the punishment seems inadequate as a deterrent to others. A disturbing aspect is that often intelligent young people have no regrets for the crime they have committed except against themselves for being too slack and being caught. One such late teenager, while waiting for the police, put his feet on the desk, sat at his ease, and said something like, "I do not have any money to pay a fine, so if you send me to gaol that will be a rest for me and will cost the country money. It will then delay completion of my qualifications and my entry into my profession."

Our present forms of punishment seem inadequate. What can we do?

SHOP IN SHOPS

We are often asked why we have shop in shops in our store. When we opened we only had one—Wedgwood. Since then the number has steadily increased and we have had to hold back from adding any more so that our overall presentation is not out of balance.

This form of trading has increased during the past twenty years and we are satisfied that it provides improved shopping facilities for our customers. We would prefer to buy their merchandise direct as part of our own buying and selling operation but the advantages cannot be overlooked. Primarily they enable us to carry a much wider selection of specific types of goods often in a higher price range than we would consider viable to offer in the same depth. As we have difficulty in repeating popular selling numbers, usually reserve stocks are held for these specialist shops so that their ranges do not flag during the season.

Another important reason is when we want to obtain the agencies for particular merchandise which may not be very easy, especially for such items as watches and fine jewellery, all of which we are now able to supply with the necessary technical knowledge.

The introduction of these shops, though an advantage to the public, creates problems for us as the savings we obtain, and the curtailed margins we receive, demand a large increase in turnover to justify the arrangement.

The personal contribution of staff, at all levels, indicates that there is still an important part for an efficiently operated family controlled business to play in the future pattern of trading in this country. It is evident the public appreciates the involvement of management at the local level and for the standard of service this encourages. This factor probably as much as any other has contributed to our success.

In 1980 our younger son, Jonathan, decided to emigrate with his family to Canada. He was always keen on the open air life and both he and his wife thought it would be a wonderful opportunity for their children to grow up in a young country that has many developing years ahead. No father likes to part with a son who has worked in the family business for nearly twenty years, especially as he was a natural merchant and a good friend maker, both in the business and with our major suppliers. However, the decision was taken and he left with the good wishes of his family and friends.

It was naturally gratifying to me to have survived the first twenty-one years of our trading in Canterbury, and this has been recognised as a very special trading period. At the time of writing, it has only just started, but it is hoped this will add another strong link to our trading success.

In this story, from early days, it must be recorded once again that Canterbury would never have been evolved without the goodwill and support of my wife and sons, and they have every right to share the satisfaction in the results of the efforts that have been made to bring it about .

A GLANCE INTO THE FUTURE

So many changes have taken place in retailing since the war that one hesitates to make predictions.

If I had my time over again I feel confident I would rather work my way up in a large successful store group or perhaps eventually start some form of business on my own, though I don't imagine it would be a department store for this would demand so much capital and expertise over such a wide range of requirements that the risk involved would be too great. Also the large store groups would claim the key sites when they became available.

Keen competition demands a high standard of merchandising and presentation making the best use of every square metre of selling space. *Specialisation* is the word under most retail headings but for myself *Fashions* in one form or another will always offer the greatest scope. Anyone contemplating establishing an independent business must be aware of the age of change that we are living in.

Coping with inflation is probably one of the most difficult problems that has altered the pattern of financing during recent years. Increased profits to justify increased capital expenditure must be encouraged by government legislation to enable companies to plough back for their profitable development.

Always be aware of the problems that can arise in expanding a successful business. Management and capital requirements have to be adjusted at each stage of a company's development. An unchecked expansion can easily result in loss of control. The unexpected disaster can occur as I have experienced. This has convinced me of the importance of adequate insurance cover which should be under constant review.

Looking back over the years it is hard for me to believe that with the help of my family we have established a department store that is known far beyond the borders of Kent with a splendid team of management and staff offering a service that many shoppers still appreciate.

I have met so many wonderful people both in and out of the store world. I think of friends under many headings—manufacturers, architects, builders, representatives of the press, leaders in the insurance and banking world, shopfitters, suppliers in one form or another and, of course, successful leaders in department stores at home and overseas. I have valued their friendship and all that I have learnt from them.

Money has never been my first objective—the thrill of doing something worthwhile has. It is hoped in recording some of my varied experiences which so often have been both exciting and challenging may bring some encouragement to others. My road to Canterbury has not been an easy one, but it has been a memorable journey.

INDEX

ILLUSTRATIONS